ANTHROPOLOGICAL PAPERS OF
THE UNIVERSITY OF ARIZONA
NUMBER 32

WOODEN RITUAL ARTIFACTS FROM CHACO CANYON NEW MEXICO

The Chetro Ketl Collection

R. GWINN VIVIAN
DULCE N. DODGEN
GAYLE H. HARTMANN

THE UNIVERSITY OF ARIZONA PRESS
TUCSON, ARIZONA
1978

About the Authors . . .

R. GWINN VIVIAN has done fieldwork at several locations in the Southwest and northern Mexico. His primary research interests are water control systems in arid areas and the Chacoan archaeology of northwestern New Mexico. He holds a Ph.D. in anthropology from the University of Arizona. In 1963 he joined the staff of the Arizona State Museum, and he has been the Museum archaeologist since 1970. His Museum research and administration are combined with teaching in the Department of Anthropology at the University of Arizona.

DULCE N. DODGEN has been employed by the National Park Service and the Heard Museum in Phoenix, Arizona. She has drawn on her numerous talents, including researching, silkscreening, and writing, in a variety of projects related to Southwestern prehistory.

GAYLE HARRISON HARTMANN holds a B.A. in anthropology from the University of California at Berkeley and an M.A. in anthropology from the University of Arizona. She has done surveying, laboratory work, photography, and excavation on archaeological projects for the Museum of Northern Arizona and the University of Arizona. She has also edited reports on various aspects of southern Arizona archaeology for the Arizona State Museum.

THE UNIVERSITY OF ARIZONA PRESS

Copyright© 1978
The Arizona Board of Regents
All Rights Reserved
Manufactured in U.S.A.

Library of Congress Cataloging in Publication Data
Vivian, R. Gwinn
    Wooden ritual artifacts from Chaco Canyon, New Mexico.

    (Contribution of the Chaco Center; no. 11) (Anthropological papers of the University of Arizona; no. 32)
    Includes bibliographical references.
    1. Pueblo Indians--Wood-carving. 2. Indians of North America--New Mexico--Wood-carving. 3. Chaco Canyon, N.M.--Antiquities. 4. New Mexico--Antiquities. I. Dodgen, Dulce N., joint author. II. Hartmann, Gayle Harrison, joint author. III. Title. IV. Series: Chaco Center. Contribution of the Chaco Center; no. 11. V. Series: Arizona. University. Anthropological papers; no. 32.
E99.P9V58   978.9'82   78-10684
ISBN 0-8165-0576-4

CONTENTS

PREFACE   vii
1. INTRODUCTION   1
2. THE COLLECTION   4
   Provenience   4
   Location and Condition of the Collection   7
   Classification Schemes   8
   Flat Carved Forms   8
   Round Carved Forms   14
   Miscellaneous Objects   17
      Wooden and Vegetal Objects   17
      Cordage   17
      Vegetal Remains, Faunal Remains,
         and Lithics   17
   Woodworking   17
   Joining and Attachment   18

3. ARCHAEOLOGICAL COMPARISONS   19
   Flat Carved Forms   19
      Other Chacoan Sites   19
      Other Anasazi Sites   23
      Mogollon Sites   24
      Other Sites   31
   Round Carved Forms   33
      Anasazi Sites   33
      Other Sites   34
   Miscellaneous Wooden and
      Vegetal Objects   35

4. ETHNOGRAPHIC COMPARISONS   37
   Flat Carved Forms   37
      Altars   37
      Masks, Tablitas, and Other Headgear   45
      Staffs and Slab Prayersticks   49
      Mask-Images   51
   Round Carved Forms   54
      Arrows   54
      Bows   54
      Lightning Lattice   54
      Prayersticks   55
      Plume Holders   55
   Miscellaneous Wooden and
      Vegetal Objects   56
   Historic Ritual Wood   56
      Pecos   56
      Hawikuh   56

   Awatovi   57
   Sikyatki   58

5. CONCLUDING REMARKS   59
   Contextual Relationships   59
   Ceremonial Use   60
   Chacoan Ritual   63

Appendix A: DESCRIPTION OF THE
              ARTIFACTS
              by Dulce N. Dodgen   65
   Flat Carved Forms   65
      Birds   65
      Possible Bird Forms   70
      Horns   73
      Oval Form with Handle   76
      Hoop Fragments   77
      Miscellaneous Forms   79
      Rectangles   82
      Discs   82
      Ovates   86
      Plaques   88
      Zoomorphic Wands   89
      Slats   92
   Round Carved Forms   106
      Bows and Arrows   106
      Lightning Lattice   110
      Prayersticks   110
      Plume Holders   111
   Miscellaneous Objects   112
      Wooden and Vegetal Objects   112
      Cordage   117
      Vegetal Remains   117
      Faunal Remains   120
      Lithics   120

Appendix B: TECHNICAL ANALYSES
              by Dulce N. Dodgen   121
   Paints   121
      Green   123
      Brown   124
      Black   124
      Yellow   125
      White   126
      Blue   127
      Red   127

Red-Purple   128
Decorative Technique   128
Decorative Style   130
Bindings   130
    Materials   130
    Construction Techniques   131

Appendix C: THE DENDROCHRONOLOGY
              OF ROOM 93, CHETRO KETL
              by Bryant Bannister and
              William J. Robinson   133

Appendix D: SPECIES IDENTIFICATION
              by Arthur E. Dennis and
              Jeffrey Zauderer   135

Appendix E: THE EXCAVATION OF
              ROOM 92, CHETRO KETL
              by Charles B. Voll   137

REFERENCES   149

TABLES

B.1.   Spectrographic Analyses of Key
       Paint Samples   122

C.1.   Dated Beams from First Story Ceiling,
       Room 93   134

E.1.   Tree-Ring Dates from Room 92   146
E.2.   Story Assignment of Room 92 Tree-Ring
       Specimens   147
E.3.   Pottery from Room 92   147

FIGURES

1.1.   Excavated portion of Chetro Ketl   2

2.1.   Ground plan of Chetro Ketl   5
2.2.   Plan and Section of Rooms 92 and 93   6
2.3.   Parts of birds   9
2.4.   Hypothetical reconstructions of birds   10
2.5.   Discs   11
2.6.   Ovate disc fragments   12
2.7.   Decorated slats   13
2.8.   "Plume circle"   14
2.9.   Arrows, prayersticks, and wooden cone   15
2.10. Artifact distribution in the western
       end of Room 93, Chetro Ketl   16

3.1.   Map of archaeological and ethnographic
       sites discussed in this report   20
3.2.   "Design board" from Pueblo Bonito   21
3.3.   Carved and painted wooden artifacts
       from Pueblo Bonito   22
3.4.   Wooden and leather artifacts from
       Sunflower Cave   24
3.5.   Painted slat bird from Bear Creek Cave 26
3.6.   Painted and carved wooden ritual items
       from upper Gila and Hueco
       Mountain areas   28
3.7.   Carved wooden bird form from upper
       Gila area   29
3.8.   Wooden artifacts from cave on Bonita Creek 29
3.9.   Effigy pahos and bird wing from
       Double Butte Cave   32

4.1.   Altar of the Cakwalenya at Mishongnovi 39
4.2.   Altar of the Oaqöl ceremony at Oraibi   40
4.3.   Altars of the Zia Querranna society   42
4.4.   Zuni altar of Eagle Down fraternity   43
4.5.   Headdress worn in women's dance at Hopi 48
4.6.   Headdress of Zuni corn maiden   49
4.7.   Hopi *mongkohos* of One Horn Society   50
4.8.   Zuni mask-image of Ko'loowisi   52
4.9.   Effigy birds from Hopi and Zuni   53
4.10. Puebloan lightning frame or lightning house 55
4.11. Prayersticks from Sikyatki   57

A.1.   Parrot head and body parts   66
A.2.   Bird heads and bills   67
A.3.   Bird tail   68
A.4.   Bird tails   69
A.5.   Bird tail fragments   71
A.6.   Possible bird parts   71
A.7.   Possible bird parts   72
A.8.   Curved fragments or horns   73
A.9.   Curved fragments or horns   74
A.10. Curved fragments or horns   75
A.11. Curved fragments or horns   76
A.12. Oval form with handle   77
A.13. Hoop fragments   78
A.14. Miscellaneous fragments of carved
       and painted wood   80
A.15. Miscellaneous fragments of carved
       and painted wood   81
A.16. Miscellaneous fragments of carved
       and painted wood and discs   83

A.17. Whole and fragmentary discs   84
A.18. Whole and fragmentary scalloped discs   85
A.19. Scalloped and semicircular disc fragments   87
A.20. Ovate disc fragments   87
A.21. Ovate disc fragments   88
A.22. Plaque fragments   89
A.23. Zoomorphic wands   90
A.24. Zoomorphic wands   91
A.25. Elongated slats   93
A.26. Slat fragments   95
A.27. Slat fragments   96
A.28. Slat fragments   97
A.29. Slat fragments   98
A.30. Slat fragments   99
A.31. Slat fragments   101
A.32. "Plume circle"   102
A.33. Slats and slat fragments   103
A.34. Slat fragments and "snake-lightning"
             fragments   105
A.35. Non-functional arrowshafts   107
A.36. Non-functional bows   108
A.37. Arrow fragments   109

A.38. Lightning lattice   110
A.39. Prayersticks and plume holders   111
A.40. Assorted sticks, paint brushes, and
             applicator sticks   113
A.41. Miscellaneous items   114
A.42. Miscellaneous items   116
A.43. Reed loops, yucca leaf ties, and
             cordage fragments   118
A.44. Miscellaneous vegetal and faunal remains
             and lithics   119

B.1. Unusual methods of binding several
            Chetro Ketl specimens   132

E.1. Type II masonry of first story,
            north wall, Room 92   138
E.2. View of Room 92   139
E.3. Plan and section of Room 92   140
E.4. Remains of ceilings, Room 92   141
E.5. Lower story, Room 92   144
E.6. Walls of lower story, Room 92   145

PREFACE

Like so many reports on the Chaco, this one has been in preparation for a long time. It has been about 30 years, but I can recall the hurried preparations we made following a telephone call from my father asking that we go to Chaco to help him excavate and record what he thought could be an important collection of painted wooden artifacts from a room in Chetro Ketl. November weather in Chaco can be pleasant, and in 1947 we were fortunate in having a number of warm days while we worked in Room 93. Much of the overburden had been taken out by the Navajo crew, but a protective layer of roofing bark and adobe had been left in place throughout the room following the initial discovery of a number of pieces of the painted wood in the southeast corner. We proceeded from that corner working slowly across the room to the west, uncovering more and more painted wood as we excavated. As each item was discovered it was cleaned, plotted on a gridded plan of the room (reproduced in part as Figure 2.10), and then removed. Some photographs were taken of particularly striking pieces in place, but the close spacing of many items and the possibility of a complete change in weather prohibited us from leaving all the artifacts as we found them until the entire floor was cleared. The complexity and superb preservation of the artifacts helped to stimulate our interest through long hours of cramped work, and at one point our task was interrupted when the fill over the undetected hatchway in the southwest corner collapsed and almost carried one of the group into the room below. When we had finished it was clear that the artifacts represented the most complete collection of painted wooden artifacts ever recovered from an Anasazi site. We had more than 200 items from the room, some notes on room fill, some photographs, and a scaled drawing of artifact location on the floor.

The history of the subsequent research is detailed in the Introduction. Other work prohibited Gordon Vivian from completing the report, though he worked intermittently for several years with Dulce Dodgen on some aspects of it. Dodgen completed descriptive Appendixes A and B, research data for comparative Chapters 3 and 4, and an initial draft of Chapter 1. Subsequently, other research on the painted wood and its function was carried out by Jon and Karen Young, and their contribution to the final product is acknowledged here. Somewhat later, C. Randall Morrison used his archival skills in bringing many of the old original notes and drafts back into order. He revised some of the original Dodgen and Young manuscripts and produced additional information on similar archaeological artifacts as well as providing us with data on bows, arrows, resins, and a number of other subjects.

Alice Holmes and Jan Bell, Associate Curators at the Arizona State Museum, suggested and located comparative specimens. Stanley Olsen, Museum zoo-archaeologist, and John Sparling, a physical anthropology graduate student, identified the few faunal remains. Gayle Hartmann arranged for Arthur Dennis and Jeffrey Zauderer of the National Park Service to identify wood species in the collection; their research appears as Appendix D. Dodgen's identification of the cordage was checked by Ann Hedlund of the Arizona State Museum and her recommendations for descriptive changes are acknowledged with thanks. Bryant Bannister's and Bill Robinson's study of dated wood in Room 93 appears as Appendix C.

Much of the success of this type of report depends on the illustrative material, and we were fortunate in having the Arizona State Museum photographer, Helga Teiwes, re-photograph the entire collection for this publication. Her careful and precise work is reflected in both the color plates and the black-and-white photographs. Sharon Urban of the Museum produced the pencil drawing of the "plume circle." Drafting was done by the Museum draftsman, Charles Sternberg. Typing of the manuscript was completed by Melinda Curry, Sue Ruiz and Margaret Wilcox. Carolyn Niethammer, Gayle Hartmann and Gail Hershberger edited various drafts. I would also like to thank the University of Arizona Press for their help in publishing this volume.

The National Park Service has cooperated consistently throughout the long and often delayed process of producing this report. The initial funding for manuscript completion was provided under Contract No. 4940P21004 with the Arizona Archeological Center in Tucson. This was generously augmented in 1973 by Dr. Robert Lister, Director of the Chaco Canyon

Research Center, Albuquerque, in order that the report could include complete photographic coverage of the specimens, as well as additional color reproductions of a number of the most striking or representative artifacts. In addition to Dr. Lister we have been assisted at one time or another in this project by the following Park Service personnel: Dr. Keith Anderson, Douglas Scovill, Carla Martin, James Rock, James Mount, Ken Neveln, Mike Jacobs and Walter R. Harriman.

Gayle Hartmann appears as an author to acknowledge her major contribution to the completion of this report. Combining the talents of researcher, writer, editor, and general taskmaster, she diligently pushed the preparation of the manuscript along while at all times showing remarkable patience with the continual delays I seemed to create.

R. Gwinn Vivian

1. INTRODUCTION

Summer rainfall in Chaco Canyon in 1947 was especially heavy and one particular storm in late August produced runoff in more than usual amounts. Runoff on the north side of the canyon from rincons or short side canyons generally follows established channels to the Chaco Wash, which drains the entire canyon. Chetro Ketl, one of the several large classic Chacoan towns located in the lower portion of the canyon, is situated near the mouth of one of these short rincons (Fig. 1.1). Investigations of prehistoric water control systems in the Chaco have shown that runoff from these rincons was diverted into canals for use in gridded fields on the wide canyon floor. These same systems also protected the large communal dwellings from flooding following storms. Much more recently the National Park Service employed a similar diversion system in the Chetro Ketl rincon for channeling floodwater away from the pueblo, but the August storm mentioned was so intense that a new channel was created and this channel carried water directly into the site. Many lower level rooms at the pueblo were filled with water that weakened the wall bases and caused the collapse of a major section of standing wall on the cliff side of the town. The National Park Service Ruins Stabilization Unit quickly began emergency operations at the site to prevent further wall collapse and loss of more of the pueblo. This work proceeded into the fall of 1947. In November of that year the Ruins Stabilization Unit crew, under the direction of R. Gordon Vivian, began work in Room 93. Long-term alluviation behind Chetro Ketl had almost completely buried the first story of the pueblo. There were, however, a number of first-story rooms with intact roofs which were only partially filled with sand and debris, and small vents in the back wall of some of these rooms provided a means for determining the extent of flood damage in structures. Vivian's investigations showed that the open first story of Room 93 had been flooded. The second-story room had never been excavated and was filled with wall fall and other debris. It was decided that the upper room should be cleared of fill to the floor in order to reduce the weight on the ceiling and on the outside walls weakened by the floodwater.

The upper layers of fill were typical of most Chacoan rooms and consisted mostly of building stone, mortar, and blow sand with minimal refuse mixed in the wall fall. No roofing beams were found, but a thick layer of juniper bark from the roof was located about 10 inches above the floor. This dry layer capped a deposit of silt and sand five to seven inches deep on the floor. Partially mixed in this deposit and partially covered by it on the floor were more than 200 artifacts, mostly fragments of carved and painted wood in an excellent state of preservation. Many of the fragments represented zoomorphic forms, primarily birds and possibly serpents, as well as plume or petal forms, plaques, slats, and discs. In addition to the pieces of painted wood, a number of other items were collected, including cordage, parts of arrows, gourd rind discs, worked sticks, worked stone, and corn husk packets. Some vegetal remains and animal bone also were found mixed with the artifacts.

Approximately one week was spent in excavating, mapping, photographing, and removing objects. They were stored in the Ruins Stabilizations Unit headquarters in Chaco Canyon, and by 1948 Gordon Vivian, who had directed the excavation of the room, had prepared an outline for a report on the collection. Some time was spent in developing ideas for an interpretive exhibit using part of the collection in the Visitors Center in Chaco, but this did not result in any lengthy description or interpretation of the collection.

In 1958 Vivian transferred to the N.P.S. Southwestern Archeological Center in Globe, Arizona, and took the Chetro Ketl painted wood with him. With the assistance of Dulce Dodgen, he began to expand on the original outline, and she took on the job of preparing a full descriptive report of all the items. Together they prepared several drafts of this descriptive section. Before she terminated her work with the Park Service, Dodgen prepared a report on the cordage and paint analysis; she had also started a section that dealt with similar painted wood in the Southwest and made some initial tests on color silk screen reproductions of all of the wood. Gordon Vivian died in 1966 and responsibility for completing the report was shifted to Chester A. Thomas, who made arrangements for two Park Service archaeologists, Jon and Karen Young, to complete the manuscript. The Youngs revised the original Dodgen descriptive manuscript and prepared a more expanded index of comparable archaeological artifacts. They also began a reference file on ethnographically recorded use of carved and painted wood. In addition to research on the wood, the Youngs attempted to reconstruct some of the artifacts from the many fragments in the collection. They had only limited success in this endeavor, but did develop a number of postulated reconstructions of some of the bird forms and went so far as to simulate a few of these. Their notes, photographs, and research have contributed significantly to the development of the final report.

Work on the report was halted again when the Southwestern Archeological Center was moved to Tucson in 1971. As a result of the cooperative agreement between the National Park Service and the University of Arizona, a number of Park Service projects were contracted to the University, and in 1972 a contract for the completion of the Chetro Ketl Wood

manuscript was made with the Arizona State Museum. R. Gwinn Vivian assumed responsibility for finishing the manuscript at this time. In 1972 C. Randall Morrison was employed as a part-time research assistant in the Museum to collect all past work on the collection into one unit and to work on the comparative sections of the report. Morrison spent about nine months organizing the data, gathering references on ethnographic and archaeological comparisons, and preparing introductory notes. In the spring of 1974, Dr. Robert Lister, director of the Chaco Center in Albuquerque, provided the Museum additional funding for the report to insure that the collection would be illustrated and that several color plates depicting the range of color in the collection could be reproduced. Gayle Hartmann was employed in 1974 to oversee the editing of the manuscript, organize the illustrative material, and assist in the final research

Fig. 1.1. Excavated portion of Chetro Ketl, looking southeast. The great kiva is at center background, and Room 93 is the roofed room at lower right (see also plan, Fig. 2.1.).

and writing phases. In 1975 Gwinn Vivian revised and expanded much of the text, excluding the appendixes.

The format and content of the present report represent modifications on the original plans for the manuscript. Gordon Vivian and Dulce Dodgen had originally contemplated an exhaustive comparative analysis of the collection that would have included not only full descriptions of all of the items, but detailed examinations of similar artifacts reported in the archaeological and ethnographic literature. It was presumed that comparison with examples of like artifacts, especially historic and recent Puebloan forms, would shed some light on the function of the wooden forms and the context in which they were used. It was assumed, coincident with their discovery, that the fragments originally represented objects of a ritual nature, and that comparative studies would form a basis for postulating their use in Pueblo ceremonialism. It was thought that this type of study could also be useful in reconstructing cultural continua from prehistoric groups to modern Pueblos. This type of research was prevalent in southwestern studies of the 1950s. The Youngs' research was directed toward somewhat the same goals, although they stressed the actual function of the objects in a ritual context. The importance of ethnographic parallels was reflected in their well-documented file on historic and modern Pueblo use of carved and painted wood.

Emphasis on similarities between the Chetro Ketl specimens, other prehistoric carved and painted wood and recent Puebloan carved bird forms, slat altars, dance paraphernalia and similar wooden objects has been developed in the report to an extent less than originally envisioned by Vivian and Dodgen or even the Youngs. Our goal was not the definitive trait comparison between prehistoric areas in the Southwest in order to postulate spheres of influence or cultural ties between the Chaco and other regions, nor a conclusive study of the ritual use of the objects to postulate the derivation of any particular Puebloan ceremony from the Chaco area.

Our goals were limited by the artifact provenience data. While the collection represents a significant ad-

dition to the bulk of material remains from Chacoan towns, it is in many ways a collection out of context. Despite efforts to reconstruct whole artifacts from the fragments and to postulate placement of the artifacts in the room, the evidence strongly suggests that the collection is incomplete and that the position of the items in the room does not reflect placement in a ritual context. Nonetheless the importance of comparative studies is acknowledged and two chapters of the report deal with comparisons, pointing toward some conclusions in those areas.

Furthermore, Room 93 represents a unit out of context in terms of the excavation of Chetro Ketl. Rooms to the east and west were excavated by Edgar L. Hewett between 1929 and 1934 for the School of American Research, and most of the excavation carried out in Chetro Ketl was directed by Hewett. Room 92, to the south of 93, was cleared by the National Park Service as were several other rooms in the pueblo. Unfortunately, no final report on those Chetro Ketl excavations was ever prepared by Hewett, and published information on the site is limited mostly to brief summaries in annual reports and periodicals. Consequently the interpretation of the use of Room 93 in terms of the prehistory of Chetro Ketl and especially the northern room block is severely limited. It is possible to go even one step further and note that data on Chacoan towns are restricted mostly to Pueblo Bonito and Pueblo del Arroyo. While some discussion can be developed on the basis of reports on these sites, the reference base is limited.

We believe that it would be imprudent to attempt extensive reconstruction of aspects of Chacoan ceremonialism in any detail using information available from Chacoan towns and Chetro Ketl in particular. We have decided to curtail somewhat such reconstructions because current investigations in Chaco Canyon will surely modify any interpretations we make now. It is our intention, therefore, to present descriptive material in detail, a broad range of comparative archaeological and ethnographic data, and some conjectural statements in the Concluding Remarks (Chapter 5) regarding the provenience of the artifacts and their use in Chacoan ritual.

2. THE COLLECTION

PROVENIENCE

The collection of painted wood described here was recovered from Room 93 in Chetro Ketl pueblo. Chetro Ketl is one of the better known prehistoric towns in Chaco Canyon, lying about one-half mile east of Pueblo Bonito. It is part of a nucleus of Chacoan towns that includes Pueblo Bonito, Pueblo Alto, and Pueblo del Arroyo. Like other towns within the canyon, it is situated on the north side of the Chaco Wash and, as was noted earlier, it was built near the mouth of a small side canyon or rincon. Chetro Ketl is one of the six largest of the 14 known towns in the Chaco Basin and it may have contained over 500 rooms. Both Hawley (1934: 7) and Coffin (in Hewitt 1936: 168) have estimated that the structure stood five stories in height in some sections. Its ground plan is the common D shape, and two great kivas are located in the plaza on the south side of the major room block. At least 12 other smaller kivas are present in the pueblo. (Fig. 2.1).

Approximately half of the site has been excavated. Most of the excavation was carried out during the early years of archaeological work in Chaco Canyon by the School of American Research and the University of New Mexico. Edgar L. Hewett directed seasonal work at the site in 1920 and 1921 for the School and then returned in 1929 to continue excavations on a seasonal basis until 1934 for both the School and the University. Most of Hewett's work was confined to the central portion of the back room block, some rooms in the eastern room block and the great kivas. Extensive testing in the refuse mounds to the east of the site and exploration of the adjoining talus unit to the west were also carried out under Hewett's direction. Limited excavations in various parts of the site subsequently were accomplished by the National Park Service, primarily as a result of ruin stabilization activities. Except for ruin stabilization reports and Hawley's (1934) published dissertation, most of the excavations and studies made at Chetro Ketl are unreported.

There is dendrochronological evidence for three periods of construction at Chetro Ketl. Structures associated with the two earliest periods have not been found, as the early-dated beams were recovered from later rooms where they had been reused. It is presumed that the early buildings were razed, and the stone and beams salvaged for new construction, a practice common in Chacoan towns. The earliest construction period probably began sometime before A.D. 900 and extended to about 950. It is assumed (Bannister 1965: 149) that what Hawley terms "unfaced slab" masonry was used during this time at Chetro Ketl as well as at Pueblo Bonito, where it has been dated to this same time period. A second construction period began sometime in the 990s and continued intermittently to about 1030. Again, no buildings from this period seem to have survived later remodeling, though they may lie below unexcavated portions of the pueblo. The masonry type used in this early structure is not known. A third and major building period at Chetro Ketl extended from about 1036 to 1040 and resulted in the construction of much of the northern room block of the presently known pueblo, including Room 93.

The masonry of Room 93 is "narrow banded with core" (Bannister 1965: 149). On the basis of his work with Chetro Ketl wood, Bannister was able to refine Hawley's dating of "narrow banded with core" type masonry to approximately A.D. 1038-1054, noting that the data suggest that "construction in the north block of rooms probably started in 1038 or 1039, and . . .two later clusters of 1043-1047 and 1051-1053 indicate continued building activity which was probably concentrated in the upper stories. By 1054 construction in this part of the ruin seems to have been essentially completed . . . ."

Subsequent construction at Chetro Ketl has been summarized by Hawley (1934: 77-8). "Between 1060 and 1090 extensive re-modeling, re-building, and new additions resulted in the growth of Chetro Ketl on the ground plan as we know it today, with the exception of the few additions made in the following period. The third and last main period, 1099-1116, was brief, a period marked by architectural degeneration." There is general agreement that the Chacoan occupation of Chetro Ketl probably had ended by about A.D. 1120. There is some evidence at the site for a later brief and limited reoccupation by McElmo or Mesa Verdian groups.

[4]

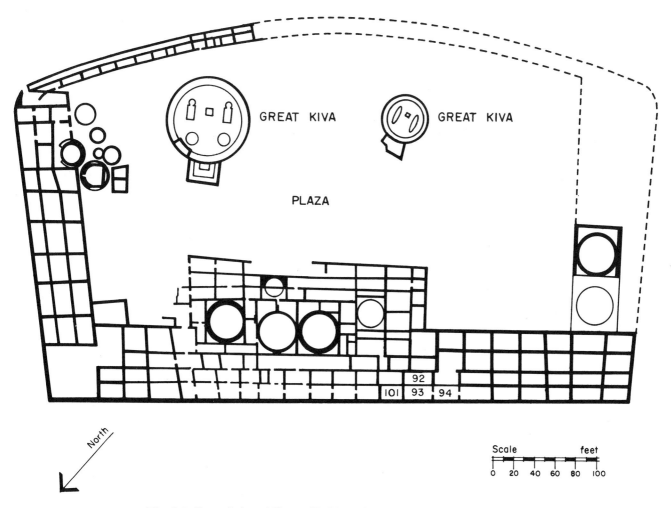

Fig. 2.1. Ground plan of Chetro Ketl (see also photograph, Fig. 1.1). Most of the painted wood was found in Room 93, and two fragments were found in Room 92; other pieces were recovered from the north room block, probably Rooms 94 and 101.

Room 93 (Fig. 2.2) is located in the back or northern room block near the western wing of the pueblo. Room 92, also shown in Figure 2.2, is discussed in Appendix E. It is in a section of the site that probably stood four or five stories high. The designation Room 93 is given both to a second-story room and the first-story room below it. Unless otherwise indicated, all references to Room 93 apply to the second-story room in which the collection of painted wood was recovered. The first and second stories of Room 93 did not differ in size, construction, masonry type, or internal features from those of adjoining rooms. The first story remains intact as a room, its ceiling serving as the floor of the second story. The remaining walls of the second story are six to seven feet high with remnants of the third story present in the northeast corner. A masonry-filled doorway opening onto the outside of the pueblo was constructed in the center of the north wall, and

vestiges of two small vents are also located in the upper corners of this wall. Doorways were present in the center of both the east and west walls, but no similar opening was located in the south wall bordering Room 92. A floor hatchway in the southwest corner opened into the first-story room and access was made easier by a large step or landing in the widened south wall of the room below.

Is is a commentary on the imponderables of excavation and the part that chance plays in our view of a past culture when the circumstances surrounding the discovery of the painted wood are considered in terms of the investigation of Chetro Ketl. The first-story room had been entered in 1880-1886 through a hole broken in the outer north wall just above the present ground surface as indicated by inscriptions scratched in the wall plaster. The room to the west, Room 94, was partially cleared by Hewett in 1921, and Room

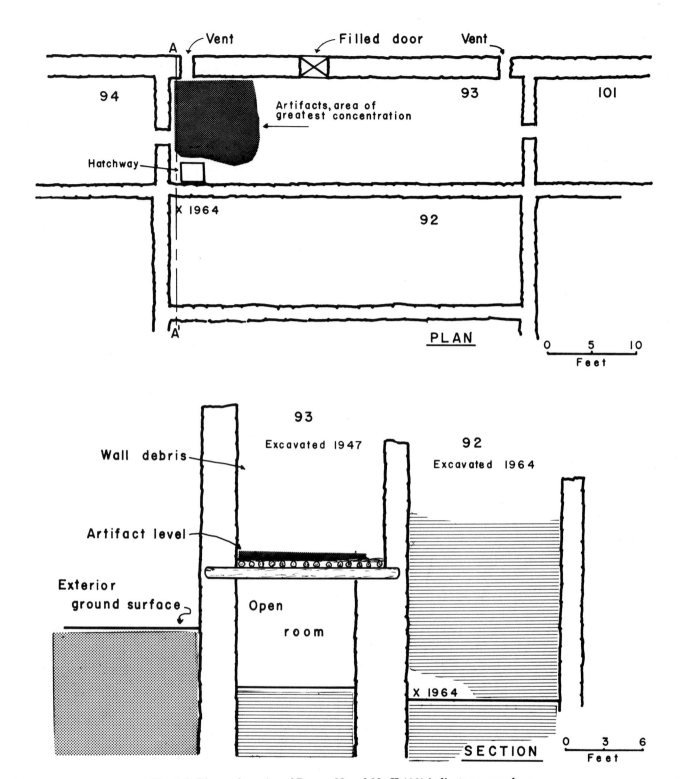

Fig. 2.2. Plan and section of Rooms 92 and 93. *X 1964* indicates area where
two fragments of painted wood were found in Room 92.

101 on the east was excavated during the 1929-1934 research directed by Hewett. In 1947 came the discovery of the wood in Room 93, and in 1964 Room 92, on the south, was excavated by the National Park Service.

LOCATION AND CONDITION OF THE COLLECTION

All of the artifactual, vegetal, faunal, and lithic debris found in Room 93 was in a layer five to seven inches thick, mixed with fine sand and silt, directly on the floor surface. In addition to being protected from ground moisture by its position above ground level and by the open space of the room below, the collection was shielded from other moisture by a thick layer of juniper bark that had fallen from the ceiling and by six to seven feet of wall debris. There were no refuse deposits in this or higher rooms, nor were vigas, construction timber, or other datable wood present in the fill.

While much of the painted wood was concentrated in the northwestern part of the room (see Fig. 2.10), fragments, many no larger than a matchstick, were scattered about the floor. Mixed with the artifacts were a few animal bones, some lithics, and various vegetal remains tentatively identified by Edward Castetter as flint corn, pumpkin rind and seed, cucurbit stem, common kidney bean, pinyon nut shells, cockleburs, and reed stems (personal communication to R. Gordon Vivian, Feb. 19, 1948). Corn, in the form of cobs, kernels, husks, tassels, and stems, was the most prevalent item. Many pieces of hard-fiber cordage and split yucca leaves tied in knots or short loops were also present in the artifact layer.

The great majority of the wooden objects in the room were fragmentary. Only six pieces were complete, showing no broken edges; all others showed some kind of fracturing. Attempts to match small and large fragments resulted in the repair of only small portions of a few objects. The remaining 60 to 80 small splinters and slivers cannot account for the many missing pieces in these objects. Interestingly, certain pieces seem to be almost selectively incomplete. For example, the collection includes birds' heads, bills, wings, tails, and possibly body parts, but none directly match or fit together. Other problematical forms are the similar but unmatching halves of an ovate (Fig. A.20) and portions of four plaques (Figs. A.30, A.31). All of these objects, and others, are incomplete; most differ from one another in basic outline and in paints, and they cannot be related positively to anything else in the collection.

The incompleteness of the items is made more interesting by the fact that at least fifteen similar fragments have been found in rooms adjoining Room 93.

Judging from form and paint, it seems likely that they belong to the assemblage from Room 93. Thirteen of these pieces of wood were found during Hewett's excavations from 1929 through 1934 in the northern room block. Their exact provenience is not known. In addition, two painted fragments similar to specimens from Room 93 were recovered from Room 92 in 1964 when that room was excavated by Charles Voll (see Appendix E). The close similarity of all of these specimens suggests that scattering of the original painted wooden objects took place when rooms in this part of the pueblo were intact or partially open.

Many artifacts found in archaeological context occur in a broken, burned, and often incomplete condition. When excavated they are usually interpreted as discarded items tossed into refuse heaps, or as complete articles left in rooms and subsequently damaged by collapse, room filling, fire, or decay. The positioning of the objects on the floor of Room 93 and the shallow fill above do not suggest a refuse area. There is no evidence for the collapse of the entire roof into Room 93, nor is there any suggestion that the room was destroyed by fire. Roof collapse on a complete collection could have destroyed some objects, but all fragments should have been present considering the good state of preservation of the collection. A few of the objects were partially burned, but burning did not appear to have taken place in the room. There was apparently little loss of the artifacts through decay, except for some soaking off of paints after contact with moisture that percolated through the room fill.

The possibility of ceremonial effacement and sacrifice may be considered as a reason for the selectively incomplete nature of the collection. Examples from the Mogollon region of the ritual "killing" of Mimbres bowls or the possible parallel of Mimbres "killing" in the cache of bows and arrows found by Hibben (1938: 36-8) in the Mogollon Mountains may be cited, but similar examples of destruction of ritual objects in the Pueblo area, either archaeologically or ethnographically, have not been reported. Sandpaintings and wall paintings are erased and altars and fetishes are put away at the end of certain phases of Pueblo ceremonies, but revered objects are not destroyed, only deposited in shrines or stored in special places.

Prehistoric vandalism cannot be discounted as an explanation for the condition of the collection. Judd (1954: 85, 335), for example, found considerable evidence for the intentional disturbance of burials in Pueblo Bonito, and a number of the wooden objects from Room 93 exhibit possible signs of intentional destruction. For instance, one of the rounded carved prayersticks (Fig. A.39 *b*) was severed with a sharp cutting instrument, and three similar objects (Fig. A.39 *c-d*) appear to have been snapped like kindling wood. At least one item (Fig. A.10 *b*) may have been destroyed by twisting and breaking, and breaks on a number of items (Figs. A.2 *a*, A.5 *d*, A.7 *g*, A.12, A.14 *c*, A.22, for example) could have been made by snapping them apart with the hands.

CLASSIFICATION SCHEMES

A number of attempts have been made to classify the painted and carved items from Room 93. Because at least two of the pieces recovered definitely represented birds (Figs. A.1 *a*, A.2 *a*), there was an early association made between many of the wood fragments and parts of birds. In addition to the obvious bird heads, single or composite items were identified as tails, wings and bills. The tendency to interpret many of the fragments as bird parts influenced some classifications of the collection and also probably led to the identification of other zoomorphic forms in the collection including horns and parts of serpents. In addition to zoomorphic forms, a number of the specimens have been referred to as flowers or flower petals. Dodgen divided the carved and painted objects into two general groups: flat carved items and items carved in-the-round. These groups were then subdivided into smaller categories primarily on the basis of shape of the artifact, and individual items within each smaller grouping were given a descriptive reference. For example, "parrot," "turkey head," and "plumed serpent or bird head" were three of the items described individually under the bird grouping of flat carved wood. The Youngs retained most of Dodgen's groupings but divided much of the painted and carved wood portion of the collection into life forms and non-life forms. Life forms were subdivided into animal, plant, and miscellaneous groups and each of these was further divided into smaller categories, many of them represented by only one item in the collection. The bird grouping of the animal category, for example, included black bird (turkey), blue bird, and green bird (parrot).

Recognizing the inherent danger of this type of classification for interpretive purposes, Morrison developed a typology for the wood artifacts based on a number of attributes including the material, the type of modification of the material (flat or carved in-the-round), the construction (composite or unitary), the contour (angular or curvilinear), the surface (painted or unpainted), the coloration (monochrome or polychrome), and the aspect (bifacial or unifacial). This system, while largely accurate, was cumbersome to use and subject to simple transcribing error. Item 2528 (Fig. A.19 *a*), a scalloped disc fragment, for example, would have been classified as FUCPMB, indicating that the specimen was flat, of unitary construction, curvilinear, and painted bifacially in a monochrome color. After a brief period of using Morrison's system it was abandoned for a more descriptive classification.

The terminology used in this chapter and in Appendix A is a modification of that developed by Dodgen. The major changes are the use of broader terms to include more items under a single category, and a shift away from zoomorphic terms wherever possible. Dodgen had grouped the specimens into broad categories of objects and had labeled a few of the general categories. This original categorization was simply extended to include all the objects, and in this way a number of new categories were developed. Carved and painted wooden objects made up the bulk of the collection. These artifacts were divided into two major categories: flat carved forms and round carved forms. Other articles from Room 93 were classified as miscellaneous wood and vegetal objects, vegetal remains, faunal remains, and lithics. All specimens, with the exception of scraps of wood, braid, and cordage, are described individually and in detail in Appendix A. A descriptive summary of the categories developed is given below for reference and for comparative purposes on a less detailed scale.

FLAT CARVED FORMS

Most of the artifacts from Room 93 were classified as flat carved forms, and this group included more sub-categories than the round carved forms. With the exception of the wands (Fig. A.23), none of the specimens were complete enough to postulate reconstruction of the entire original form, but the flat carved objects seem to represent parts of a composite article in most instances. Suggestions of the composite nature of many of the original items are present in such specimens as the oval form with handle (Fig. A.12).

Similar composites are represented by birds' heads, bills, and tails (Figs. A.2, A.3), and the multiple slat forms (Fig. A.25). In addition to the fact that most of the forms were composites of parts, many individual parts were constructed of two or more pieces of wood. For example, some bird tails (Fig. A.5), rectangles (Fig. A.16), and ovates (Figs. A.20, A.21) are comprised of joined sections of wood that constitute a single element.

Flat carved forms are in most instances fashioned from thin sections of wood and are usually painted, often on both sides. The composites were most commonly joined by bindings and ties of various fibers, though an adhesive resin was used on several of the pieces. Materials other than wood utilized in fashioning the artifacts were limited to the tanned hide topknot of one bird head (Fig. A.2 *b*) and the reed or bulrush stem binding on the handle of a wand (Fig. A.23). Various forms were identified within the flat carved category. They are summarized below.

Fig. 2.3. Parts of birds. *Clockwise from bottom:* tail (Fig. A.3); head (Fig. A.2 *b*); head (reverse of Fig. A.2 *a*); bill (Fig. A.2 *c*); head (Fig. A.1 *a*).

Birds (Figs. 2.3, 2.4, A.1-A.7). As presently categorized, verifiable and possible bird forms constitute a small number of the total artifacts recovered (Fig. 2.3). Other forms may represent bird parts. The Youngs, for instance, classified what are here called plaques (Fig. A.22) as possible body parts of "black birds." Elements included in the birds category of Appendix A include heads (Figs. A.1, A.2), bills (Fig. A.2), tails (Figs. A.3-A.5), and wings (Fig. A.6). The parrot head (Figs. 2.3, A.1 *a*) is probably the most noteworthy example from the entire collection and may have consisted of a single element, though the Youngs postulated a composite form for this specimen (Fig. 2.4). Other head fragments are less clearly defined as to type of bird or method of construction, though the Youngs utilized one head (Fig. A.2 *a*) in the reconstruction of the "basket bird" (Fig. 2.4) and

tentatively identified the bird as a turkey. Bird tails (Figs. 2.3, A.3-A.4) consist of fan-shaped and usually scalloped-edge pieces striped with color and with wooden attachments or tie holes. Another group of elements identified as bird tails (Fig. A.5) differ appreciably from the fan-shaped group. In many respects these latter elements are like the artifacts identified as slats. Bird wings (Fig. A.6 *a-d*) are even more tenuously identified and consist of only parts of two sets of wings. Painting, scalloping on the edges, and form were the primary attributes used for this identification. A number of fragments like these that were too large not to be illustrated and described, but too incomplete to determine accurately their original shape, were simply categorized as possible bird forms (Figs. A.6-A.7) on the basis of their vague similarities to other bird forms.

[9]

Fig. 2.4. Hypothetical reconstructions of birds. *Left,* bird with parrot head (cf. head, Fig. 2.3; tail, Fig. A.4 *d*). *Right,* "basket bird" (cf. head, tail, Fig. 2.3; wings, Fig. A.6; hoop, Fig. A.13).

Horns (Figs. A.8-A.11). The term "horn" was believed to be more representative of the shape of these artifacts than the term "curved objects," employed in some of the original descriptions. By using this term, however, there is the suggestion that these items constitute another category of animate forms in the collection. This may not be the case, though the shape is strongly reminiscent of bison horns. Examples in the collection are basically of two types: a short, broad, heavily curved version (Figs. A.8-A.9), and a longer, narrower, crescentic version (Figs. A.10, A.11 *a*). In addition, there are a number of tips of these forms that may be representative of either the long or short versions. The number of attachment holes in most of the objects suggests that both types had appendages. All of the examples were painted; the short type was most commonly solidly colored, while the longer version was more often divided into two different colored strips. The Youngs classified several of the short, green-colored specimens as leaves.

Oval Form with Handle (Fig. A.12). The artifact is one of the more complete examples from Room 93, though it probably represents only a portion of a composite object. The Youngs utilized this specimen as the base for the reconstructed "basket bird" (Fig. 2.4). It has not been classified with any of the other artifacts, although the oval shape is reminiscent of the ovate category.

Hoops (Fig. A.13) Four short fragments curved and painted wood probably represent parts of a single hoop constructed of two or more thin pliable laths sewn together after being bent into a circle. Paint was applied after the laths were attached together. There is no evidence for other attachments to the hoop, although the Youngs used these fragments in their reconstruction of the "basket bird."

Miscellaneous Forms (Figs. A.14-A.15). The twelve objects illustrated comprise a category only in terms of their unrelatedness to each other (except for paired items *a* and *b*, and *c* and *d* in Fig. A.15) and to other objects recovered from Room 93.

Rectangles (Fig. A.15 *h-1*). This particular form, like slats, appears to have been manufactured only as a part of a composite and not as an element that was utilized by itself. Attachment perforations in all of the examples and binding in some of the items indicated that a number of rectangles were sewn together to form a strip or band. Both sides of the existing examples are painted, suggesting that the pieces were fixed to wand laths (Fig. A.23).

Discs (Figs. 2.5, A.16-A.19). Three types of carved and painted discs were identified. These were round discs (Figs. A.16 *a-g*, A.17 *a*), perforated and appended discs (Fig. A.7 *b-e*), and scalloped discs (Figs. A.5, A.18-A.19). The round and scalloped discs are all shaped from single pieces of wood (item *a* in Fig. A.17 was split in manufacture and mended with bindings). Perforations in the center or on the edge of many specimens suggest that most were probably appended to or suspended from another element. Two of the complete scalloped discs (Figs. 2.5, A.18 *d-e*) were originally called flowers. In general, decoration on round and scalloped discs consists of contrasting center and encircling colors. The perforated and appended discs do not conform entirely to the disc category and were originally labeled horns. Remaining fragments indicate that they were composed of three pieces of wood and may not have been totally disc-shaped. Item *c* in Fig. A.17 suggests that the perforation in the disc may have been closed at the top forming a circular hole and not a hooked projection as is suggested by items *b*, *d*, and *e*. The method for appending these discs is clearly unlike that used with the round and scalloped types, suggesting a different use in composite forms. Decoration of this disc type was similar to rounded and scalloped types.

Ovates (Figs. 2.6, A.20-A.21). Ovates are thin oval wood slabs decorated on both surfaces. The two specimens recovered represent the most elaborate painting in the collection. Both objects were formed of two or more sections of wood bound together into an oval shape. These artifacts are similar to the oval element in the oval form with handle artifact, with the major exception that all perforations and ties on ovates are for joining the parts of the oval and do not appear to have been used for appending a handle. Neither is

Fig. 2.5. Scalloped discs (*top row, left to right:* Fig. A.18 *a, b, c; second row:* Fig. A.18 *d, e*); scalloped semicircular fragments (*third row, left and center:* Fig. A.19 *b, a; bottom:* Fig. A.19 *c*); semicircular fragment (*third row, right:* Fig. A.19 *d*).

Fig. 2.6. Ovate disc fragments (*left:* Fig. A.21; *right:* Fig. A.20 *a-b*).

there any evidence to suggest that the ovates were suspended. Resin near the center of the largest ovate (Fig. A.21), however, was interpreted by Dodgen as possibly having been used as an adhesive for a handle.

Plaques (Fig. A.22). This is not an entirely appropriate term for these objects, although a similar item recovered in 1936 from a village site in Chaco Canyon, Bc 50, was classified as a plaque or tablita (Brand and others 1937: Frontispiece, 96). The four examples recovered all have essentially the same shape, consisting of an oval to round eared plaque with a basal rectangular extension of unknown length. An appended scrap of wood near the top of one plaque and perforations on the others in the same location indicate that an additional piece was attached to the top of the plaque. Dodgen has suggested that the unpainted striped areas on the ears may have been the location of slotted appendages or large quills of attached feathers.

Wands (Figs. A.23-A.24). One almost totally reconstructed wand (Fig. A.23) out of a group of three represents the most complete composite item in the Room 93 collection. These objects were originally identified as zoomorphic wands and the heads at the top of the slats were considered by Dodgen to represent serpents. In addition to representing the most intact examples from the collection, the wands, with their multiple differing parts joined by sewing and resins, served as an indicator of the probable composite nature of most of the other fragmentary objects recovered.

Slats (Figs. 2.7, 2.8, A.24-A.34). The greatest number of items in the collection were those identified as slats. Some of the best-preserved examples are shown in Fig. A.25 and an assortment of types in Fig. 2.7. These include 83 artifacts represented by single pieces or attached sets of two or more pieces. The fact that this particular form was the most common element used in the construction of the carved and painted wooden objects is demonstrated not only by the large number of individual pieces, but by the use of slats in the construction of several more complete objects in the collection. The striped bird tails (Fig. A.5 *a-d*), the base of the oval form with handle (Fig. A.12), an ovate (Fig. A.20), and the wands (Figs. A.23-A.24) all are constructed totally or in part of joined slats.

Attributes common to most of the slats are their elongated shape, a tendency to taper at the proximal end, curving or other shaping of the distal end, side

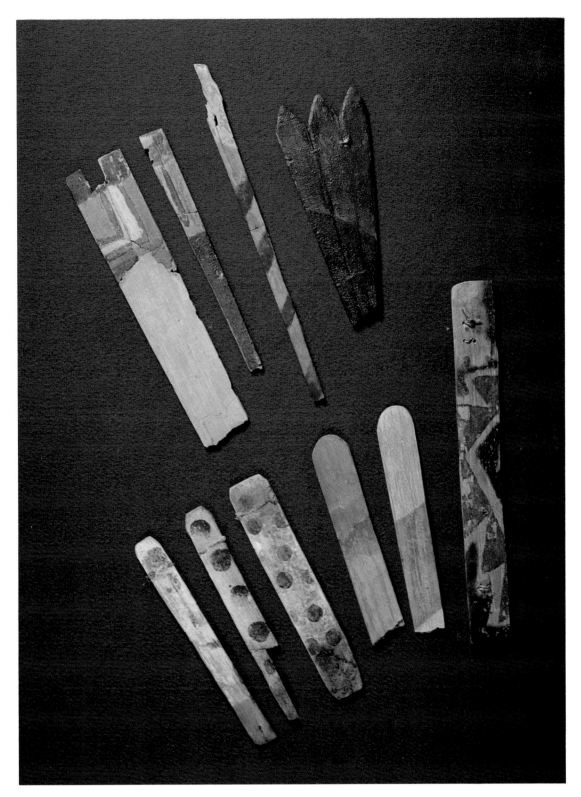

Fig. 2.7. Decorated slats (*top row, left to right:* reverse of Fig. A.26 *a;* Fig. A.26 *b, e;*
Fig. A.28 *g; bottom row:* Fig. A.29 *c, d, e;* Fig. A.30 *a, b;* Fig. A.33 *e).*

Fig. 2.8. "Plume circle" (Fig. A.32 a).

perforations for attaching ties at the distal end, and central perforations and notching of the proximal end for attachment. Slat shape and the method of attachment suggest that composite forms constructed of slats were fan-like, or possibly circular as in the "plume circle" example (Figs. 2.8, A.32). One example (Fig. A.34 e) may have served as the primary lath for construction of a wand as its features resemble rather closely the two wand laths. Most slats were painted; in most instances motifs and coloring were repeated on both sides of the slat. Dodgen identified individual slats as plumes and petals, and one partially reconstructed composite form (Figs. 2.8, A.32) was described as a plume circle. There is little evidence that slats were used in the composite construction of bird or floral forms, though one particular shape (Fig. A.34 h-j) identified by Dodgen as snake-lightning may represent a zoomorphic form. It stands out among the other slat elements and could be considered as a separate form.

ROUND CARVED FORMS

The second major grouping of the carved and painted wood is represented by considerably fewer forms and individual elements. Only five types of artifacts were defined in this group: arrowshafts, bows, a lightning lattice, prayersticks, and plume holders. The majority of these objects were not carved in-the-round, but were constructed of rounded rather than flat elements. Some of the arrowshafts (Fig. A.35), in fact, consist of round elements combined with flat carved elements which, under other circumstances, might have been identified as slats. The only forms in this category that can be considered to have been carved in-the-round are the prayersticks and the cone plume holder (Figs. 2.9, A.39 a-f). In addition to differing from the flat carved group by including round elements, more artifacts in this group are single rather than composite forms. Thus, objects such as the bows, prayersticks, and plume holders served as the total form, not parts of composite forms. Many of the elements retain traces of paint, though compared to the flat carved forms, these artifacts are not highly decorated.

Arrows (Figs. 2.9, A.35, A.37). The fragmentary arrows in the collection were classified by Dodgen as non-functional and functional. Non-functional arrows (Figs. 2.9, A.35, A.37 a-b) were constructed of solid wood mainshafts and foreshafts with flat carved wood elements to simulate feather fletching. All specimens were painted. Fragments of functional arrows (Fig. A.37 c-i) included reed mainshafts and solid wood foreshafts. The fletched portions of most mainshafts retained remnants of fletching quills. Some painting occurred on a few of the functional arrows.

Bows (Fig. A.36). Portions of five bows were recovered from Room 93. Dodgen listed all as non-functional. These objects were classified as bows on the

[14]

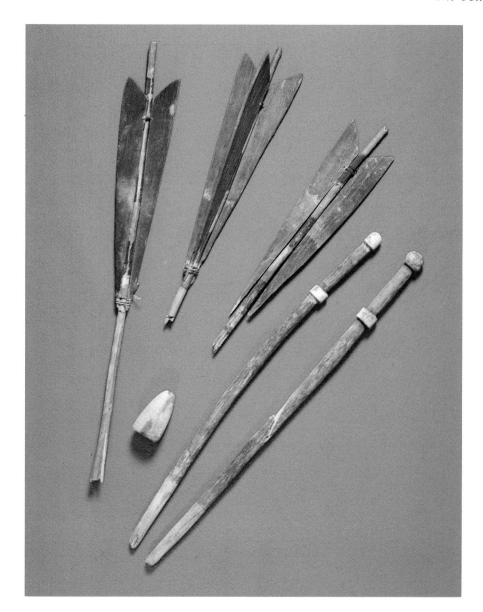

Fig. 2.9. Arrows (*left to right:* reverse of Fig. A.35 *b*; reverse of Fig. A.35 *a*; reverse of Fig. A.35 *c*); prayersticks (Fig. A.39 *a, b*); cone (Fig. A.39 *f*).

basis of the shape and curvature of the item, and the presence of a bowstring nock on the end of one specimen. All had been wrapped completely with cordage and then covered with resin.

Lightning Lattice (Fig. A.38). Twenty-seven perforated and flattened sticks of similar shape were identified tentatively as parts of a lightning lattice. If the sticks were joined through the perforations so as to construct a diamond lattice, the constriction of two sticks at one end of the lattice would presumably cause the lattice to extend, thus shooting out like lightning. Twenty-two of the sticks were burned at one end. The lattice can be constructed so that the burned ends occur only on one side.

Prayersticks (Figs. 2.9, A.39 *a-e*). Five objects found in Room 93 have been referred to by Dodgen and others as pahos or prayersticks. This identification is based primarily on the use of the term prayerstick for similar objects from other archaeological locations. Objects identical to the specimens in Figure A.39 *a* and *b* were found in Pueblo Bonito and were called ceremonial sticks by Pepper (1920). The term "ferrule stick" has also been used for these knobbed and ringed artifacts. The specimens in Figure A.39 *c* through *e* may not belong to the same class of artifacts as specimens *a* and *b*. They are larger and unpainted, and their original length may have exceeded the normal limits for most prayersticks.

Fig. 2.10. Artifact distribution in the western end of Room 93, Chetro Ketl.

Plume Holders (Figs. 2.9, A.39 *f*, *g*). Two artifact forms were identified as plume holders, though the basis for this identification is slight. The specimen in Figure A.39 *f* is a cone-shaped form made of yucca or agave stalk that was partially hollowed in the basal portion and perforated longitudinally. A strand of sinew in the perforation suggested the possible attachment of feathers or down. The second form of holder (*g*) includes 35 rounded, small sticks that were burned on one end and split longitudinally at the opposite end. Feather barbules were found in the split ends of two of the sticks.

MISCELLANEOUS OBJECTS

Wooden and Vegetal Objects

This grouping includes artifacts that were probably used in the construction of composite carved and painted forms, including painting of decorated elements, and some that may have been used in association with the composites. Several of the specimens may not be artifacts or may not have been associated originally with the objects described in the preceding categories. Summaries of individual groups are not given here, inasmuch as these summaries would essentially parallel those given in Appendix A. In general, the kinds of items represented in this grouping conform to those that would be expected as paraphernalia of Pueblo ritual, as for example the curved wrapped sticks (Fig. A.41 *a*), and paired sticks (Fig. A.41 *e-f*), and the cornhusk packets (Fig. A.41 *h-j*). Artifacts identified in this category include assorted sticks, paint brushes and applicator sticks, curved wrapped sticks, paired sticks, twig hoops, twig loop, cornhusk packets, carved cucurbita rind, reed cigarette, twigs, reed and yucca loops, and matting.

Cordage

More than 170 pieces of cordage were recovered from Room 93 (Fig. A.43). These included string or twine of sinew, bark, yucca fiber, and cotton. The use of cordage in the collection is reviewed below in the section on joining and attachment, and an analysis of the kinds of cord recovered is given in Appendix B.

Vegetal Remains, Faunal Remains, and Lithics

In addition to the items described in the categories above, a few plant remains, some scraps of bone, bits of feather and tanned hide, and several simple stone tools were found in Room 93. These items were more reminiscent of refuse than any of the other objects found in the room. They have been described in Appendix A because of their association with other artifacts in the room.

WOODWORKING

A strong tradition of wooden sculpture is characteristic of the American Southwest, where wood is available, and simple carving in-the-round was practiced to some extent among the early Pueblo peoples, so far as preservation has allowed such evidence to be known. At least two examples are known from Chaco Canyon. A snake fashioned from a cottonwood root, probably by only slightly altering the original root shape, was recovered by Judd at Pueblo Bonito (1954: 278); and a small wooden frog was found at Kin Kletso (Vivian and Mathews 1965: 101-2). Because the Chetro Ketl collection is incomplete, pieces carved in-the-round, such as bird bodies to which flat tails, wings, heads, and bills were attached, could have existed. The concept of assembling flat carved pieces to produce three-dimensional representations of life forms and other symbols appears to be a successful adjustment to the material, rather than a limitation imposed by it. Generally speaking, it appears that flat carving of wood was more typical of the prehistoric pueblos, and that the carving in-the-round typical of modern Zuni and Hopi kachina dolls is a recent economic adjustment (Dockstader 1954: 104-5).

Evidence of probable carpentry techniques can be discerned from examination of the surfaces and edges of the pieces when correlated with our knowledge of prehistoric woodworking tools. Stone axes, blades, saws, and a variety of sandstone abrading tools were used for splitting, trimming, shaping, and smoothing large and small timbers into the desired forms and shapes. Use of the abundant, fine sandstone in Chaco Canyon for tools undoubtedly accounts for the thinness and smoothness of most of the pieces. Examples of these tools include several thin slabs, worn as though used as saws, and several pointed implements and flat tablets from Pueblo Bonito. From Pueblo del Arroyo six long, narrow files of the same material were recovered (Judd 1954: 118-26). Carpentry techniques used on the production of wooden planks found at Chetro Ketl have been described by R. Gordon Vivian (1949), and it may be presumed that similar woodworking was employed on the smaller forms found in Room 93. (See Appendix D for reference to the wood species used in the artifacts.)

The average thickness of the flat wooden objects from Room 93 is 0.35 cm; the range is from 0.15 cm to 0.7 cm. Edges of most of the objects have been either sanded smooth or are too heavily covered with paint to reveal edge-cutting techniques. Straight edges appear to have been sawed from both sides and then broken off. Most edges were finished; the majority are smoothly rounded and, less frequently, flattened or squared. As expected, the majority of flat pieces are carved with the greatest dimension parallel with the wood grain; only nine (Figs. A.1 *b*, *e*; A.3; A.4 *a-b*; A.28 *a*, *c*; and A.34 *f-g*) are cut diagonally across the grain.

Three objects were constructed by splicing separately carved and finished sections of wood together with sinew. The large oval base of the object in Fig. A.12 is composed of four slats stitched together. Shaping appears to have taken place before the slats were joined since the resultant outline is uneven and poorly matched. Two of the black striped tail fragments (Fig. A.5 *b-c*) and the two ovates (Figs. 2.6, A.20, A.21) also appear to have been formed from separately carved sections; adjacent edges were sanded smooth before splicing. Four pieces in the collection (Figs. A.1 *d*, A.2 *a*, A.17 *a*, and A.22 *b*) clearly have repaired breaks rather than splices. Sinew bindings hold together pieces that have split apart along the grain, probably during carving. Broken edges interlock and paints are applied over repair stitches in all four cases.

JOINING AND ATTACHMENT

Nearly all of the flat carved pieces are joined to one or more elements to form composite objects, or they show evidence of having once been so attached. The general method of joining the wooden pieces is by tying with cordage or other flexible material through perforations in the elements. Sinew is utilized in 173 instances, hard plant fiber in 35, and split twig in six. In most instances the method of tying or binding is relatively simple. The cord is looped one or more times through a hole in each wooden piece and then secured in one of several ways. It may be tied in a single knot or one end may be tucked under one loop or wrapped several times around a loop. In addition, both ends may be tucked into one hole and trimmed on both sides, or both ends may be tied in a knot *inside* one hole. Overhand, granny, and square knots were used. In eight instances the method of tying is more complicated. These methods, for which verbal description alone would be inadequate and unclear, are illustrated and discussed in more detail in Appendix B.

Probably all of the small (generally 1-2 mm diameter) perforations for the fiber bindings were drilled and then punched through the wood, but this was not always apparent because of the tight bindings in many holes and thick paint coverings. Striations around and inside of small holes are visible in only a few objects. The large holes on either side of the oval base of the

oval form with handle (Fig. A.12) appear to have been drilled first then enlarged by reaming or carving. Perforations on the multiple parts of the lightning lattices (Fig. A.38), all appear to have been drilled; under magnification two show fine sand around the orifices on one side and inside the holes, adhering in such a way as to suggest that the sand was wet when ground into the wood.

Most joined pieces seem to have generally symmetrical edges, but in at least one case (Fig. A.22 *a*) an appended fragment was slightly beveled along the edge that contacted the major piece, apparently to control the angle of projection. The fragment shown in Fig. A.1 *d* is thinner on the upper end of one surface. Apparently this was done to facilitate its fit to another piece by a parallel-side slot. It was held in place by a binding through two holes in the thinned, unpainted surface. The ends of wooden inserts are fitted into slots cut into the bird tails illustrated in Figs. A.3 and A.4 *d*, and held tightly in place with sinew ties. This construction feature may also have been employed on the smaller bird tail in Fig. A.4 *b*.

Examples of the use of pitch or resin as an adhesive are rare, though traces of resin appear on a number of the objects. Both sides of the squared end of the small black and white tail or wing (Fig. A.6 *e*) are covered with an uneven coat of resin. Its texture suggests its function as a glue rather than a painted band. Resin on the wands (Figs. A.23, A.24) may also have served to help hold the crosspieces to the primary slat. Finally, the small areas of resin on both sides of the large painted ovate (Figs. 2.6, A.21) could have served a similar function, but clear evidence is lacking.

The examples of attachment cited above have been of pieces that were apparently joined firmly into a rigid shape. The fragments of the matched wings (Figs. 2.4, A.6 *a-d*) furnish the best example of a possible flexible or movable joint. The two sections of each wing were first joined by two sinew ties, then apparently reinforced on one side by oval shaped pieces. This could have been a rigid material, but a support of textile or leather is possible. Within this oval-shaped, unpainted area on both wing fragments (Figs. 2.4, A.6 *d*) there are traces of a fine clay-like substance that could have been an adhesive used to attach backings to the hinge areas of the wings. Another small bird tail (Fig. A.4 *b*) has an unpainted area around the attachment perforations and presumably could have been joined similarly.

3. ARCHAEOLOGICAL COMPARISONS

Although wood was used in the manufacture of numerous items prehistorically, it is not commonly well preserved in open archaeological sites except occasionally as an element of habitation construction. Few wooden items have survived and the number of preserved wood artifacts that may have been used in a ritual context is limited. However, some wood artifacts, presumably utilized in ritual, have been found in the Southwest. The artifacts described below have been reported in the Anasazi and Mogollon literature. No attempt was made to record all of the numerous examples of the more simple single, double, or crook prayersticks or *pahos* that have been reported. Nor were wooden artifacts that had no apparent similarity to the Chetro Ketl specimens described. Attention was focused instead on composite wooden forms or simple forms that were painted or carved. Comparative examples are presented in terms of increasing distance from Chaco Canyon and follow the major divisions described for the collection in Chapter 2—flat carved forms, round carved forms, and miscellaneous wooden and vegetal objects. Site locations are shown in Figure 3.1.

FLAT CARVED FORMS

Other Chacoan Sites

Sites considered in this category include those in Chaco Canyon, the immediate vicinity of the canyon, and the Aztec Ruin. Examples of painted and carved wood have been reported from towns, villages and McElmo pueblos in the canyon area and from the Aztec Ruin, a townsite on the northern limits of the Chaco Basin. In general, flat carved and painted wood from Chacoan sites is not well documented in reports, but there is reason to believe that the number of fragmentary examples is larger than has been reported. For example, though no attempt was made to investigate the collections made by Pepper at Pueblo Bonito or Morris at Aztec, their occasional references to "altar fittings" recovered from their excavations suggest that undescribed examples of this type of artifact are present in the collections.

A number of specimens were recovered from Pueblo Bonito by Judd and Pepper. While Pepper removed a large number of wooden objects and frag-

ments of objects during his excavations at Pueblo Bonito, he failed to describe many of them. For example, he reports (Pepper 1909: 369, Table 5) that Room 1 produced 194 pieces of worked wood, the second largest number of wooden objects from a single room in this townsite, but no further description of the individual items is given. There is also some confusion about the provenience of several specimens. For instance, Pepper (1920: Table 5) lists two painted slabs from Rooms 32 and 99 in Pueblo Bonito but describes only the object from Room 32. An illustration (Pepper 1920: Fig. 101) of a "painted board" from the debris "near Room 63" could possibly be the Room 99 board, although these two rooms are widely separated in the site. One additional flat painted wood specimen from an undescribed room (Room 169) is illustrated but not described in detail. None of the illustrated or described specimens exactly duplicates any of the objects found in Room 93 at Chetro Ketl.

The only complete wooden artifact reported by Pepper (1920: Pl. 8 *a*) is the Room 32 design board (Fig. 3.2), which was associated with a large number of carved prayersticks. The board was essentially square (16.5 cm by 17.5 cm) and thicker (1.7 cm) than most of the Chetro Ketl flat objects. It was painted on both sides with design elements that were basically similar. One flat surface was decorated in an interlocking, serrated fret design painted in black and green on a red background. The design was carried over the edges to the opposite side where a similar interlocking fret design, without serrated edges, was painted in black and deep carmine on a red background. Designs on both sides were outlined in orange. The only other modification on the board was a hole drilled through one corner for possible suspension. Pepper (1920: 159) suggested that the board may have been an altar slab. The design style was similar to that painted on an ovate form (Figs. 2.7 *b*, A.21) in the Chetro Ketl collection.

The second painted board, from near Room 63, was not described but was illustrated by Pepper (1920: Fig. 101). Two edges appear finished, so it may be assumed that the shape was slat-like, though dimensions are unknown, and it is not known if the object was painted on both surfaces. Design elements were geometric, interlocking frets with some serrated edges,

Fig. 3.1. Archaeological and ethnographic sites discussed in this report.

and judging from the illustration, at least three colors were employed in the painting. Another undescribed object from Room 169 is pictured as a disc with slightly angular scalloping on about three-quarters of the circumference (Pepper 1920: Fig. 139). A possible attachment is shown on the unscalloped edge, though means for appending the attachment is not apparent. The object appears to have been perforated in the center and was painted in three single bands of red, yellow, and green.

Although none of the objects recovered by Judd from Pueblo Bonito matched specimens found by Pepper in terms of the elaborate painting, Judd does illustrate a wider range of flat carved and painted wood. Three of the best preserved objects include two half discs (Judd 1954: Fig. 75 a-b) decorated with black paint (Fig. 3.3 a-b). Specimen a, which had a circular section removed from the center of the disc, is similar in shape and painted decoration to a semicircular piece from Chetro Ketl (Fig. A.32). A third object (Judd 1954: Fig. 76) was a portion of a flat "arrow" (Fig. 3.3 c) that resembles quite closely the slat arrow from Chetro Ketl (Fig. A.14 c). This object retained traces of orange and green paint on both surfaces and was perforated for possible attachments. The original shape of most of the other specimens has been so altered by decay and wood shrinkage that close comparison with the Chetro Ketl specimens is difficult. Several short sections of wood that may have been pieces of wide slats are illustrated by Judd (1954: Pl. 78), and a number of oval or rounded pieces that vaguely resemble the ovates and plaques of the Chetro Ketl collection are also shown. Similarly, one small piece, i, in the Judd illustration has a scalloped edge reminiscent of the Chetro Ketl bird wings (Figs. 2.4, A.6 a-d). Most of these items were painted on both surfaces in green. Two of the items were decorated with diagonal blue lines.

In addition to the above specimens, which Judd referred to as altar fragments, a number of utilitarian wooden items he found at Pueblo Bonito are of interest because of painting or shape. Three fragmentary perforated discs shaped from single pieces of juniper were identified by Judd (1954: 153, Fig. 42) as spindle whorls, but they closely resemble the round Chetro Ketl discs (Figs. 2.6, A.17-A.18). One of the Pueblo Bonito artifacts is decorated with differing patterns on each face in red, yellow, light green, and blue. The shape of one additional utilitarian item (Judd 1954: Pl. A.38 m) resembles the upper portion of the Chetro Ketl wands (Fig. A.24 a), though no painting or perforations for attachments are present in the Pueblo Bonito specimen.

There are only limited examples of flat carved and painted wood from Pueblo del Arroyo, a townsite just

Fig. 3.2. "Design board" from Pueblo Bonito
(Pepper 1920: Pl. 8 a).

west of Pueblo Bonito. The most notable was a painted wooden sandal last (Judd 1959: 131, Fig. 29) prepared from a "tablet of cedar" and painted in a black geometric design on a green and red background. Judd considered this object to have been a possible altar piece and noted (1959: 131) that other "bits of painted wood from Rooms 44 and 62, too small to suggest either shape or size, may also have been parts of altar pieces." One additional item from Pueblo del Arroyo, a perforated slat of juniper that was described and illustrated by Judd (1959: 131, Fig. 28) as a handle, was not painted but may have been a component of a composite ritual wooden form.

Carved or painted flat wood objects from the Aztec Ruin, a Chacoan town on the Animas River northwest of Chaco Canyon, are only sketchily reported. A wooden disc on a cord and a "thin, rectangular slab, perforated at one corner and at mid point of one side" were found by Morris (1919a: 46) at Aztec, but apparently neither of these items was painted. Several fragments of painted alder or cottonwood bark found in a room formed a band about 6 cm wide and more than 25 cm long. The decorated side was painted with a green and reddish brown strip on each edge of the bark, leaving the center unpainted. Morris (1919a: 47) notes that, "A narrow black line in the form of a serpentine curve traverses each colored zone from end to end." Six items from Room 73 were

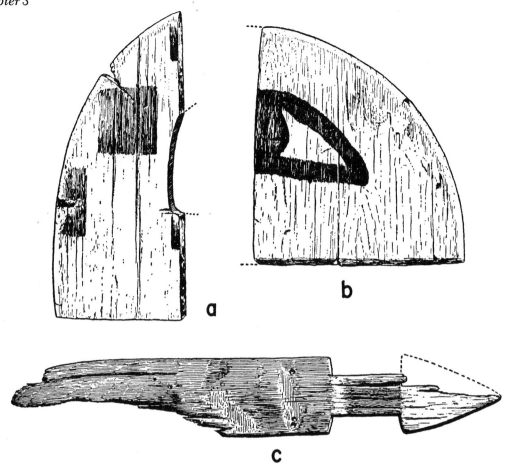

Fig. 3.3. Carved and painted wooden artifacts from Pueblo Bonito. Half discs,
a-b (Judd 1954: Fig. 75 *a-b*); portion of flat "arrow," *c* (Judd 1954: Fig. 76).

considered by Morris (1928: 313) to be portions of wooden altar fittings. These included "five small slabs of wood, a flattened stick painted black, [and] split willow painted red." The most striking objects recovered from Aztec were two painted wooden sandal lasts similar to that found at Pueblo del Arroyo in Chaco Canyon. Morris reported on these items in his La Plata report and their exact provenience at Aztec is not given. Only one is illustrated (Morris 1939: 132, Pl. 145) and it shows different geometric designs on each side of the last. Morris notes here that "against broad, unpainted strip across center of back was sewn a flat stave, opposite end of which presumably was thrust into earth to hold sandal form upright among altar fittings." The Pueblo del Arroyo specimen also had a broad, lightly painted zone across the center of the last, but Judd reported that the design covered this area and he described no perforations for attachments. The two lasts from Aztec were found "in a rubbish dump, together with other painted, wooden altar fittings" (Morris 1939:132).

Excavations at Kin Kletso, a McElmo pueblo in Chaco Canyon, produced only one specimen of painted wood. This object, a small strip of wood or possibly bark, was painted on both surfaces in a bright chalky green. Vivian and Mathews (1965: 101) considered the item to have been used in a ritual context.

One of the more complete collections of painted and carved wood from Chaco was found in a refuse deposit on the floor of Room 1 at Tseh So (Bc 50), a village site on the south side of Chaco Canyon opposite Pueblo Bonito and Chetro Ketl. At least seven pieces of wood were recovered and were described by the authors (Brand and others 1937: 96) as effigy forms. The objects were shaped from cottonwood that had been thinned to approximately the thickness of a shingle. The authors report that "the subjects were depicted both by outline and interior painting. This painting was primarily turquoise green and dead black, supplemented by white, dark red, and brown." The forms that were recognizable included "some sort of bird, a dragon fly, a human face, and possible portions of some animals." The frontispiece of the Tseh So report illustrates one of the objects which reportedly represents the form of a tablita of a human face. This object more closely resembles a fragmentary plaque similar to those from the Chetro Ketl collection (Fig. A.22). The decay and breakage of this item seems to have only fortuitously produced a human likeness in profile. This specimen is painted green and has a black and white eye motif near the center. Two bird wings (Brand and others 1937: Fig. 4 *a-b*), identified only on the basis of shape, may represent a soaring bird, but are unlike those found at Chetro Ketl. The Chetro Ketl specimens are shorter, do not have a pronounced curve, and have scalloped edges. At least two of the Tseh So objects (Brand and others 1937: Fig. 4 *c-d*) differ from the Chetro Ketl items in that they appear to have been fashioned by cutting out shapes rather than creating shapes by combining several single elements into a composite form through tying and gluing. None of the forms, with the exception of the "human face" plaque, closely duplicates specimens found at Chetro Ketl.

The small number and fragmentary nature of carved and painted flat wooden objects from other Chacoan sites limits a comprehensive comparison with the Chetro Ketl specimens, but several general observations can be made. At least two single elements, sandal lasts and square boards, found in other Chacoan sites are not present in the Chetro Ketl collection. Conversely, bird heads and horns, present at Chetro Ketl, are not reported from other sites. Fragmentary plaques, ovate forms, and discs are represented in several of the collections, and slats seem to be common elements, though in general the Chetro Ketl slats appear to be narrower than those found at Pueblo Bonito. There is more evidence for composite forms at Chetro Ketl, but this may reflect a lack of descriptive detail on items from other sites. The use of cottonwood at Tseh So and juniper at Pueblo del Arroyo is an interesting variant in woodworking contrasting with the use of pine at Chetro Ketl. There is seemingly more use of geometric motifs in specimens from other Chacoan sites, though the style of painting on the Tseh So artifacts rather closely parallels that of the Chetro Ketl wood. Colors utilized are similar, but orange, reported from Pueblo Bonito, was not used on the Chetro Ketl items. Finally, similar items from other sites usually appear as fragments in refuse deposits in abandoned rooms.

Other Anasazi Sites

Painted flat carved wood from other Anasazi sites is rare, and the few examples that have been reported are, for the most part, dated in the Pueblo III period. The earliest dated specimens are two simple pieces reported by Bartlett (1934: 35) from Medicine Cave (NA-863) in the San Francisco Mountains near Flagstaff. This site was dated in the middle Pueblo II period. One of the objects is a roughly plume-shaped thin section of wood with four perforations near the narrow end. A thin band of red paint crosses the wide, broken end. Edges on the item are rounded. The second piece is an irregularly shaped fragment with

one small and one large notch along opposing edges. A small area on one surface retains traces of a green malachite paint.

The most notable collection is the Sunflower Cave cache from Marsh Pass, west of Kayenta, Arizona (Kidder and Guernsey 1919: 145-7, Pl. 60-61). This cache, which included 26 wooden and two hide sunflowers, 25 wooden cones, and one painted bird carved in-the-round (Fig. 3.4), was found in a partial corrugated vessel in the cave floor. The wooden flowers are constructed of individual petals cut from thin flat slats of wood each of which is inserted into a groove encircling a cylindrical wooden center of cottonwood. The petals are held in place by a "black, pitchy gum" (Kidder and Guernsey 1919: 146). The petals are painted white or yellow, 21 of the flowers being yellow, five white. Many of the specimens have more than one coat of paint and three of the white flowers were originally yellow. The centers of the flowers, formed by the wooden cylinder, are painted black. The number of petals in the flowers ranged from 19 to 35; the outer diameter ranged from 7.6 to 16.3 cm. The bird is described under the section on round carved forms. Kidder and Guernsey (1919: 147) report that Fewkes examined the cache materials and believed that "the bird . . . formed part of an altar equipment similar to that of the Hopi flute altar. The 'sunflowers' were perhaps attached to the sides of helmet masks like those worn by the personators of Hopi Kachinas."

Other items from the Anasazi area have been found at Mesa Verde, Glen Canyon, and Jemez Cave. Two wooden slabs excavated at Spruce Tree House at Mesa Verde have been described by Fewkes (1909: 43, Fig. 16) as possible priests' badges, tablita parts, or altar slabs. These long, rectangular slabs are not painted but do have perforations at each corner on one end and two perforations on each side near the middle of the slab. Fewkes noted that these perforations could have served as binding holes and that the slabs may have been used as a cradle board rather than a religious object. The Glen Canyon specimens comprised two small pieces of flat carved wood collected from site NA-6456 in the lower Glen Canyon and dated in the 12th or 13th century (Adams, Lindsay, and Turner 1961: 51, Fig. 53). One is roughly square (approximately 2 cm on a side) with rounded corners and the other is a broken rectangular fragment with notching near the center. These items were not described or further identified. A small fragment of a wooden "gaming piece" decorated with "pencil-line-like marks" on one side was reported by Alexander and Reiter (1935: 47, Fig. 14) from Jemez Cave in New Mexico. This same site produced a fragment of a "sandal last (?)" shaped from thin soft wood and carefully smoothed on one side and end. No painted decoration was present.

Fig. 3.4. Wooden and leather artifacts from Sunflower Cave.
Wooden sunflowers, *a-c*; leather sunflower, *d*; wooden bird, *e*;
wooden cones, *f* (Kidder and Guernsey 1919: Pl. 61).

Mogollon Sites

Compared to the quantity of flat carved and painted wood from Anasazi sites, this type of artifact is plentiful in the Mogollon culture area. Virtually all of the items found have been recovered from dry caves, and in many instances the artifacts were on the surface or stacked together suggesting ritual use of the cave. This use of caves in the Mogollon area was probably common. For example, Lambert and Ambler (1961: 20) report that U-Bar Cave in the Alamo Hueco Mountains of New Mexico's panhandle was "used for ceremonial purposes rather than for habitation. . . [and produced] non-utilitarian artifacts such as pahos, 'tablita' fragments, [and] other pieces of painted wood. . . ."

Although deposits of painted wood have been recovered from sites of the Jornada, Mimbres, Cibola, and San Simon branches of the Mogollon culture area (Wheat 1955), their occurrence is mostly restricted to sites in a mountainous zone in southwestern New Mexico and southeastern Arizona drained by the Gila River and its tributaries, primarily the San Francisco and Blue rivers. This is predominantly Wheat's Mimbres area (Wheat 1954: Fig. 1), and the overlap into adjoining areas is slight. Mimbres branch sites

with carved and painted wood include the Alamo Hueco caves reported by Lambert and Ambler (1961), the Reserve area caves and cliff dwellings on the San Francisco River (Martin and others 1952; Martin and others 1954), the Bonita Creek cave (Wasley 1962), and the upper Gila (Silver City area) caves described by Hough (1914) and Cosgrove (1947). The Mimbres also includes Hough's Bear Creek Cave and the cliff dwellings at Gila Cliff Dwellings National Monument on the West Fork of the Gila River, where Gordon Vivian recovered several pieces of painted wood. The Hueco Mountains near El Paso, Texas, and Feather Cave in the Capitan Mountains of southcentral New Mexico are outside the Mimbres area and cave sites in these mountains are usually associated with the Jornada branch of the Mogollon.

In general the Mogollon specimens postdate A.D. 1000, though examples from O Block Cave and Cordova Cave in the Reserve area were dated in the Pine Lawn phase (ca. 150 B.C. to ca. A.D. 500) and other pre-Reserve phases.

Descriptions of flat carved and painted wood from the Mogollon region have frequently used the Spanish word *tablita* (or, equally correct, *tableta*), "small, thin board." Cosgrove (1947) was apparently the first to make use of this term in an archaeological context for describing artifacts from the Hueco Mountain area, though Hough (1914: 106) postulated that some of the specimens from the upper Gila region were parts of headdresses. Tablitas may be defined as thin, flat carved wooden objects, slats or slabs, usually painted or otherwise decorated, that occur either singly or as composites of two or more joined pieces. Most appear to be ritual in character, suggesting parts of historic Pueblo wooden ceremonial paraphernalia such as headdresses, altar pieces, and wands. Cosgrove (1947: 134) noted that "the name *tablita* has been rather arbitrarily restricted to objects made from thin strips of wood assembled to make miniature or full-sized headdresses, similar to those of the present-day Pueblo. The bird or flower symbols may have been either attached to headdresses or used independently as shrine offerings." The reference to shrine offerings suggests that Cosgrove did not limit the term to headdresses, though he noted that some tablita fragments "have no drill holes or marks to show, how, or if, they were intended to be attached to the dancer's head." Wasley (1962: 397) has commented on the general inappropriateness of this term for some archaeological items, a point we agree with, and it is used in this section only because of the precedent set by past Mogollon researchers.

Most tablitas were constructed from sections of lath cut from the bloom stalk of the yucca (usually *Yucca elata*), agave (*Agave palmeri*), or sotol (*Dasylirion wheeleri*). Tablitas consist of a number of separate pieces of lath tied or sewn together into a composite form. Cosgrove (1947: 132-4) has provided the best details on tablita construction, and the following remarks are abstracted from his description. Rectangular sections of lath were cut from the dry bloom stalk, scored and broken into desired lengths and sanded on the ends. Sides were not sanded but the edges were usually fairly even as a result of the straight grain of the material. Finished sections of lath ranged from 1 to 11 inches long, 3/4 to 1-3/4 inches in width, and 1/16 to 1/8 inch in thickness. Some lath was apparently used in single elements such as the split-stick wands described later, but most was used for constructing composite forms. These forms were built from the rectangular lath or lath that had been cut "into forms suggesting flower petals, feathers, or the complete wing of a bird" (Cosgrove 1947: 133). When shaping was finished, edges or ends of the piece were drilled or punctured for tying or sewing with a fiber or occasionally a cotton cord. Pitch or mesquite gum was occasionally used to hold elements together and "in 1 specimen . . . the laths are laid diagonally on top of each other, sewed and cemented together with pitch, making a stiff 2-ply board" (Cosgrove 1947: 133).

Not all wood used in these tablitas was of lily or amaryllis bloom stalk. Cosgrove (1947:132) reports a thin plate of juniper wood used in one form recovered from the upper Gila, and the tablitas found at Cordova Cave on the San Francisco River were all fashioned from unidentified wide pieces of wood that were split from slabs. Surfaces were not smoothed after splitting although some edges were smoothed. Thicknesses ranged from 0.1 to 0.8 cm. These specimens were rectangular in shape with two sets of holes in each board located near the center and midway between the middle and ends of the form. Several pieces of flat painted wood from other sites in the vicinity of Cordova Cave, including O Block Cave, Cosper Cliff Dwelling, and Hinkle Park Cliff Dwelling, were lath-like in shape but appear to be carved from wood and not bloom stalk. The painted bird offering from the Bear Creek Cave pictured by Hough (1914: Pl. 21) is so large that the material used in its construction probably was not bloom stalk. Cosgrove (1947: 135) reports that this artifact was made from yucca lath, but inasmuch as Hough had to depend on a photograph of the specimen for illustration and description, it is doubtful that construction material was known to Cosgrove. Another item reported by Hough from the Silver City area employed bloom stalk and a gourd rind disc.

Individual tablita elements, in addition to finished sections of plain lath, have been described as flower petals, feathers, and bird wings. Composite forms have been described as flowers, birds, plume or bird pahos, terraced objects, and tapered objects. One wooden kachina has also been reported by Lambert and Ambler (1961).

Some short sections of lath tapered at one end and rounded on the other, found in both the Mimbres and Jornada areas, have been interpreted as flower petals. Definite flower forms have been described by Wasley (1962) from a cache in a cave on Bonita Creek, a tributary of the Gila River in southeastern Arizona. This cache included five nested sets of joined petals strung together with cord. Although Wasley (1962: 384) referred to each nested set as a "flower," he noted that probably "each of these 'flowers' in reality represented a string of several flowers of the same type and color, with each individual set of petals representing a single flower." Each separate flower was constructed of eight or more separate petals fashioned from agave stalk. The flowers formed were concave in shape. Four of the five groupings consisted entirely of triangular-shaped petals; the fifth included 10 separate flowers with rounded petal edges and one flower with triangular petals. All petals were perforated with three holes, one near the pointed end and two on the lateral edges near the center. Agave fiber cordage was used to sew the petals together. Two sets of flowers were painted on both sides of the petals; one blue, the other green. A number of "wooden buttons" found in the top flower of the green set were interpreted as representing the androecium of the flower.

Flat, circular flowers or "sun discs" formed of single sections of lath or half-circles bound together were reported by Hough (1914: 106, Fig. 221; 129, Pl. 26) from the upper Gila. Some of these specimens were painted, usually with a light center color and bordering darker color. A similar unpublished round plaque or disc with concentric circles of yellow and green was found by Dodgen in the Hough collection in the U.S. National Museum.

A number of single elements of carved and painted flat wood from the Mogollon area have been identified as parts of birds. Lambert and Ambler (1961: Fig. 49) illustrated a number of round-ended and tapered slat fragments from the Alamo Hueco caves that might be single feathers. Ellis and Hammack (1968: 37, Fig. 5) report fragments of painted lath, from the outer chamber of Feather Cave in southcentral New Mexico, that "may have been a part of a bird representation, the end of one slat slit to suggest feathers." The pieces illustrated show rectangular sections of lath

bound with yucca cordage at right angles to form possible wings. Designs in red, black, and green were painted on this lath. Hough's collection from the upper Gila included single slat plumes, groups of plumes ("plume pahos") sewn together and attached to a single wider slat, and single element bird wings. The upper Gila plumes were tapered at one end and either fully rounded on the other end or curved on one side and end. Hough's bird wings were slightly curved or straight on both ends of the lath. Hough also identified painted designs on some long slats as bird designs, thereby interpreting the identification of certain pieces of plain lath on the basis of painted design rather than shape. This interpretation probably resulted from his familiarity with a striking painted bird representation recovered from Bear Creek Cave (Hough 1914: Pl. 21). This composite form (Fig. 3.5) was complete and consisted of two slats of flat wood sewn together at right angles with yucca cord. The uppermost piece was a rectangular slat with slightly rounded corners. The outline of a bird as seen from above, including the head, body, and tail, was painted on this board. The lower slat, which comprised the bird wings, was rectangular with one straight edge and one slightly curved edge. The curved edges of the slat were painted with a design suggestive

Fig. 3.5. Painted slat bird from Bear Creek Cave (Hough 1914: Pl. 21).

of the tips of feathers. Hough (1914: 105) guessed that the bird represented a woodpecker and noted that "the colors used in painting this object are white, black, salmon, yellow, red, blue, and green, showing greater variety and a greater discrimination in shades of color than in a majority of specimens from this locality."

Wasley (1962: 381) describes a "cruciform pendant representing a bird" from the Bonita Creek cache. This object was cut from agave stalk and is 5.7 cm long and 3.9 cm wide at the cross arms. Both sides and all edges were painted with a bluish green pigment (Wasley 1962: Fig. 10 *g*). Wasley (1962: 388-9) noted that "this particular cruciform outline was commonly used as a stylized bird representation, and without much doubt that is what was intended in this instance."

Cosgrove (1947: Frontis. *b-c*; Fig. 126 *a-e, h-j, l*) illustrates several items from the upper Gila and Hueco Mountain areas that he refers to as bird wings and feathers. The feathers, which are part of what Cosgrove considers a tablita (Fig. 3.6 *b*), consist of short tapered sections of yucca slats with rounded or squared ends. The bird wings are primarily composite forms of joined sections of slats carved to simulate the curve of a wing. One of the seven rectangular tablitas illustrated by Martin (Martin and others 1952: Fig. 155 *f*) from Cordova Cave is smaller than the others and curved on one side and end, producing a shape suggestive of a wing. This piece, like all of the Cordova Cave tablitas, is a single element and not a composite form. Gordon Vivian found two similarly curved rectangular tablitas in excavations at the Gila Cliff Dwellings National Monument.

No bird tails are reported from the Mogollon area, but two of Hough's bird pahos (Hough 1914: Figs. 217-20), and a tablita (Fig. 3.6 *b*) illustrated by Cosgrove (1947: Frontis. *b*, Fig. 126 *c*) from Mule Creek Cave on the San Francisco River, could represent the open fan of a bird tail. All consist of joined plume slats in a fan shape. The tips of all plumes are painted, and the bases are attached to some type of slat crosspiece.

Definite birds were represented in the Mogollon collections of carved wood, but as round, not flat, forms. Hough (1914: 103-4, Figs. 211-213, 216) illustrates several examples, including "ceremonial staffs having bird effigies carved on the upper end" and a more tabular bird (Fig. 3.7) that may have been tied to a staff. Cosgrove (1947: 134-5, Fig. 126 *f*) described a round wooden bird from Doolittle Cave in the upper Gila area that somewhat resembles Hough's ceremonial staff birds and the painted wooden bird found by Kidder and Guernsey (1919: 145, Pl. 61) in Sunflower Cave in northeastern Arizona.

Many slats appear to have been used in the construction of terraced objects. The best examples of this type of artifact were recovered from the Bonita Creek cache (Wasley 1962: 388, Fig. 10), where three were found (Fig. 3.8). Wasley (1962: 387) wrote:

> Each consists of a vertical lath forming the apex of the terrace and five horizontal laths increasing in length from top to bottom and centered so that the finished object is stepped on both sides. In each one, the vertical lath, or top piece, is painted a pale green (malachite pigment) all over the front surface, the lateral portions of the front surfaces of the first and fourth horizontal laths are painted this same green, the lateral portions of the second horizontal lath are painted black, and the third and fifth horizontal laths are unpainted.

> One specimen has an additional element consisting of a stick fastened vertically to the back of the unit at the center of the fifth lath and between the first lath and the top piece. It extends from the center of the top piece to 5 cm. below the bottom of the fifth lath.

Cosgrove (1947: Fig. 125, *l-o*) shows two possible terraced objects from the upper Gila, and another complete specimen from Mule Creek Cave (1947: Fig. 126g), in which the terracing is produced as negative or cut-out space within a rectangular shape rather than as a positive form.

A variation on the terraced object shape occasionally produced tapered objects. No complete specimens are illustrated, but the best examples (Cosgrove 1947: Fig. 126 *m-n*), which are from the Hueco Mountains, show a triangular-shaped flat framework of lath to which strips of lath that decrease in length from the base to the apex of the triangle were sewn.

One wooden kachina was found in U-Bar Cave in the Alamo Hueco Mountains of the New Mexican panhandle. Two rectangular sections of yucca lath joined along the long sides with yucca cordage form the body of the effigy. This body section is stabilized near one end by a narrow lath crosspiece that extends beyond the body, creating arms. Short sections of lath, one attached at right angles to the end of each arm, form the hands of the kachina. Lambert and Ambler's (1961: 77) description of the artifact is given below.

> The front of the body is decorated as follows: the masked head is black (carbon paint) and the eyes are depicted by two blank circular areas, in the center of which two black dots have been gauged. A crescent of turquoise surrounds the lower half of the left eye. The left side of the body and left arm are painted a turquoise green (malachite), and the right side and arm are painted red (ochre). Fingers are reproduced by painting four black lines on each "hand." The entire back is embellished by irregular splashes of black paint, perhaps meant to be rain drops.

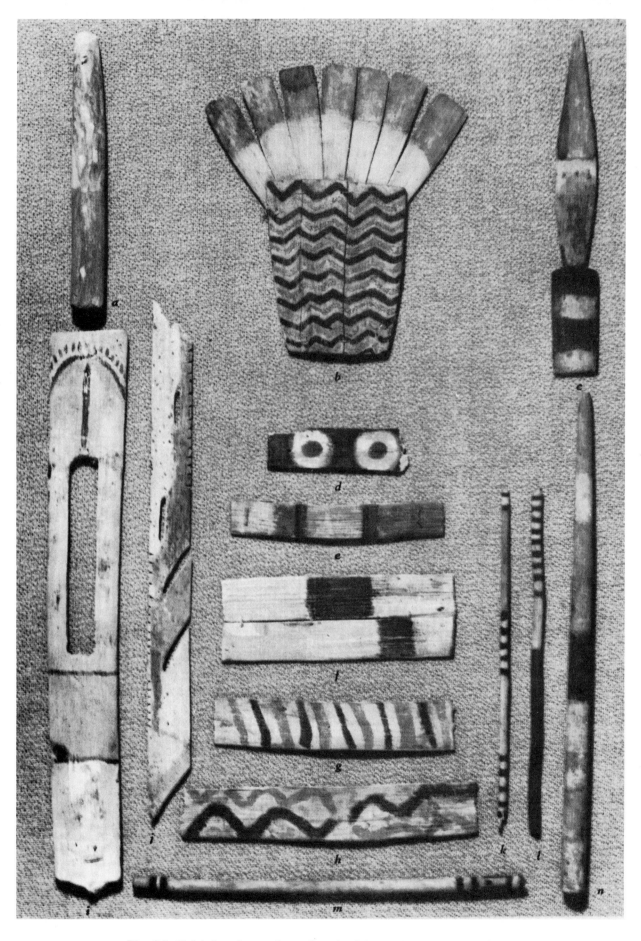

Fig. 3.6. Painted and carved wooden ritual items from upper Gila and Hueco Mountain areas. Painted stub pahos, *a, n;* wooden tablita, *b;* fragments of wooden tablitas, *c-h;* painted split-stick wands, showing sewing, *i-j;* painted sticks, *k-m* (Cosgrove 1947: Frontis.).

No other flat, painted wooden kachinas have been reported in the Mogollon area, but Cosgrove (1946: 134, Figs. 125 *g*, 126 *o*) does illustrate a strip of lath with a "flexed arm in red with the hand painted green," and a composite lath form painted with a face characterized by "diamond-shaped eyes, triangular nose, and square mouth." Both were from caves in the upper Gila Area.

Most of the composite forms and many of the individual pieces retain painted decoration. Colors represented on Mogollon painted wood include black, white, red, blue, green, and yellow in varying values and intensities. Most decorative motifs are geometric or curvilinear, the former including squares, triangles, diamonds, and zigzag lines. Positive and negative dots are common. Most of the pieces show only one decorative motif; that is, a lath will be covered with only zigzag lines or squares and not have two or more motifs employed on the same piece. Solid colored spaces also were commonly used. In addition to paint, Martin (Martin and others 1954:202) noted that "some thin boards from Hinkle Park Cliff Dwelling, without decoration, are marked with gum."

In addition to fragmentary or complete composite forms, many single pieces of whole or broken finished lath have been found. Because most of this lath is perforated with small holes on the edges or ends, it has been presumed that they represent pieces of a composite form or tablita. However, Cosgrove did classify

Fig. 3.7. Carved wooden bird form from upper Gila area (Hough 1914: Fig. 216).

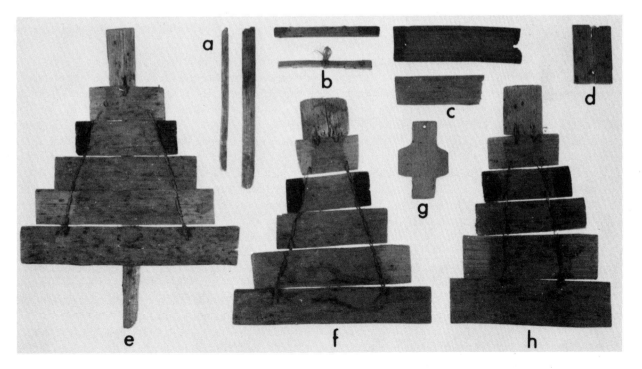

Fig. 3.8. Wooden artifacts from cave on Bonita Creek. Terraced wooden objects, *e, f, h;* wooden pendant, *g;* elements from other terraced objects, *a, b, c, d.* Height of *e,* 22 cm (Wasley 1962: 388, Fig. 10).

some single-element lath as split-stick wands (1947: 132, Frontis. *i-j*; Figs. 41, 124). Although fashioned of the same bloom stalk material as tablitas, these artifacts do not show evidence of having been elements of a composite form. Instead, they appear to have functioned singly and, according to Cosgrove, may have been carried in the hand rather than being a part of a headdress. He drew this conclusion from the fact that the butt ends of some lath artifacts were tapered or otherwise carved or gave evidence of wrapping that suggested a handle for gripping. The length of the wands ranged from 22 to 68 cm, and width varied from 2 to 4.5 cm. Wands were decorated with painted designs in the same colors used on tablitas, though a specularite purplish paint not found on the tablitas was used on one wand. Another wand had zigzag lines burned rather than painted on the surface. Unlike tablitas, wands were also decorated with notching, cutting, and bored holes on the edges and centers of the lath.

Although the concept of preparing flat, shaped wood objects with painted decoration was shared in the Anasazi and Mogollon areas, similarities in the artifacts produced in the two culture areas are not particularly striking. This class of artifact appears to be older in the Mogollon culture area. As has been noted, some of the specimens from Mogollon sites, particularly O Block and Cordova caves in the Reserve area, predate the occurrence of painted wood in Chaco Canyon by at least 500 years. Though much of the wood from the Mogollon area is not dated securely, researchers who have reported on painted wood specimens from the Mogollon generally do not date them much before the Reserve-Tularosa phases (A.D. 1000-1300), placing their occurrence in the Mogollon within the time period that they are present in the Chaco. Most of the specimens from the Reserve area and the upper Gila probably date in this three-century span. The Bonita Creek cache was dated in the latter part of this time period, and possibly Cosgrove's material from the Hueco Mountains in Texas dates at about the same time. Painted wood from U-Bar Cave in the Alamo Hueco Mountains may date this early but was tentatively attributed to the Animas phase (post-A.D. 1350) by Lambert and Ambler (1961:21). It would be difficult, therefore, to attribute the occurrence of painted wood in the Chaco to the development of this artifact class in the Mogollon culture area, though it is recognized that some pieces from the San Francisco River area pre-date the Chaco collections. It is more certain that this tradition in woodworking persisted in the Mogollon after the abandonment of Chaco Canyon.

The use of caves for storing painted wood artifacts in the Mogollon has been noted. A number of researchers also have assumed that these caves served as shrines or locations for ceremonies. Lending support to this assumption are the identified shrines at U-Bar Cave (Lambert and Ambler 1961: 16-7) and Feather Cave (Ellis and Hammack 1968). Because poor preservation may account for the lack of painted wood in Mogollon open sites, it should not be assumed that this type of paraphernalia was not stored or used in habitation sites. Though caves and rockshelters serve as shrine areas for contemporary Pueblo peoples and were used in the past in the Anasazi area, ceremonial goods, including painted wooden objects, were apparently stored and used in pueblo rooms.

Lightweight construction of forms composed of several elements characterizes both Anasazi and Mogollon painted wood artifacts, but the assembly and finishing differed, primarily as a result of the materials employed. Most of the Anasazi artifacts were fashioned from thin wood boards worked down from slabs or shingles of pine, Douglas fir, and other soft woods. Most of the Mogollon specimens were constructed from the bloom stalk of sotol, yucca or agave, which did not have the durability of wood. In addition, while long shapes could be fashioned from this material, artifact width was controlled by the size of the bloom stalk. Wide forms had to be created, therefore, by splicing together several widths of lath. As a result, Mogollon flat painted wood artifacts were usually composed of more pieces than their Anasazi counterparts, entailing more sewing, tying and gluing. Based on descriptions of Mogollon wood, it also appears that finishing of lath by sanding or abrading was not common in the Mogollon. Decoration on many of the tablitas from the Mogollon was applied directly to unfinished surfaces of the stalk slats.

Sewing techniques are not reported in sufficient detail from most of the Mogollon area to permit good comparison with the Chacoan specimens. Where data are available there are some similarities and some differences. The separate petal components of the flowers from Bonita Creek (Wasley 1961: 384), for example, were connected with a continuous cord looped through the holes in each piece. Those few disc or flower forms from Chetro Ketl that consisted of more than one element were attached by separate bindings. The same was true of the plume forms (Fig. A.28) found in Room 93 at Chetro Ketl. Holbein stitching was used in the Bonita Creek terraced objects, a technique employed on the Chetro Ketl specimens shown in Figure A.16 *j-l*. Yucca fiber and sinew was used predominantly in Mogollon tablita construction; cotton cordage was used sparingly.

While there is a greater range of finished shapes in the Chetro Ketl collection, both the Chetro Ketl and Mogollon specimens are dominated numerically by slats. In addition, some Chetro Ketl forms, like the

Mogollon artifacts, were composed of joined slats. Both Chacoan and Mogollon slats are characterized by tapering at the proximal end, shaping by rounding or curving at the distal end, and side perforations for attachment ties. The impression gained by observing slat elements from both areas is that many were used in fan-like composites. The complete plume object (Fig. 3.6 *b*) illustrated by Cosgrove (1947: Frontis. *b*, Fig. 126 *c*) is suggestive in particular of some of the Chetro Ketl slat composites, as are the bird pahos recovered by Hough (1914: 105-6; Figs. 218-20) from a cave near Silver City. These are most similar to the forms from the Chetro Ketl collection illustrated in Figures A.29-A.30.

No items in the Chetro Ketl collection resembled the terraced objects from the Bonita Creek cache, though construction of the Chetro Ketl wands was somewhat similar in that cross slats were affixed to a single vertical slat. Composite bird wings identified in the Chetro Ketl collection are reminiscent of a pair of joined bird wings from the Cosgrove collection from Mule Creek Cave in the upper Gila (Cosgrove 1947: Fig. 126 *l*). The latter are made of multiple slats sewn together horizontally to form what appear to be hinged, curved wings.

Shapes found in the Chetro Ketl collections not present in the Mogollon area include flat bird heads, horns, ovates (though some of the Mogollon curved slats may have been elements of ovates) and plaques. A few examples of bent slats from the Mogollon may have formed artifacts similar to the Chetro Ketl hoops, though the parallel is tenuous. The Chetro Ketl wands are composite forms rather than single-element forms as described by Cosgrove for the Mogollon, but like the latter they may have been hand held. Flat discs were found in both culture areas, though they seem more common in the Chaco, relatively few being reported from Mogollon sites. The Bear Creek Cave discs (Hough 1914: Fig. 221, Pl. 26 *1-4, 6, 8*) are especially like some of the Chetro Ketl examples (Fig. A.18).

While the reconstruction of many of the Chacoan forms is unsubstantiated, there is evidence that some, like a few examples from the Mogollon area (most notably Hough's "Painted Bird Offering" [Fig. 3.5], and Lambert and Ambler's "Wooden Katchina"), were assembled using joined flat shapes to achieve a three-dimensional effect. Unlike the more realistic Chacoan forms, however, Mogollon three-dimensional composites are more stylized and abstract.

As in Chacoan collections, Mogollon flat shaped wood was decorated by painting for visual effect and depiction of motifs useful for interpreting the character of the item. The range of colors used was virtually the same, though the use of specularite for obtaining a glistening purple has not been noted in Chacoan col-

lections. As in the Chaco, black and green seem to be the most prevalent of colors used. Interestingly, black is the only color used on items from the Pine Lawn phase in O Block Cave and the plainware level of Cordova Cave in the Reserve area. Red, white and green occur in later levels of these and other caves in the area (Martin and others: 1954: 200-2). Design elements are similar in both areas, and the use of solid colors on single elements is also a trait typical of Chaco and the Mogollon, as is the use of unpainted areas as part of the painted design. Though some anatomical features are depicted in painting on Chacoan specimens (bird's eyes, bird's beaks, etc.) the full depiction of life forms found on some Mogollon items such as the bird offering (Fig. 3.5) and Cosgrove's human arm and face are not found in the Chetro Ketl collection or in other Anasazi specimens. Similarly, notching, silhouetting (as in cutouts), and burning were not used in the Chaco as decorative techniques.

Other Sites

Haury (1945: Fig. 128) has published six wooden artifacts (Fig. 3.9) found by Frank H. Cushing at Double Butte Cave near Tempe in southern Arizona. All are flat, carved, and painted but only partially resemble the painted wood discussed in the preceding pages. Five of the items are single-element effigy pahos, and the sixth is a flat form carved and painted to resemble a bird's wing. Haury (1945: 200) believed that this latter piece (Fig. 3.9 *f*) was intended for use in a composite-wooden bird, noting that "this is suggested by the tenon at the base used either for insertion into the mortise in the body of the bird or for attachment otherwise." Feather symbols were painted on one side of the wing in black on a white surface, while the reverse was painted with red, green, black, and white. It is interesting that attachment of this piece was presumably by a tenon into a mortise and not by tying or sewing, the common method of attachment in Mogollon and Anasazi pieces. The tenon-mortise technique also suggests that the flat wing may have been inserted into a rounded form and not a flat shape. The type of wood used in this artifact was not reported.

The five effigy pahos consisted of two similar pairs and a single odd specimen. Haury classified these artifacts as pahos on the basis of shape and their occurrence with other round, wooden pahos in the cave. The four paired pahos (Fig. 3.9 *a, b, d, e*) were fashioned from sections of agave bloom stalk that were notched at one end to offset "the head from the tapering body" (Haury 1945: 198). Method of decoration was the basis for dividing the four pahos into paired sets. Two (Fig. 3.9 *a, b*) were covered with a black paint containing specularite over which geometric designs were applied in yellow and green. This set was also embellished with short oblique holes cut through

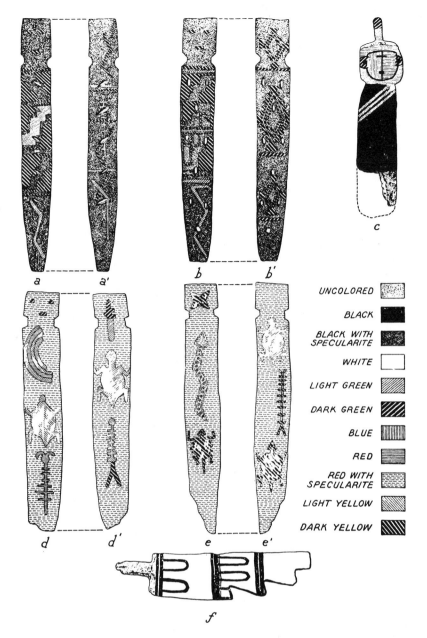

UNCOLORED

BLACK

BLACK WITH
SPECULARITE

WHITE

LIGHT GREEN

DARK GREEN

BLUE

RED

RED WITH
SPECULARITE

LIGHT YELLOW

DARK YELLOW

Fig. 3.9. Effigy pahos and bird wing from Double Butte Cave. Length of *a*,
10½ inches (Haury 1945: Fig. 128).

one paho, and small round holes through the other; these apertures originally may have held feathers. The second set (Fig. 3.9 *d, e*) was coated with a red paint containing specularite on which representational designs had been painted. These designs, painted in yellow, red, and green, included a rainbow, star, horned toads, centipedes, and a serpent. This set was not perforated.

The fifth effigy paho (Fig. 3.9 *c*) was somewhat similar in shape but had a topknot on the head, and the base was apparently not tapered. This specimen was flat but was carved from cottonwood. In referring to this item, Haury (1945: 200) stated: "The face treatment of the Double Butte effigy is unquestionably intended to represent a mask, a feature with which all kachina dolls are supplied as well as the living impersonators of the supernatural beings at festival times." This feature, in addition to the shape of the object, led Haury (1945: 198) to describe the effigy as a "prototype of those [kachinas] currently used." Decoration was applied in black, red, blue, green, and yellow paint.

These effigy pahos do not closely resemble any of the flat carved and painted artifacts that have been described. The head portions of the paired sets are vaguely suggestive of the heads on the Chetro Ketl wands (Fig. A.23), but the latter artifacts are composites, unlike the single-element Double Butte pahos. Neither are these pahos similar to the U-Bar wooden kachina described by Lambert and Ambler (1961: 77-8, Fig. 50). Haury's use of the term "paho" succinctly serves to denote the major difference between the Double Butte artifacts and most of the Anasazi and Mogollon material described earlier. While a few of the single-element Anasazi and Mogollon *flat* wood specimens may have served as pahos, most of these items were probably used as ceremonial paraphernalia and not as offerings *per se*. In discussing pahos, Hough (1914: 91) stated:

> The paho stands for the human supplicant, and is formed in accordance with this idea, painted, dressed, furnished with food, money, medicinal plants, etc., and feathers that, by the *orenda*, or magic power, of flying creatures carry petitions to the gods. The paho is thus the central feature of the sacrifice, and may be of any form or material or any object thought to be pleasing to or appertaining to a particular supernatural being whose characteristic personal offerings have been determined and fixed by the traditional usage of the religious organization.

Cultural affiliation of the Double Butte material was not firmly established, though Haury thought that the pahos had a Pueblo character and that there were few analogies with recent Pima articles. It is possible that the Double Butte pahos can be attributed to the postulated Salado occupation of the Hohokam area of southern Arizona, which ended around A.D. 1400.

ROUND CARVED FORMS

Only a limited number of artifacts from Room 93 were round carved forms. These were classified as arrows, bows, lightning lattice, prayersticks, and plume holders. In general, similarity between Chetro Ketl round forms and those from other southwestern sites is greater than similarity of flat carved forms. There is also less diversity in the Chetro Ketl round carved forms compared to similar southwestern artifacts. No effigy figures carved in-the-round were recovered from Room 93, although this type of artifact has been reported from sites in most southwestern culture areas, and is known from other Chacoan sites (Vivian and Mathews 1965: 101-2; Judd 1954: 278,

Fig. 78). Comparisons in this section have been grouped under only two headings: Anasazi Sites and Other Sites.

Anasazi Sites

This section includes Chacoan as well as other sites in the Anasazi region. Comparisons follow the descriptive format for round carved forms used in Appendix A.

Functional arrows have been found in most Anasazi sites including Chacoan towns and McElmo villages in Chaco Canyon. The most prevalent type consists of a reed mainshaft with a hardwood (frequently greasewood) foreshaft, and feather fletching. Most are nocked, and many were painted near the butt end, possibly as a cresting device. Wooden points were probably as common as stone points, if not more so. The foreshafts and mainshafts of functional arrows from Room 93 do not differ appreciably from any other Anasazi specimens.

The non-functional or replica arrows from Chetro Ketl are rare, however, and symbolic wooden fletching is not duplicated in other Chacoan or Anasazi sites to our knowledge. Arrows with entirely solid wood shafts occur only in late prehistoric sites or among historic tribes (Martin and others 1952: 341). The few non-functional arrows reported from other sites share the characteristics of impractical size, structural weakness, and crude workmanship compared to their functional counterparts. Morrison's study of the Chetro Ketl arrows determined that cresting was identical in two of the non-functional arrows and consisted of two dull green bands and a black band under the fletching. The other two non-functional arrows had the fletching area of the shaft painted totally black, though one had traces of green paint overlying the black. This suggested that the two green-black-green crests marked arrows of a set. This assumption was strengthened by the fact that these two arrows were three-fletch, while the other two were two-fletch.

Bows and bow fragments have been reported from many Anasazi sites, including the classic Chaco towns of Pueblo Bonito, Pueblo del Arroyo, and the Aztec Ruin. Those from Aztec and Pueblo del Arroyo appear to be functional bows, as are several reported by Judd from Pueblo Bonito. Judd (1954: 250-1) does report, however, on five "boys' bows" from Room 209A at Pueblo Bonito that at least superficially resemble the non-functional bows from Chetro Ketl. Unlike the Chetro Ketl bows, though, a hard wood (oak) was used in their construction, they were not flattened on both sides, and none were completely wrapped with sinew or cordage, though several had partial wrappings. Non-functional bows have been reported from a number of Anasazi areas including Tsegi Canyon

(Guernsey 1931: 99) and the Ridge Ruin (McGregor 1943: 273), but this type of artifact seems much more common in the Mogollon region.

Identification of the lightning lattice is tentative and not based on other known archaeological specimens, though ethnographic examples are known (see Chapter 4). No complete set of perforated and slightly charred sticks resembling this artifact have been found in other Chacoan sites, nor have references to duplicates been located in the literature.

The five prayersticks from Room 93 included two carved prayersticks and three prayerstick butts. The latter are undecorated and generally resemble many carved sticks found in southwestern sites that have been tentatively identified as prayersticks. Following Hough's (1914: 91) classification, the carved prayersticks from Chetro Ketl are roundel pahos. This type has also been referred to as ceremonial sticks, ceremonial staffs, and ferrule sticks. Unlike twig or stub pahos (Hough 1914: 91-3), roundel pahos are usually longer and rod-like, better finished, and more elaborately carved on one end. The carving usually involves a knob or spatulate shape (both occasionally perforated) on the end with one or more raised cylindrical rings about 10 cm below the carved end. The intervening space is either cylindrical, barrel-shaped, or less often, flat. Though many of these pahos have had the bottoms broken off, those that are complete (including the two Chetro Ketl specimens) indicate that the sticks were slightly tapered to a rounded point opposite the carved end. The longer variety of crook pahos (Hough 1914: 93), and especially the type with the end flattened and bent over to approach the staff but not tied to it, may also fall into the roundel category; in this case the crook would merely represent another method of shaping the top of the paho.

Probably the most varied collection of roundel pahos found in an Anasazi site was uncovered by Pepper in Room 32 at Pueblo Bonito, where 375 were found. Pepper reports others from Pueblo Bonito and Judd (1954:268) recovered 16 more, bringing the total from this site to over 400. Pepper (1920) divided the Pueblo Bonito ceremonial sticks into four types on the basis of end carving. These included double knob, crook or bear claw, spatulate, and wedge-shaped types. The latter type was sometimes bound with buckskin and cord.

Pepper's classification applies to most examples of this widespread kind of prayerstick, including the two Chetro Ketl examples (Fig. A.39 *a, b*). This type appears to occur primarily in late Pueblo III sites, but its presence in Chaco Canyon at Pueblo Bonito and Chetro Ketl may be earlier. It is reported from a variety of classic Pueblo III sites, including Aztec Ruin (Morris 1919a: 46; Richert 1964: 18-9), Mesa Verde (Fewkes 1916: Fig. 11; Nordenskiöld 1893: Pl. XLII

1-6), Mummy Cave (Morris 1941: 228), Johnson Canyon (Morris 1919b: 178, Pl. 44 *f*); and Betatakin (Judd 1930: 59). While the two from Chetro Ketl were painted, very few others reported, including only one of the more than 400 recovered from Pueblo Bonito, retained any trace of pigment.

Chetro Ketl plume holders consisted of a cone variety and split stick variety. Parallels with the split stick type were not sought in the literature as the identification of all split sticks from sites as plume holders would not only be unwarranted but impossible. The only Anasazi wood cones that resemble the Chetro Ketl specimens (Fig. A.39 *f*) were those found at Sunflower Cave (Kidder and Guernsey 1919: 146). The Chetro Ketl cone (4.3 cm high and 2.5 cm in maximum diameter) fits well into the range of dimensions of the 25 Sunflower Cave cones which are 4.4 to 5.1 cm high and do not exceed 3.18 cm in diameter. The Chetro Ketl cone has a concave base, is perforated top to bottom, and has a notch at the apex. Eighteen of the 25 Sunflower Cave cones are concave at the base and perforated tip to base. The Chetro Ketl cone shows traces of brown resin on the outer surface, while the Sunflower cones are all a rich, dark red ochre covered with a coat of "resinous varnish." These wood cones may have functioned in a manner similar to the stone and clay cones found in many southwestern sites. Lange (1944: 446-8) has discussed sandstone and clay cones in the Southwest.

Other Sites

Arrows were used as both utilitarian and ritual objects in the Mogollon and have been found in functional and non-functional (frequently miniature) forms. Functional arrows have been reported from sites in the general Mimbres branch region, where Hough (1914), Hibben (1938), Cosgrove (1947), Martin, (1952, 1954), Lambert and Ambler (1961), and Wasley (1962) all recovered whole or fragmentary examples. Similar reports for Jornada branch sites have been made by Mera (1938), Ferdon (1946), Cosgrove (1947), and Ellis and Hammack (1968). Other sites peripheral to the Mimbres and Jornada branch regions that have produced functional arrows include the Canyon Creek Ruin (Haury 1934), Double Butte Cave (Haury 1945), and Winchester Cave (Fulton 1941).

Many of the functional arrows reported probably were utilized in a ritual context inasmuch as the majority have been found in cave deposits associated with ceremonial paraphernalia. Cosgrove (1947: 65) noted the probable ceremonial significance of functional arrows found in caves in the upper Gila, and arrow shrines have been reported from several caves. Arrow Grotto in Feather Cave was so named because the major deposit in the upper room consisted of "36 reed arrows with painted basal portions and some remains of fletching, [that] had been forced at various angles into a lateral crevice . . . above the floor" (Ellis and Hammack 1968: 26-7). A similar shrine is pictured by Lambert and Ambler (1961: Fig. 10) from U-Bar Cave in the Alamo Hueco Mountains.

These functional arrows closely resemble their Anasazi counterparts, consisting of a reed mainshaft and hardwood foreshaft. The majority of these arrows do not have stone projectile points attached to the foreshafts, suggesting that the use of a functional arrow in a ritual context did not require the expenditure of a stone point.

Most non-functional arrows found in Mogollon sites are miniature in form. They often accompany miniature bows and in such circumstances are often tied to the bow (Hough 1914: Fig. 205; Cosgrove 1947: Fig. 123; Martin and others 1952: Fig. 152). Non-functional miniature arrows occur as compound forms, as single sections of reed, and as single hardwood shafts. Fletching is present on some of the specimens, and most of these small arrows have been referred to as "arrow pahos." None of the non-functional arrows found in Mogollon sites had fletching replicated in wood, as did the Chetro Ketl specimens.

Bows, especially miniature bows, are also quite common in Mogollon sites. Grange (Martin and others 1952: 339-42, 347-50) classified the bows from Tularosa and Cordova caves on the basis of length, designating bows in excess of 87 cm as functional, 87 cm to 35 cm as ceremonial, and less than 35 cm as miniature. Brown (Martin and others 1954: 187-8) found this classification useful and applicable for bows found in other sites in the Reserve area, but noted that additional criteria such as diameter and body shape were useful for classifying bow fragments. Decoration may also be considered another criterion for distinguishing non-functional from functional bows (Hough 1914: 100, Fig. 204, illustrates a decorated bow from Bear Creek Cave), though functional bows could have been elaborately decorated. The Chetro Ketl specimens resemble the Mogollon ceremonial type. The bows recovered by Wasley (1962: 389, Fig. 11) are reminiscent of the Chetro Ketl artifacts, and Grange (Martin and others 1952: 350) has listed several other Mogollon sites that have produced ceremonial bows.

Though a few large or functional bows have been reported from shrine areas (Ellis and Hammach 1968: 26), smaller bows, especially the miniature forms, constitute the majority of bows found. This is in contrast to arrows, most of which are usually of the larger functional variety. Simple (as opposed to compound) miniature arrows of reed or hardwood may have been overlooked or misidentified from some excavations, but there is an overriding impression that large arrows

and miniature bows constituted the standard offering in Mogollon shrines. It is probable that large functional arrows were considerably more expendable than large functional bows.

No complete or fragmentary artifact resembling the lightning lattice could be found in the Mogollon archaeological literature.

As has been noted earlier, the roundel-type paho or prayerstick found in Room 93 at Chetro Ketl was described by Hough (1914: 96, Pl. 20) from the upper Gila area, especially Bear Creek Cave. Cosgrove (1947: 128) recovered several roundel pahos from his work but noted that "all specimens were found in the southwestern part of the Upper Gila area, over half coming from the San Francisco district." Martin did not report this type from the Reserve area caves, nor were any found in the Bonita Creek cache. Their absence from the Hueco Mountain caves, Feather Cave, and other Jornada area caves is noteworthy. Lambert and Ambler (1961: 77) recovered the carved top of a paho from the Alamo Hueco area that they believed may have been of the roundel type. Haury (1945: 198, Fig. 127 *a*) has described one complete specimen from Double Butte Cave that has a pointed top rather than a knobbed or spatulate end. This is in contrast to those illustrated by Hough (1914) and Cosgrove (1947)˙ which strongly resemble the Chacoan specimens. In general, this type of paho appears to be somewhat more common in the Anasazi area than in the Mogollon.

The single wood cone from Room 93 partially resembles the eight cones from the Bonita Creek cache (Wasley 1962: 385, Fig. 7). All the Bonita Creek cones are larger than the Chetro Ketl specimen, ranging from 6.5 to 7.5 cm in height. Concave bases are present in all of the Bonita Creek specimens, but none have perforations completely through the center. Five have small perforations in the flat tops of the cones, and three have larger oval perforations through the bottom, one of which continues through the top but is off-center. Three of the Bonita Creek cones show "faint traces of some foreign material which may or may not be a pitchy or resinous substance" (Wasley 1962: 385).

MISCELLANEOUS WOODEN AND VEGETAL OBJECTS

None of the miscellaneous wooden and vegetal objects reported herein is peculiar to the Chaco or Room 93 at Chetro Ketl. An exhaustive comparison of these Chetro Ketl items with others from the Southwest will not alter the significance of the Chetro Ketl collection nor add greatly to its understanding.

The following brief comparative summary considers only the more diagnostic miscellaneous items from Room 93 and is not complete in its coverage.

Peeled, unpeeled, painted, and unpainted sticks (Fig. A.40), presumably of ritual use, are fairly common in the collections of perishable material from southwestern sites. Close parallels to the Chetro Ketl specimens have been illustrated in numerous monographs, including Hough (1914: Pl. 25), Kidder and Guernsey (1919: 185, Pl. 84 5-8), Morris (1919a: 45-6), McGregor (1943: 273), Cosgrove (1947: 128-9, Figs. 118, 119 *k*, *m*), and Martin and others (1952: 354, 357, 434-5; 1954: 198-200, Fig. 100).

The two small twig hoops from Room 93 have counterparts from other sites, though these are usually larger than the 2.5 cm diameter of the Chaco specimens. The five twig hoops from Tularosa Cave (Martin and others 1952: 358, Fig. 164), for example, range in diameter from 14.9 to 5.0 cm. Hough (1914: 59, Pl. 12) reports similar twig hoops from Tularosa and Eagle Creek caves, and Cosgrove (1947: 119, Fig. 111 *f*) recovered one small ring-paho of devil's claw (*Martynia*) with the ends bound together with yucca cord. The latter specimen contained feather fragments. A ring made of a flat strip of wood (cottonwood or willow) 5 mm wide was recovered by Steen (Steen and others 1962: 86, Pl. 3 *q*) from the lower ruin of Tonto Cliff Dwellings. The ends of the strip were overlapped and bound with agave fiber to form a circle 3.5 cm in diameter.

Among perishables from the West Ruin at Aztec, Morris (1919a: 62) noted "small husk packages, globular, flat rectangular, tied with strips of husk." Presumably these resembled the cornhusk packets found in Room 93. Hough (1914: 92-3, Figs. 189-190) illustrates twig pahos with bundles of corn husks containing food attached. They each appear to be a single strip of husk, rolled and tied at each end.

Grange's (Martin and others 1952: 351-4) discussion of reed cigarettes presents a concise summary of the distribution and morphology of reed, cane, or ceremonial cigarettes. Grange does note the presence of reed cigarettes at the Aztec Ruin. Reed cigarettes are also described by Martin and others (1954) and by Lambert and Ambler (1961).

Painted sections of reed were not found in Room 93, but are reported from the site of Leyit Kin in Chaco Canyon. Dutton (1938: 72, Table VI) reported "two small reeds painted a turquoise color [which] probably represented part of some ceremonial object, such as a *tablita*" from Room 7. It is not clear why Dutton interpreted the reeds as tablita fragments.

4. ETHNOGRAPHIC COMPARISONS

At the risk of oversimplification it may be said that among all the Pueblo groups there exist certain societies or fraternities, usually but not always masculine, the primary function of each of which is the periodic celebration of some particular esoteric ceremonial ritual. These ceremonies vary from brief observances to extended performances lasting as long as nine days and nights. Some are relatively simple, while others involve a very elaborate paraphernalia, including masks, costumes, altars, wall paintings, and a wide variety of ritual objects [Smith 1952: 4].

The discussion developed in this chapter is based on two assumptions: that the occupants of Chetro Ketl and other towns in Chaco Canyon were Puebloan peoples whose descendants inhabit some of the modern Pueblo villages, and that the majority of the items found in Room 93 at Chetro Ketl were not utilitarian, but ritual artifacts. The above quote from Smith provides a means for introducing several of the contexts in which wood has been used ritually by historic and modern Pueblo peoples. As stated in the Introduction, it is not the intent here to use ethnographic data to postulate specific ritual use of the objects from Room 93 nor to infer the derivation of any particular Puebloan ceremony from the Chaco area. Rather, a survey of recent Puebloan material is viewed as a means of increasing awareness of how wood has been used in a ritual context, thereby providing additional opportunities for comparative interpretations.

Comparisons are made following the format established in previous chapters: flat carved and painted wood, round carved and painted wood, and miscellaneous wooden and vegetal objects. This method of classification will not correlate necessarily with the construction of recent ceremonial paraphernalia. Both flat and round carved forms may be incorporated in a single ritual item, so a division by form could hamper recognition of the ritual object through our concentration on parts rather than the whole. We have proceeded, however, with the established format believing that the Chetro Ketl material is described and illustrated sufficiently in Appendix A to permit comparisons on several levels.

FLAT CARVED FORMS

Altars

We speculate that the majority of flat carved and painted wood used in recent Pueblo ritual is employed in altars. In discussing altars, White (1942: 330) notes:

Two of the most conspicuous features of ceremonial paraphernalia and setting among the Pueblos (at least among the Keres, Zuni, and Hopi), are (1) pictures or diagrams made of meal, ochers, powdered pigment, etc. commonly called "sand-paintings," or "dry-paintings," on the floor of ceremonial chambers, and (2) carved and painted wooden frames which are placed, as a rule, upon the meal-and-pigment diagram, at one end, and at right angles to the floor diagram. Other ceremonial paraphernalia, such as effigies of birds and animals, figures of anthropomorphic gods, medicine bowls, fetiches, etc., are laid upon the meal-and-pigment painting and upon the floor near it . . . . The word "altar" has been used somewhat loosely, by ethnographers to designate (1) the meal-and-pigment painting, (2) the carved and painted wooden frame, and (3) both painting and frame together. The Indians are more definite. The eastern Keres call the meal-and-pigment painting ya·Ba·cınyı; the wooden frame is called aĭtcın.

The antiquity of altars has not been established and will presumably remain a problem for some time (Smith 1952: 322-33 provides an excellent discussion of the topic), though references to cave shrines with wooden sticks arranged in upright positions (Lambert and Ambler 1961: 16, Fig. 10) may provide a clue. Descriptions or illustrations of more recent wooden altars exist for Jemez, the majority of the Keresan pueblos, Zuni, and the Hopi towns. Their presence in Tewa villages is questionable, and Parsons (1932: 279, fn. 46) reports their possible use at Tiwa-speaking Isleta.

In reviewing the literature we have arrived at the untested assumption that Hopi altars may come close to representing the more basic and possibly older form of Pueblo altar. Zuni altars, on the other hand, appear to us as the most stylized and hence possibly the most recent development of this ritual form. Keresan and Towa altars seem to fit somewhere between the Hopi and Zuni altars in terms of this hypothesized evolutionary sequence. Though it may prove incorrect, we have used this evolutionary concept as a means for reviewing the basic details of Pueblo altars, and discussion proceeds from the Hopi to the Keres and Towa and finally to Zuni. It should be noted that our ethnographic coverage has been affected by the quantity of comparative data available. In brief, it can be said that as one progresses from the Hopi villages toward the Rio Grande in the east data become more meager.

Data on Hopi altars were selected from Fewkes (1899, 1900, 1924), Voth (1901, 1912), Dorsey and Voth (1901), and Stephen (1936). Most Hopi altars appear to be constructed around a sand ridge into which ritual objects, including carved and painted wood slats, are inserted in an upright position. In some instances this ridge with accompanying ritual items apparently constitutes the entire altar. For example, the Marau altar illustrated by Voth (1912: Pls. V, X, XIII) consists of a row of many small closely spaced vertical sticks (representing the deceased members of the Marau order) that form a backing to several carved wood slats set into the sand ridge. These slats include wide slabs representing corn stalks and zigzag lightning sticks. Anthropomorphic figurines are placed at either end and slightly in front of the sand ridge. These figurines, the sand ridge, and the items inserted into the ridge form a slightly curved backdrop for a number of ritual items placed on the floor. Fewkes (1900: Figs. 43-44; 1924: 392, Pl. 5) illustrates examples of this type of altar.

This altar arrangement may be elaborated upon through the incorporation of a rigid slat frame parallel to and above the sand ridge. This frame consists of two vertical slats set on the floor near the ends of the sand ridge and joined near the top by a horizontal crosspiece. When the frame is set on the floor, the open space below the crosspiece and between the vertical slats is filled with short slabs, small sticks, and feathers, all of which are inserted into the sand ridge (Fig. 4.1). Carved stone or wood idols may also be set under the frame near the ends of the ridge. In discussing the Blue Flute and Drab Flute altars at Mishongnovi (which incorporate the slat frame described above), Fewkes (1900: 993-6) noted that similar altars at Shipaulovi did not have the horizontal or transverse framing slat. Removal of this crosspiece essentially would reduce the altar to a series of sticks and slats flanked by two somewhat higher slats.

A variation on this frame altar consists of several spaced horizontal slats or rods tied between the uprights. These rods form a framework upon which to tie decorated slats and slabs of wood, painted altar cloths, idols, and similar items. Voth's (1903: Pl. I) illustra-

tion of the Oaqöl altar serves as a good example of this type (Fig. 4.2). Frequently space is left under the bottommost horizontal crosspiece for the usual objects to be set in the ridge of sand.

Excerpts from Stephen's journal regarding the installation of the Mamzrau ceremony altar at First Mesa in 1891 provide an excellent account of the use of flat carved and painted wood. Stephen (1936: 866-911) reports that on the first day of the ceremony "near the ledge on the west end of the kiva floor about in the centre, they make a ridge of the sand, thirty inches long, six inches wide at base and rounded up to quite a narrow edge; they smoothed it with their hands. From Sa'liko's bundles they produced a lot of prayersticks and other fetich objects and set them up erect along the crown of the sand ridge." In addition to crook and round prayersticks and prayer feathers, the altar paraphernalia included two "flat pieces carved in curves and painted brown" and two flat prayersticks. On the fourth day the altar arrangement was completed with the addition of an upright screen over the sand ridge and a sand painting in front of the ridge. The parts of the wood screen were brought into the kiva and covered with a quilt until used.

> Su'pelā takes off the quilt and brings out a lot of large painted slabs . . . (altar wood). These are of spruce wood . . . and were made very long ago. This is quite evident, they are hewn, and Su'pela says long ago with stone tools . . . . He also says the first decoration was laid on long ago and that he and the other chiefs only renew it, strictly following the old lines, and this too is quite evident, many coats of pigments are visible. There are five of these large slabs, four poles and one or two other smaller pieces. They are bored with several holes along the sides at intervals and through these Su'pelā connects two sets together with strips of yucca . . . . Sa'kabenka went out and brought in two great lumps of wet clay . . . . These were set at each end of the ridge . . . . The men then set two of the cubical stone seats, behind each lump of clay, then set the two long poles up to the roof; these upper ends they fastened to the rafters with yucca strips. A shorter and lighter rod was fastened with yucca across these two uprights as a brace about five feet above the floor, and a few inches above this crosspiece another rod was hung in two loops . . . . Across these was tied with yucca to the frame a cotton curtain (Pl. XXIII), and on the second lowest crosspiece two wooden figurines were set and tied with yucca strips around the neck and fastened through the fabric, their feet on the rainbow.

The upright framework was removed late on the eighth day and the sand ridge objects were removed on the ninth or last day of the ceremony.

Fig. 4.1. Altar of the Cakwalenya at Mishongnovi (Fewkes 1900: Fig. 44).

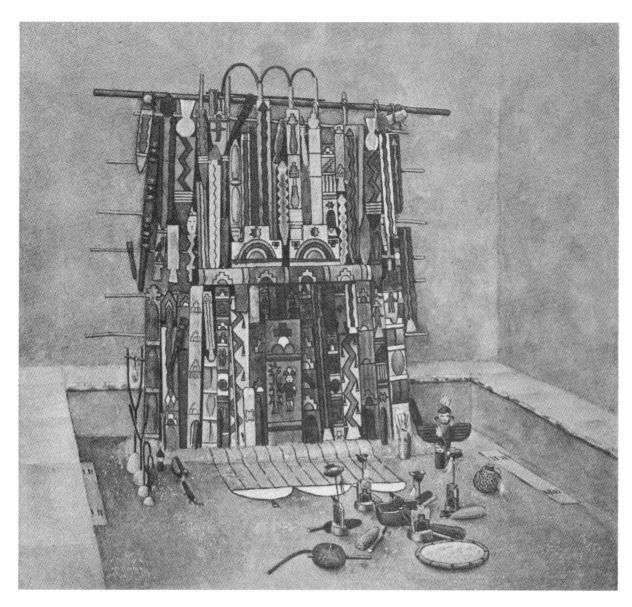

Fig. 4.2. Altar of the Oaqöl ceremony at Oraibi (Voth 1903: Pl. I).

In addition to frame and sand ridge altars, the Hopi painted screens consisting of a rectangular wood framework covered with a piece of cloth or hide. The covering was painted and the framework was often decorated on top with simple cotton clouds and along the sides with wooden flowers. These screens apparently could be used by themselves (Fewkes 1899: Pl. XXVI; Dorsey and Voth 1901: Pl. XXVIII) or as part of an altar (Stephen 1936: Figs. 313-314).

For the Keresan pueblos we have drawn on White (1932a, 1935, 1942, 1962) and Stevenson (1894) for illustrations depicting wooden altars at Acoma, Santo Domingo, Santa Ana, and Zia. White (1932b) and Goldfrank (1927) report wooden altars at San Felipe and Cochiti, but do not provide detailed descriptions or illustrations. In general, the components of Keresan altars appear more stylistically uniform than Hopi

altars, but variation, with the possible exception of Zia altars, is present. In almost all instances the basic form of Keresan altars consists of two vertical framing slats joined by one, and occasionally several, crosspieces. Unlike Hopi frames, a bottom crosspiece is present on many altars, especially those illustrated from Zia. This crosspiece appears to serve the same function as (and possibly has replaced) the sand ridge, for the various slats and slabs of wood contained within the framework are affixed to or inserted in the bottom horizontal bar. Zia altars almost consistently utilize straight-sided slats (frequently anthropomorphic) in the frame (Stevenson 1894: Pls. XIV, XVIII, XXII), but other shapes including crooks, arced rainbows, zigzag lightning, trees, and birds are present in other Keresan frames (White 1932a: Pl. 1; 1925: Figs. 15, 35; 1942: Figs. 40-42).

Unlike Hopi frame altars, Keresan frames apparently were not dismantled following a ceremony, but because their construction permitted it, were removed intact. Stevenson (1894: Pls. XVIII, XXI, XXIII) shows several complete altar frames leaned against or hung on room walls (Fig. 4.3). The bottoms of the framing vertical slats are inset or tapered for inserting into slots or holes in the floor or into holes in a timber base that was set in the floor (White 1952: Fig. 44). Illustrations of Santa Ana altars (White 1942: Figs. 40-42) show this bottom crosspiece.

Parsons, who was consulted for information on Jemez, illustrates (1925: Pl. 4 *d*, 7 *a-b*) native drawings of the altars of the Fire and Arrowhead societies, which, she notes (and we concur), "are strikingly like the altars of Sia." Two of the altars consist of alternating flat "lightning arrows" and "*tablita* crowned figures" seemingly inserted into a base board. The end slats, zigzag lightning sticks, are no higher than the other slats. The winter solstice altar of the Fire society consists of two "spruce trees in painted wood, 3 to 4 feet from the ground" with an arced rainbow between them. Similar tree shapes are common in Santo Domingo altars (White 1935: Figs. 15, 35, 44) where they, like the Jemez trees, form the outer framing elements of the altar.

Zuni data were obtained from Stevenson (1904). Wooden altars at Zuni display much greater homogeneity in form than is present at Hopi or even the Keresan villages. We have designated these altars as double frame to distinguish their construction from Keresan and Hopi single frame altars (Fig. 4.4). All altars illustrated by Stevenson (for example, Pls. CIV, CXVI, CXXV) are composed of a backdrop consisting of two vertical upright slats or "tablets" which frame and contain a solid wood panel or slab that extends from the floor upward to near the top of the uprights. No base board is present, the panel being held entirely by the vertical uprights. One or two horizontal cross bars are present near the top of the altar and are inserted into the vertical slats. These slat crosspieces are most often shaped as arced rainbows or scalloped cloud designs. Extending out from the base of the two uprights are two squared boards that lie flat on the room or kiva floor. Two additional upright slats are inserted into the ends of these boards, forming a front and second frame for the altar. These uprights are not joined by horizontal boards, however. Many of the altars have additional uprights (often curving snake or zigzag lightning figures) set between the two pairs of vertical framing slats. The tops of the upright slats or tablets often are surmounted by the round faces of Ku'p̌ishtaya (lightning makers) with cloud symbol headdresses. All of the uprights are carved and painted as are the horizontal framing boards on the backdrop. The wood screen between the two back uprights apparently is composed of a number of

carved and painted boards that are joined in such a way as to create the illusion of a flat sheet of wood decorated with cut-out designs. A similar effect is achieved in some Keresan altars (White 1935: Fig. 35; Fig. 41) but most Keresan altars are constructed of spaced slats. The space on the floor between the two sets of uprights or the two frames on the Zuni altars is apparently reserved for *mi'li*, corn fetishes, during rituals and other paraphernalia is placed in front of the structure, not between the uprights. In addition to this altar arrangement, all wood altars illustrated by Stevenson included two wide wooden slats formed as a cross (the "star of the four winds") suspended like a mobile from the ceiling over the altar. Similar items have been reported from First Mesa at Hopi (Stephen 1936: 788, Fig. 424). Several Zuni altars are also pictured with decorated planks or boards extending across the room at ceiling height above the altar (Stevenson 1904: Pl. CXXVI).

Considerable variation in recent wooden altars is apparent, but several characteristics are consistent. In almost all instances the structure serves as a backdrop for a dry-painting or ritual objects laid out on the floor before it. The objects placed in front of the altar are generally low in profile and rounded or curvilinear in shape, such as small netted gourds, pottery bowls, shallow basin baskets, *tiponi*, ears of corn, and prayersticks. In contrast to these items, the components of wood altars are usually tall and more angular in shape and include not only the slat frame but long flat prayersticks, lightning sticks, and painted slats and slabs of wood set within the frame. These objects, when set in an upright position, help to form a backdrop or curtain for the ritual stage, thereby focusing more attention on the floor items. The backdrop requires boundaries to enhance this function so that most altars are framed at the edge with tall vertical slats. An upper horizontal slat joining the vertical uprights often serves as the top framing device, while the floor becomes the lower boundary. While the need for boundaries prescribes the general framing structure of the altar, the open space created within the frame may be used in a variety of ways, thereby permitting expression of individual ceremonial requirements. This should not imply that the items used in the construction of the wooden altar are less important for having served as a background for floor items. Rather, they serve a dual purpose—as ceremonial paraphernalia for a specific ritual and as a means for offsetting the floor items. Smith (1952: 322) has conjectured that kiva wall murals served essentially the same purpose as wood altars and may have predated them.

If the Chetro Ketl items represent components of a slat altar or altars, their size, shape and form should have contributed to providing the necessary backdrop described. Though our impression is that much of the Chetro Ketl wood did not resemble historic or recent

Fig. 4.3. Altars of the Zia Querranna society (Stevenson 1894: Pl.XXVIII).

Fig. 4.4. Zuni altar of Eagle Down fraternity (Stevenson 1904: Pl. LVIII).

altar elements, there are, nonetheless, a number of tantalizing resemblances. The closest similarities between Chetro Ketl specimens and recent altar parts are seen in the various "slat" objects (Figs. A.25-A.27, A.29-A.31, A.33) from Room 93. Most of the Chetro Ketl slats are perforated along the edge for attachment to other slats (for examples of joined slats see Figs. A.25 *a, g;* A.27 *e;* A.28 *a, g*), suggesting that if they were used in an altar they constituted parts of a solid screen or panel. We have noted that solid wooden screens are typical of Zuni and some Keresan altars, while the Hopi achieve the same effect through the use of painted cloths in some altars. Interestingly, the joined slats in Figure A.25 *a* are notched to form diamond-shaped cut-outs in the solid shape, a characteristic of some recent altar screens. The tapered form of many of the Chetro Ketl slats, when joined, would have produced fan-like shapes not entirely consistent with the more usual square or rectangular altar frame. We have noted the occasional occurrence, however, of semi-circular screens in Keresan villages (White 1935: Fig. 7; 1942: Fig. 42), so that the shape is not entirely without contemporary analogues.

A number of the Chetro Ketl slats (Figs. A.26, A.27 *b*, A.30, A.31) do not have side attachment holes in surviving portions and may never have had them. We have indicated that many Hopi altars consist of a frame under which are placed numerous wooden sticks and slabs. These are all individual pieces. Fewkes's (1924: Fig. 6) drawing of the "Altar of the Basket Dance, Owakülti, at Sitcomovi" provides a superb example of the range of flat wooden forms that occur in Hopi altars. Almost any of the wooden elements noted in Figures A.26, A.27, A.30, and A.31 could have been used in a similar fashion. The wide slat in Figure A.26 *a* is particularly reminiscent of a Mamzaru altar slab illustrated by Stephen (1936: Figs. 470-471). It is notable that this slat and its probable counterpart (Fig. A.26 *b*) have small perforations at the top. Inasmuch as the upper portion of these two slats is unpainted and perforated, a transverse attachment (a slat crosspiece?) is possible. The most notable look-alike among the Chetro Ketl items is the snake-lightning stick represented by three carved pieces (Fig. A.34 *h-j*). Long. thin zigzag sticks representing snakes or lightning are found in almost all Pueblo altars.

Though stylistically there are at least one specific parallel and several general ones to historic altar parts, the majority of the Chetro Ketl slats may have been too short to have served effectively as a screen. A rough survey of slat measurements provided by Stephen (1936) has shown that on the average the height of Hopi tablets and sticks placed in sand ridges ranged from 25 to 60 cm. The complete Chetro Ketl slats in Figures A.29 and A.33 average 12 to 19 cm in length. The upright framing slats on a Flute society

altar shown by Stephen (1936: 426) is estimated to be about 120 cm high and 10 cm wide. The slat fragment shown in Figure A.25 *a* is 15.5 cm long and 3.25 cm wide. On the other hand, there is the possibility that Chetro Ketl slats were tied to a framework at several levels to create a screen or panel. Fewkes (1924: Fig. 6) shows a number of short slats attached in this manner to a Hopi altar frame.

We have focused on the Chetro Ketl straight-sided slats that most closely resemble recent altar parts. Much of the Chetro Ketl wood consists of curvilinear pieces, however, a shape that is more rare in recent altars. We have already noted that, though infrequent, curvilinear screens do occur in some Keresan altars. The Kwinic Hakawa Cikame society altar at Santa Ana, for example, which is illustrated by White (1942: Fig. 42), is composed of a screen in the shape of a half circle. More often, the use of curvilinear shapes is limited to particular elements that make up a part of the altar. The most common use of curvilinear shapes is in scalloped cloud designs and arcing rainbows. These are often found as the top crosspiece on slat altars (White 1942: Fig. 42; Stevenson 1904: Pl. CXVI; Parsons 1925: Pl. 4 *d*; Stephen 1936: Fig. 426). Essentially none of the artifacts in the Chetro Ketl group, including the plume circle (Fig. A.32 *a-b*), resemble cloud or rainbow shapes on recent altars.

Circular and oval forms are even less common, but they do occur on Hopi and Zuni altars. A circular moon is attached to an arced rainbow on several Zuni altars (Stevenson 1904: Pls. LVIII, CXVI), and the heads of the lightning makers on the upright slats of Zuni frames are circular (Fig. 4.4). Keresan altars appear to incorporate circular or oval forms more often, though these are usually half circles and half ovals. The altar of the Flint society at Santo Domingo (White 1935: Fig. 15) is embellished with two half-oval faces, and the altar of an Acoma medicine society (White 1932a: Pl. 1 *b*) is decorated with a number of half-oval cloud faces. Parsons (1925: Pl. 5 *b*) shows two small circles with face markings that appear to be suspended from the horizontal crosspiece on the Jemez Eagle society altar. Several of the circular and oval shapes in the Chetro Ketl collection (Figs. A.12, A.16-A.21) are only represented by fragments, but enough whole or almost whole specimens exist to suggest that complete circles and ovals were intended. The method of attachment of these artifacts in most cases is also unlike recent examples. In addition, historic and modern ovals and circles almost consistently are marked with simple faces, while the Chetro Ketl pieces are decorated primarily with geometric designs.

Birds figure prominently in Puebloan ritual and are used in altar arrangements but usually as round forms and not flat shapes similar to the Chetro Ketl birds (Figs. A.1-A.6). White (1935: Figs. 15, 35) illustrates the use of flat birds in Santo Domingo altars. The profile of an eagle's head surmounted the top crosspiece of the Boyakya altar, and the upper bodies of two eagles, also in profile, were incorporated into the Flint society altar screen. These latter eagles were framed by slats leaving an open space around the flat figure. Features were painted on, a technique reminiscent of the Chetro Ketl "parrot" (Fig. A.1a). The two carved birds shown on the Zia Querranna (Kwiraina) society altar by Stevenson (1894: 113) surmount posts on the sides of the altar but are carved in the round (Fig. 4.3). A more recent depiction of the altar (White 1962: 169, Fig. 19) shows the two birds (desert sparrow hawks) carved as single flat shapes. Several Zuni altars illustrated by Stevenson (1904: Pls. LVIII, LIX, CXVI) include small birds attached to the tops of altar uprights or to the hanging "star of the four winds." It is not possible to tell from the illustrations, nor does Stevenson indicate, if the birds are two-dimensional, but modern examples of similar birds on Sha'läko altars at Zuni are carved in the round. The anthropomorphized bird A'chiyalä'topa, "the being with wings and tail of knives," more commonly known as a "thunder bird," is also present on a number of Zuni altars and is shaped from flat wood. Both the latter figure and the small altar birds have wings and tails represented, but all are carved from a single piece of wood and are not made up of joined parts. This is in contrast to the separate tail and wing pieces in the Chetro Ketl collection (Figs. A.3-A.6). Hopi altars also include birds, but these all appear to be carved in the round. Most often they are placed in front of the altar with other ritual objects (Stephen 1936: 791, Figs. 426, 428).

Anthropomorphized slats, consisting of rounded or angular heads carved at the top of the slat, are present in many Pueblo altars (Stevenson 1894: Pl. XXII; Parsons 1925: Pl. 7 a-b; Stevenson 1904: Pl. CXXII; Fewkes 1924: Fig. 6). These heads are frequently created by simple notching near the top of the slat and the application of eye and sometimes mouth marks. Terraced cloud headdresses are present on some of the more elaborate examples. The heads on the Chetro Ketl zoomorphic wands (Figs. A.23-A.24) resemble some of these figures, especially the Hopi examples (Fewkes 1924: Fig. 6). The attached projections on the heads of the Chetro Ketl specimens do not resemble cloud terraces, however, as much as they do the headgear of the Tewa *kossa* (Parsons 1929: 127, Pl. 18) or the Keres *koshare* (White 1935: Fig. 6; 1932b: Fig. 2 b).

We discovered no recent altar element that resembled the Chetro Ketl plaques (Fig. A.22), and only one instance of the use of horns on an altar was found. Fewkes (1924: Fig. 6 p) shows three curved, flat (?) objects attached near the top of the "Altar of the Basket Dance, Owakülti" that he describes as "horns worn on the head of Owakül Maid." These items look like the horns in the Chetro Ketl collection (Figs. A.8-A.11). Three small plume-shaped objects tied above the Owakülti horns resemble the tapering slats with pointed ends (Fig. A.28 a-f) from Chetro Ketl. Horns are also depicted on the Hopi altar cloth painting of the Ho-Katcina illustrated by Voth (1901: Pl. XXXVIII).

Masks, Tablitas, and Other Headgear

Smith (1952: 293-4) has provided a succinct statement on Pueblo masks:

Among the entire catalogue of Pueblo ritual paraphernalia, probably the most important single item is the face mask that is usually worn by participants who impersonate kachinas or other supernaturals, and sometimes also by other persons . . . . The man may wear also an elaborate costume, but the mask is the important thing, and from it the wearer not only derives "power" but even in a sense is invested with the spirit of the actual kachina, with the result that he becomes the kachina for the time being, endowed with all its powers and attributes. Usually, though not always, kachina impersonations are masked, and masked dancers appear at nearly all the villages, although in most of the eastern ones white people are not permitted to see them, and as a consequence very little information is available concerning them there. A number of drawings and descriptions have been collected from some of the eastern villages, however, and an enormous mass of material on the subject has been published for the western villages of Hopi and Zuni, where also the masks are much more elaborate than in the east.

The data and debates regarding the antiquity of masks in the Southwest also have been summarized by Smith (1952: 308-10), and we have limited our review of his summary to his convincing argument for the pre-Hispanic use of masks among Pueblo peoples.

Roediger (1961: 158-64) has classified Pueblo masks into three categories: half masks, face masks, and helmet masks. The first type consists of a leather band that covers the face from hairline to mouth and from ear to ear. A horsehair beard attached to the bottom covers the mouth and chin. This kind of mask allows the dancer to be clearly understood "when he accompanies his movement with song." The face mask also fits only over the face, but the leather covering extends below the chin. As in the half mask, the wearer's hair covers the top and sides of the face covering. The helmet mask covers the entire head and extends to near the shoulders, resembling a leather bag placed over the head. In general, helmet masks in the western pueblos have rounded tops, while those in the eastern pueblos are flat (Roediger 1961: 163). Bunzel (1932: 857-8) divides masks into only two types, helmet and face, but notes that the face mask may cover only the upper part of the face or only the chin. Parsons (1939: 339) reports that "masks are of two types, the false face and the cylinder which covers face and head."

In addition to classification by shape, a more important distinction is made by Pueblo peoples between permanent and personal kachina masks. The following excerpts from Bunzel (1932: 848) summarize this distinction:

> One type is ancient and permanent . . . . These masks are held as tribal property and are handed down through the generations. Each one represents a named and individualized god, one of the priestly rulers of the village of the katcinas . . . . The masks are kept in sealed jars in houses from which they are never taken except for their public ceremonies . . . . These permanent masks are never made over into the likenesses of other katcinas. Under exceptional circumstances they may be renewed, but the old mask is not destroyed. This type of mask is found among the Hopi (in addition to personal masks) and, so far as I have been able to learn, is the only type found in the Keresan villages . . . .

> There exist in Zuni, in addition to these ancient and permanent masks, others which are individual property, which a man has made to serve as his personal fetish so long as he lives, and as his guarantee of status after death. These are the masks that are used' in group dances, and which I have therefore designated as the masks of dancing katcinas, to distinguish them from the priest katcinas.

The basic mask usually is constructed of leather, cowhide having more recently replaced deerskin, elkskin, and buffalo hide. Gourd and wicker are used in a few masks, but Parsons (1939: 340) notes that wood is never used. In addition to painting, various materials are used in decorating the mask. A superstructure may be created from "feathers, unspun cotton, sheepwool for hair, flowers, horns, and wooden slab or tablet, or with side or back slabs or feathers. Ears, gourd or wooden snouts, a tongue flap, bulging eyeballs of buckskin stuffed with cotton, wood, and seeds may be attached. There will be a large collar or ruff of fur or feathers or spruce" (Parsons 1939: 339).

Smith (1952: 293) has noted that "literally hundreds of different masks are known to exist, each of them distinguishable by certain characteristic markings which serve to identify the particular

supernatural that is portrayed." This great variation is made possible through the infinite combinations of materials and designs used for ornamenting masks. Materials used on masks include flat carved and painted wood elements.

Before proceeding to a brief survey of historic and recent wooden mask parts, we believe it is important to note Bunzel's (1932: 858) observation that the only part of the mask that is permanent is the basic shape (i.e., face or helmet shape). She reports, "All else is removed, even in the case of ancient masks. The mask is made up anew each time it is worn. The old paint is scraped off and it is freshly painted. The features which were removed at the last wearing are renovated and put back or replaced by new feathers. With the exception of the permanent masks, the mask may be made, by the use of suitable paint and feathers, to represent any katcina wearing that particular form of mask." This statement is in slight contradiction with an earlier excerpt from the same report in which Bunzel (1932: 848) remarks that permanent masks may be renewed "under exceptional circumstances," implying that their renewal is not routine. Presumably renewal refers to repainting and refurbishing of fragile parts (e.g., feathers, spruce ruff). What is not clear from either statement is whether more durable parts on masks, such as wooden tablitas, horns, and ears, are removed. Apparently if the mask is a personal one and can be used for impersonating various kachinas through changing the outward appearance, this would be possible. In the same vein, wooden attachments presumably could' be removed from permanent masks only if they were broken or damaged and needed repair or replacement.

Most mask parts constructed of flat wood are either appendages representing head parts such as ears, horns, and snouts, or superstructures, most commonly tablitas. Several artifacts in the Chetro Ketl collection (Fig. A.15 a-d) bear some resemblance to ears on historic and recent masks. The specimens in Figure A.15 a and b, in fact, are referred to as ears in Appendix A because of their shape, the decorative motif suggestive of the inner curve of an ear, and the attachment holes on the straight side of the element. In addition to square and semi-circular shapes, rectangles are the most common ear form on pueblo masks (Parsons 1925: Pl. 15 c-d; 1920: Figs. 16-17; White 1932b: Fig. 4; Stevenson 1904: Pl. LXX; Stephen 1936: Figs. 115, 244). Rectangular ears on recent masks are usually more rounded or more squared than the examples in the Chetro Ketl collection (Fig. A.15 a, b), but the latter specimens fall well within the range of rectangular shapes. A number of illustrations show the short side rather than the long side of the rectangle attached to the mask, thereby creating a more protruding ear. This type is especially notable on Zuni masks such as Pau'tiwa (Stevenson 1904: Pl. XXVIII).

Less common ear shapes on recent masks include terraces (White 1932a: Pl. 2; White 1932b: Fig. 4; Voth 1901: Pl. LI), rabbit-like ears (White 1935: Figs. 23-25), ears of corn (Parsons 1929: Fig. 7), and triangular ears, represented only on Tewa masks in the literature surveyed. Parsons' drawings of Tewa masks are all done by native artists and are rather simple. It may be that these triangular ears are actually simple horns, a type of mask adornment that is seemingly not represented on Tewa masks. Lightning sticks are relatively common as elements on tablitas, but in at least one instance (White 1935: Fig. 21) they were used in place of ears. Petal-shaped forms similar to the tapering slats with carved ends (Fig. A.28 a-f) from Chetro Ketl were inserted into a round wooden plug to form a fan-shaped ear on the Hopi mask of Au'halani (Stephen 1936: Fig. 32).

Wooden ears are often perforated for inserting earrings, feathers, and evergreen sprigs (Stephen 1936: Fig. 244; White 1942: Fig. 19; White 1932b: Fig. 6; Parsons 1920: Fig. 16). The flat, wooden, painted earrings of the Hopi kachina So'owuqti illustrated by Stephen (1936: Fig. 115) are square but their appearance suggests a possible similar use for some of the smaller discs (Fig. A.18) from Room 93.

The use of flat wood for noses or snouts appears limited, these appendages (when present at all) being most often represented by shapes carved in the round. Stephen (1936: Fig. 244) does illustrate one kachina mask, Cho'sbushi, with a long, lath-like nose (with a nose pendant!), and presumably this style is present on other masks. No Chetro Ketl artifacts were suggestive of this item.

Horns on masks are placed on the top or attached to the side. Side horns in all of the examples in the literature surveyed were of a simple curve type (bison horn shape in profile), the arc of the curve varying from slight to deep. This type occurred in all but the Tewa pueblos with relative frequency (Parsons 1925: Pl. 14 f; White 1932b: Fig. 7; 1942: Fig. 19; Stephen 1936: Fig. 32; Stevenson 1904: Pl. CIII). Our limited Tewa sources and the lack of data on Tewa ritual paraphernalia may account for this fact, or as noted earlier we may be misrepresenting features shown on native drawings of Tewa masks. Simple curved horns are less commonly placed on the tops of masks (White 1932a: Pl. 15; White 1932b: Figs. 5, 6). The length of these horns varies considerably, as does the width of the base where it is attached to the mask.

Most horns on the tops of masks were from deer (Parsons 1929: Fig. 12; White 1935: Fig. 21), antelope (Parsons 1925: Pl. 15 a; White 1935: Fig. 22), and occasionally mountain sheep (Parsons 1925: Pl. 14 b;

Roediger 1961: Pl. 15). These are either the natural horns secured to the mask or representations in flat wood. Branched horns (i.e., deer, antelope) are common in the eastern pueblos, but were not noted on Zuni or Hopi masks in the literature surveyed.

The Chetro Ketl horns (Figs. A.8-A.11) compare closely with many examples of the simple curve type. The shape and, in a few cases, coloring of horns on some Zuni masks such as Sayathila, Sayatasha and Sha'läko (Stevenson 1904: Pls. XVI, LIV, LXI) are especially similar. No horns or other shapes in the Chetro Ketl collection are suggestive of deer or antelope horns. Enough examples of horns in the Chetro Ketl material retain holes along the base (Fig. A.8 a, b, d; Fig. A.9 a; Fig. A.11 a) to suggest that most if not all horns were affixed to another form. In at least two cases (Fig. A.8 a; Fig. A.9 a) the other form was of wood and not leather, possibly ruling out their use on masks. In Appendix A it is noted that the curve of the horn is continued in the attached fragment on these two pieces.

Lightning sticks, as noted above, occur frequently on tablitas, occasionally in place of ears, and in some instances as "mask back sticks" which are attached around the edge or at the back of the mask. Stephen (1936: 529, Fig. 298) illustrates two such sticks from First Mesa, noting that "there is the usual diversity in the carved stick at the back of the mask . . . which are lightning sticks of diverse forms, flat prayer-sticks, etc. (Fig. 298). These back sticks are said to represent objects in old times seen on the altar." A good example from Laguna is shown by Parsons (1920: Fig. 7). Like snake-lightning altar sticks, these forms resemble the Chetro Ketl snake-lightning (Fig. A.34 h-j).

As Pueblo ritual paraphernalia, tablitas occur both on masks and as separate dance headgear, but in both instances they are associated with ritual dance. Smith (1952: 308) states that tablitas "are usually approximately square in over-all dimensions, with an upper margin in curved or stepped outline, embellished with extensions and protuberances in the form of conventionalized flowers, feathers, lightning-sticks, and the like, their faces painted with similar conventions. They are used to a greater or lesser degree in nearly all the Pueblo villages." (For examples see White 1942: Fig. 22; Parsons 1920: Figs. 8-9; 1929: Pl. 27; 1925: Pl. 15 c-d; Stevenson 1904: Pl. LXXIV; Dorsey and Voth 1902: Pl. LXXXII a). Dance tablitas usually extend over the head to just above the ear, but the outer edges of mask tablitas often extend to near the bottom of the mask as long slats attached to the side of the mask, thereby providing more stability for the tablita. Because their form is otherwise essentially the same in both instances, no further distinction is made between the two in the following discussion. Most modern

Fig. 4.5. Headdress worn in women's dance
at Hopi (Fewkes and Owens 1892: Pl. 1).

tablitas appear to be made from single sheets of wood
(White 1935: Pl. 8), but earlier versions probably were
constructed from joined slats and then painted over to
create a smooth surface.

As Smith has noted, the overall tablita shape is
almost always square, though curvilinear outlines,
most frequently cloud shapes, are found on the top
margin (an interesting parallel with the general
outline of many slat altars). A variation of this theme
is illustrated by Fewkes and Owens (1892: Pl. I), who
show a crown-like headdress worn in a Hopi women's
dance, La-la-kon-ta, at Walpi (Fig. 4.5). This headdress consists of three flat semi-circular pieces of wood
that encircle the head. A horn protrudes from one side
and on the other "a fan-shaped body made of slabs
and colored red" is held in place by a wooden button
attached to the crown. The ends of the slabs are
painted black with white spots. These slabs are
especially like the slats in Figure A.28, most
particularly specimen *g*.

Curved tablitas, in which the outer circumference
follows the same arc as the curve that fits over the
head, were rare in the literature surveyed. The most
notable example located was that of the Hopi Sio
Shalako Maiden pictured by Roediger (1961: 116, Pl.
18). This mask, which was reconstructed from an an-
tique mask at the Laboratory of Anthropology, Santa
Fe, consisted of nine slats carved in terraced and

rounded cloud shapes and embellished with painting
and feathers. The slats were affixed by pegs and
thongs to an arced wood frame that fit over the head.
We have identified this headdress as a tablita, though
it was the only one we found that was made up of
spaced slats. White (1942: Fig. 16, no. 1) pictures a
tablita from Santa Ana that is slightly fan-shaped, the
top of the headdress being wider than the base. This
particular tablita is constructed of at least three and
possibly four joined pointed wood slats that compare
with some of the shaped slats (Fig. A.27) from Chetro
Ketl. In this instance the slats only constitute elements
of the tablita. Fewkes (1899: Pl. XXV *b*), however,
illustrates a tihu (Hopi kachina doll) of the "Big-head"
kachina with joined pointed slats representing feathers
in a fan-shaped headdress. The pointed slats in this
case are like the tapering slats with carved ends (Fig.
A.28 *a-f*) in the Chetro Ketl material. The use of slats
to represent feathers in headdresses may be limited to
kachina dolls, as real feathers are apparently the rule
in the adornment of masks (White 1942: Figs. 17, 19).

Fewkes (1899: Pl. XXV *c*) also illustrates the
Kwátaka kachina *tihu*, whose headdress is a bird. The
bird's body, head, and tail appear to be carved in the
round and in part constitute the head of the kachina.
The curved wings are carved from flat wood and attached to the body. Voth (1901: Pls. LIX, LXIII)
pictures the Hahai-i kachina *tihu* and the imperson-
ator, showing crow's wings attached to the side of the
mask. These wings are of flat carved wood in the *tihu*,
but they appear to be actual bird's wings on the im-
personator's mask.

We make these observations because the Chetro
Ketl plume circle (Fig. A.32 *a-b*) has been interpreted
by some persons as possibly representing a plume
tablita, though a case is made in Appendix A for this
object having originally been a complete circle. Although parallels to this form are extremely rare in recent tablitas, and slat feathers appear limited to *tihu*,
the possibility that some of the Chetro Ketl items,
especially slats, were used as tablita parts cannot be
discounted. Similarly, other artifacts from Room 93,
such as the small discs, could have been suspended
from tablitas or otherwise attached to masks.

The above review covers the great majority of instances we found of flat wood being used on masks or
other kinds of ritual headgear. Two other minor items
are noted. Stephen (1936: Fig. 245) depicts a mask of
the Hopi cross perched kachina, the top of which is
crowned with two crossed slats resembling the Zuni
"star of the four winds." The method of attachment is
not clear.

While most tablitas are shaped to fit directly on the
head, the headdress worn by the corn maidens in the
tHla′hewe ceremony at Zuni (Stevenson 1904: Pl.
XXXVIII) rests upon a miter set on the dancer's head

(Fig. 4.6). Stevenson (1904: 194, fn. a) describes the headpieces as "a circle . . . formed by a slender bit of wood and four additional pieces . . . attached to the band at equal distances coming together at the other ends, forming a sort of miter . . . A tablet similar to those carried in the hands stands out from the center of the miter." The strip of wood encircling the head is quite narrow in the illustration, but a similar band illustrated by Stephen (1936:Fig. 248) and used in a "caplet of clouds" on First Mesa is much wider. Four willow hoops covered with cloth or skin are attached to the circular wood lath in this latter item. The Chetro Ketl hoop fragments (Fig. A.13) may have served a similar purpose, though attachment holes for upright pieces were not present on the pieces in the collection.

Staffs and Slab Prayersticks

Among the Pueblo Indians, hand-held objects are common items of ritual in dance and other aspects of ceremonies. In addition to prayer feathers and evergreen boughs, hand-held objects include standards, staffs, prayersticks, and dance boards. Most of these items are wooden or wooden in part.

Standards (Hopi *na'chis*, Keres *kastotcoma*, etc.) consisting of long poles to which are attached painted gourds, skins, feathers, and in the east a ceremonial sash, are described by Smith (1952: 194) as representing the emblem or badge of Pueblo societies. There appear to be distinct differences in use between the eastern and western pueblos, but inasmuch as these objects do not employ flat carved wood, we do not discuss them further here.

Many Pueblo staffs bear a resemblance to standards but are, in general, shorter and seem to be associated more with individual ritual office rather than being representative of a society. Parsons (1939: 325), for example, refers to staffs as "sticks of office." Most resemble the description provided by Smith (1952: 201): "they are usually 4 to 5 feet in length, with a bouquet of feathers at the top, and sometimes corn ears, crooks, feathers, or spruce twigs attached at a lower point on the shaft. They are carried vertically." There are other sticks of office, however, that do not resemble these short standards, but rather are shaped of flat wood.

Position or status, for instance, is represented among the Hopi by a slab-type stick of office—the *mongkoho* (Fig. 4.7). The mongkoho is a narrow rectangular board; those illustrated by Stephen (1936: Figs. 21, 430) range from 35 to 55 cm in length and from 5 to 8 cm in width. They are carved at one or both ends with V-shaped notches and terraces and may also have short lateral cuts on the sides. Feathers are frequently suspended from the sides. Voth (1901: Pl. LV) shows one with an ear of corn tied to the slab,

Fig. 4.6. Headdress of Zuni corn maiden
(Stevenson 1904: Pl. XXXVIII).

Fig. 4.7. Hopi *mongkohos* of One Horn society (H. R. Voth Print, Bethel College Historical Library, North Newton, Kansas).

and Stephen (1936: Fig. 2J) pictures another with an ear of corn carved in bas relief on one side. All have two holes drilled along one edge, through which a cord is fastened. Parsons (1939: 325) described the mongkoho as a "chief stick . . . used or made for the Hopi Town chief, for various kachina, Aholi, Aototo (Oraibi), and Auhalani (Walpi), and for every member of the Agave and Horn societies. This stick, carried horizontally by a cord and carved with terrace cloud or, for Walpi Agaves, with Water Serpent, is very sacred." Similar boards were not noted in the literature for other pueblos, and nothing in the Chetro Ketl collection closely resembled the mongkoho.

Parsons (1939: 270) has written that "there is no ceremonial, as far as I know, outside of Tiwan and Tewan towns in which, in some connection, prayersticks are not offered or used. Indeed, it can be said that Pueblo ceremonial consists of prayer-stick-making and offering together with prayer and other ritual." Prayer-sticks come "in a variety of forms, but are always composed of one or more feathers attached to some small object such as a piece of string, a long stick, two short sticks, a small cylinder, annulet, or the like" (Smith 1952: 189). Our interest is in a less common

style of prayerstick—the flat carved form, or, following Smith (1952: 195), the "slab prayer-stick." At least some of these slab prayersticks were meant to be carried in the hand during dance or other ritual, while others apparently were meant only for altar use or placement in shrines, or both. For example, the small (three inches long), slab "Antelope" prayerstick shown by Stephen (1936: Fig. 48) probably was not carried in dance ritual. Other slab pahos, however, are used in dance at Hopi and Zuni and have been described by Smith (1952: 195) as being "made from a flat slab of wood of rectangular outline, with a short straight handle at the bottom, and painted on its obverse with any one of a variety of designs." The rectangular shape of these wands appears slightly longer than mongkohos. Feathers and sometimes grasses are attached to the edges. Hopi designs are usually "painted corn and cloud symbols and in some cases portraits of kachinas or other supernaturals. The Zuni examples have simple geometric figures, such as crosses, circles, crescents, and the like" (Smith 1952: 196). Slab prayersticks are especially common at Hopi where they are carried in many of the summer dances of the women's societies. After the dance performance they are usually placed on the altar in the kiva. Voth (1912: Pl. XVIII) illustrates several of such pahos that were used in the Oraibi Marau ceremony.

The zoomorphic wands (Figs. A.23-A.24) in the Chetro Ketl collection somewhat resemble these dance pahos. A handle is presumed on the Room 93 artifacts because of the special binding, but it is unlike those on Hopi or Zuni specimens. In addition, we found no recent examples with attached slats such as are present on those from Chaco. Stephen (1936: Fig. 180 *a*) does illustrate an interesting example of a Hopi dance wand that is shaped like a flat *tihu*, in this instance "Lightning horn man." This figure has two wavy zigzag horns extending above the head that bring to mind the attached straight protuberances on the Chetro Ketl pieces, though the latter are tapered and not wavy in outline.

Dance wands, common in eastern pueblos, may have a function similar to the Hopi and Zuni dance slab prayersticks, but their shape is rather different. Those illustrated for Jemez (Parsons 1925: Pl. 4 *b*) and Santo Domingo (White 1935: Pl. 8, *Upper*) consist of wide rectangular to almost square boards with small handles tied to the board. Decoration consists of painting and serrated or terraced top margins.

If the Chetro Ketl zoomorphic wands were hand held in dances or other ritual activities, several additional items in the Chacoan collection may have been used in a similar way. For example, two of the four Chetro Ketl plaques (Fig. A.22 *a, d*) have basal extensions or handles (?); almost certainly the other two fragmentary examples were similarly equipped. The length of these extensions is not known, but it is conceivable that they were sufficiently long to have been held in the hand during dancing. Similarly, the "oval form with handle" (Fig. A.12) is so constructed as to suggest that it was hand held. The Youngs' hypothetical reconstruction of one of the bird figures (Fig. 2.4) employs this artifact, and in their reconstruction the handle is wrapped for carrying, like the zoomorphic wands.

Do dance wands function as flat prayersticks, and should the Chetro Ketl items with handles be considered as slab prayersticks, dance wands, both, or neither? The following quotation from Smith suggests that the functional division drawn between these items by ethnographers and archaeologists, and possibly at times by the users themselves, may not be clear cut. Smith (1952:196) writes, "In some cases flat slabs with handles are used, not as *pahos* or wands, but as society standards or *na'chis*. An example of this usage has been reported for the Owakül ceremony at Oraibi, where the object used as a *na'chi* is said to be called *paho*, thus suggesting an identity between the two classes of objects."

It would appear that there may be overlap in the use of flat carved and painted wood in Pueblo ritual, single items being used in a variety of ways. A number of flat prayersticks resembling some of the Hopi dance pahos may not be used in dance ritual at other pueblos. The Zuni "elder war god" tablets found on altars and in shrines have the Hopi wand shape, including the same handle, but there is no indication that they are used in dance. Designs on these boards are cut out and not painted. Stevenson pictures one of these tablets in the elder god of war altar (1904: Pl. XXI) and in shrines on Twin Mountains and Corn Mountain (1904: Pls. CXXXVII, CXXXVIII, CXXXIX). A prayerstick from San Felipe illustrated by White (1939b: Fig. 17) looks like some of the Hopi slab pahos, except that it does not have a handle. It is rectangular, painted with a simple mask design, has a feather attached and is terraced at one end. White gives no indication, however, that this type of prayerstick is used in Keresan dances.

Other flat prayersticks are patterned after the zigzag snake or lightning sticks, which, as noted earlier, are common on many Pueblo altars. Parsons (1925: Fig. 12 *a-b*) shows two fine examples from Jemez that she refers to as "War-god lightning sticks"; White (1932b: Pl. 2 *a*, Fig. 16 *a*) illustrates two from San Felipe; and Voth (1901: Pl. LX) shows two in a shrine north of Oraibi. Finally, Stevenson (1904: Pl. LXXXI) depicts a "pleasure dance" at Zuni wherein two male dancers hold long zigzag slat objects similar to these lightning sticks.

Mask-Images

In discussing Pueblo ritual, Parsons (1939: 347) noted that "between mask and image there is a type of effigy which may be called mask-image, such as the Horned Water Serpent image, the bird images of Zuni and First Mesa, the deer, antelope, and buffalo heads of Cochiti and probably of other towns . . . ." Some mask-images are of particular interest, not so much because they employ elements of flat wood, but because they are used as moving effigies in ceremonies. As we noted earlier, many of the Chetro Ketl specimens constitute parts of compound objects, and it has been theorized that some of them may have been constructed as movable forms.

One of the best examples of the recent use of moving effigies by Puebloan peoples is the ritual associated with the horned and plumed serpent. At Zuni the plumed serpent effigy, Ko'loowisi (Fig. 4.8), is used during a kachina initiation ceremony that corresponds to the Hopi Powa'mû. At Hopi the horned water serpent, Pa'lülükoña, is used in the horned water serpent dance, which Parsons (Stephen 1936: 288) has described in an explanatory note in Stephen's journal as "a dance which might be asked for by any man, as in the case of the simple kachina dances." Parsons further indicates that similar ritual occurs at Isleta, Jemez, and probably in the northern Tewa villages.

Construction of this mask-image is essentially the same at Zuni and Hopi, and Stevenson's (1904: 94) description for Zuni is applicable for both:

> The figure of Ko'loowisi, which is constructed of deerskin, is about 5 feet long and 8 inches through the thickest part of the body . . . . A rod of cottonwood extends through the fetish, symbolizing the spinal column . . . . Hoops of slender pieces of cottonwood, representing the ribs of the serpent, extend from the neck to the lower end. A deerskin tongue, colored red, hangs from the mouth, which is provided with teeth. Plumes stand from the top of the head, which is made of a gourd . . . . The head of the fetish passes through a tablet [wood] ornamented with cloud symbols (see plate XIV).

The Hopi effigy described by Stephen (1936: 291-303) is similar, though cotton cloth was substituted for deerskin and a cotton cloth was used in place of the wooden tablet. In addition, the Hopi effigy had a turquoise-colored gourd horn attached to the top of the head.

Stevenson (1904: 94-102) has chronicled the use of the effigy in the initiation ceremony at Zuni. The mask-image is brought in the evening to the room where the ceremony is conducted. At a point in the ritual the head is projected through the hatchway for all to see. Water is then poured through the body of the effigy, emptying into bowls held by persons in the room. This is followed by shelled corn and finally grass seeds which are collected in baskets.

Hopi use of the effigy is somewhat different, and Stephen (1936: 305-7) has described a horned serpent dance at First Mesa held in 1893 in which several serpent effigies, including a horned "struggling effigy," were used.

Fig. 4.8. Zuni mask-image of Ko'loowisi (Stevenson 1904: Pl. XIV).

Fig. 4.9. Effigy birds: Hopi, *a, b* (Hough 1914: Figs. 214, 215); Zuni, *c* (Stevenson 1883: Fig. 493).

After singing the Pa′lülükoñ songs for five minutes, the cloth curtain was unrolled and suspended from a roof beam, while, as last night, several men got behind it, some to blow the gourd trumpets, others to manipulate the six Pa′lülükoñüh [serpents]. One donned the mask of Hahai′wuqti and another took the struggling serpent in his arms, first passing the loop attached to the hoop at the base over his neck . . . .

When all is ready, those in front begin another Pa′lülükoñ song and at the first note all the six serpents are thrust through the six circular sun designs [in] the curtain . . . . Then Hahai′wuqti . . . passes along in front of the projecting, moving serpents and stooping down holds her breast to each, and each serpent in turn lays its lips against the mammae, imitating the action of a mother suckling a child, for she is their mother . . . .

Hahai′wuqti, having passed across the curtain suckling the serpents, once or twice, passes across again, holding the basket of meal before each serpent, and each of them dips its head in the basket as if eating the meal offered . . . .

During all this time the trumpeting continues behind the curtain, and the struggling serpent continues its struggle in the hands of the manipulator.

As this second stirring song ceases, the serpents are withdrawn and the hinged sun designs close, the curtain is at once rolled up and laid on the floor in front of the growing plants, and the seven serpent effigies are laid at the fireplace.

In addition to the serpent effigy or effigies, several other mechanical mask-images or puppets may be used in this ritual. Small moving birds apparently used in ceremonies are reported from Hopi and Zuni. Stevenson (1883: 372, Fig. 493) collected a painted bird from Zuni with moveable wings controlled by a string, and Hough (1914: 104, Figs. 214-215) illustrates similar birds from Hopi and Zuni (Fig. 4.9). Robert Elder of the National Museum of Natural History, Washington, D.C., has written that several dozen similar Zuni birds are in the Museum's collections and that "they range in size from about 3-6 inches long [and are] painted mainly in black, white and yellow. Unfortunately their moveable features are not operable because of partial disassembly" (personal communication to Gayle G. Hartmann, Oct. 9, 1974).

Stevenson mentions a moving bird, Su′ti^tki, used in announcing the coming of Ko′loowisi. This bird is attached to a pole and is brought to the roof of the chamber in which the ceremony is held. "The pole is projected through the hatchway, and by an ingenious arrangement of cord the bird is made to run back and forth, while a second man uses a whistle of most curious workmanship that is hidden under his blanket. The bird is supposed to chirp and warble, notifying those in the [room] of the coming of Ko′loowisi. Finally the bird halts at the far end of the pole" (Stevenson 1904: 100).

Stephen does not describe the use of a moving bird at the Hopi ceremony, but he does illustrate (Stephen 1936: Fig. 193) two bird puppets attached to the ends of sticks. These bird puppets were part of the paraphernalia of the horned water serpent dance.

Stephen (1936: 335-6, Figs. 195-196) also illustrates and briefly describes another puppet, Shala′kmana, associated with the horned serpent dance. Shala′kmana is an anthropomorphic figurine consisting of a wooden head with a tablita-like headdress and hinged moveable arms. The body, which is attached to a long neck, consists of a "crinoline of willowhoops set close together with string fastening [that] descends in conic form from neck to ground" (Stephen 1936: 335). A mantle covers this framework and strings are used to manipulate the arms and body.

ROUND CARVED FORMS

Comparison of the Chetro Ketl specimens with recent Puebloan round forms is limited to the categories discussed in Appendix A. We have used this approach because there are only a few round carved forms in the collection, and the forms present are identifiable in most instances.

Arrows

Both functional and nonfunctional arrows are considered here. The use of arrows in recent Pueblo ritual is extensive and intensive, and we have not considered the subject in detail. Ritual arrows are most commonly used in dances and as shrine or altar paraphernalia. In many instances they are associated with bows, but they may also be used by themselves. For example, Parsons (1939: 546, 632, 646, 841) notes that arrows are carried in ceremonial dances at Isleta, Hopi, Zuni and Taos. These are full-size, feather-fletched arrows that may be characterized by special pairings. It is more common, however, for arrows to be carried with full-size or short bows in Pueblo dances (for examples see White 1942: Fig. 33; Parsons 1920: Fig. 3; Parsons 1929: Pl. 30; Stevenson 1904: Pl. XLII).

Arrows are also used as offerings on altars and in shrines, but these usually appear to be miniature forms. Parsons (1939: 305) discusses the use of miniature arrows, bows and shields as offerings, noting that they are employed especially during winter solstice ceremonies. Dorsey and Voth (1901: Pl. XVIII) do illustrate a normal sized arrow and "old bow" used in the "small Soyal altar" at Oraibi, but most reports (Parsons 1925: Fig. 12 c; Voth 1912: Pls. XX a, XXXII; White 1942: Fig. 51; White 1932b: Pl. 15 t) illustrate or describe small forms. These small arrows range from unmodified feathers and simple sticks attached to bows (White 1942: Figs. 51, 54 b) to miniature compound arrows with full feather fletching (Voth 1912: Pl. XXX a).

Although the construction of recent Pueblo arrows used in ritual frequently cannot be determined from published accounts, many appear to be compound arrows similar in construction to the Chetro Ketl functional arrows. Some, however, appear to be simple one-piece forms. We found no instances of the use of wood fletching in imitation of feathers in the literature reviewed.

Bows

Bows, like arrows, are common paraphernalia in Pueblo ritual and are used in similar fashion. When carried in dance they are usually full size or somewhat shorter than normal, but seldom are of miniature form. They may be carried with or without arrows. Most illustrations of dance bows show a simple curved shape similar to the Chetro Ketl examples. Whether all ritual bows were originally constructed solely for ceremonial use is difficult to determine, but we believe it is safe to say that most recent forms are nonfunctional.

Small or miniature bows are used on altars (Stevenson 1904: Pl. CVIII) or as offerings in shrines (Parsons 1925: Fig. 12 c; White 1942: Fig. 54 b). Like arrows, miniature bows vary considerably in craftsmanship and complexity. The presence of a large bow on the Oraibi small Soyal altar has already been noted.

Lightning Lattice

The reconstruction of the Chetro Ketl lightning lattice illustrated in Figure A.38 is based on the presence of two complete elements and the use of lightning frames or lightning houses in recent Pueblo ritual. The use of the lightning frame in Pueblo villages has been summarized by Parsons (1939: 378): "The 'lightning house' or frame is the familiar European set of sticks which fold up or extend into a series of lozenges. It lies in front of the War god images (Walpi) and is used by kachina (Hopi, Zuni, Cochiti), by Buffalo dancers (First Mesa), in the Acoma Flint society, and in the Hopi Snake society. Snake men shoot lightning frames toward the east or the sun in making ritual circuits, or within kiva they shoot the frame, four times, toward the hatchway, swinging the rhombus also, to represent lightning and thunder."

Stephen (1936: Fig. 182) has illustrated and described lightning frames used at Hopi. The elements were long, flat, rectangular sticks connected through perforations near the center and each end. An eagle wing feather was attached to each outer joint. "A knotted bit of buckskin is the hinge at each end, and at centre, and each end is also bound with sinew and yucca. The alternate halves are painted green and yellow. One frame of eighteen pieces has fourteen pieces 30 inches long and four, 18 or 20 inches long. At the tip is a wood imitation of a stone arrow point" (Stephen 1936: 308). The length of the wood elements used varied considerably. Stephen reports two frames with sticks 4.5 inches long, and another with 9-inch sticks. A number of Voth's photographs (Voth 1901: Pl.XLVIIIb; Dorsey and Voth 1902: Pls. CXXXIV a, CIX b) showing the lightning frame in use at Hopi also reflect considerable size differences. White (1962: 319, Fig. 55) illustrates a "lightning snake" from Zia that appears to be constructed of smaller and more rounded sticks (Fig. 4.10). Feathers are attached to the ends of the sticks and a wooden arrowpoint is affixed to the end of the device. The complete Chetro Ketl specimens fall within the size range of the Hopi examples, though the sticks are somewhat narrower than those illustrated, more closely resembling the Zia specimens.

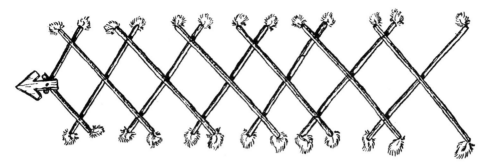

Fig. 4.10. Puebloan lightning frame or lightning house (White 1962: Fig. 55).

A major characteristic of the Chetro Ketl specimens is the burning on one end of the sticks. Twenty-two of the 27 pieces were burned. In our review of the Pueblo literature we found no reference to igniting the ends to produce an additional theatrical effect, and such an action would quickly render the item inoperable when joint attachments burned. It should be noted, however, that the joints are not at the extreme end of the stick but slightly toward the center. Wadded cotton, textile, or pitch placed on the ends of the sticks might burn for some time before destroying the joint attachment.

Prayersticks

Five artifacts in the Chetro Ketl collection were identified as prayersticks, only two of which are complete. As was noted in Chapter 2, it is uncertain whether any of these items actually were utilized as prayersticks. Despite their near universality in Pueblo ritual (Parsons 1939: 270), prayersticks are not necessarily always associated with other ceremonial items, and in fact are commonly deposited alone or with other prayersticks or prayerfeathers. Their possible absence from Room 93, therefore, would not be unusual.

The search for ethnographic examples of ferrule sticks led us to a consideration of ritual stick swallowing or sword swallowing. Few of the artifacts used have been illustrated, but the upper portion of a Zuni sword pictured by Stevenson (1904: Pl. CIX) appears to be knobbed and several rings are painted on this rounded stick. A thin carved blade of wood is attached to the base of this stick, and it is presumably this portion that is swallowed. Equally elaborate specimens from Jemez (Parsons 1925: Pl. 4 *a*) and Zia (White 1962: Fig. 14) have the upper or handle section painted and embellished with zigzag lightning arrows.

Stick swallowing is reported by Parsons (1939: 442) for Hopi, Zuni, some Keresan villages and Jemez. Swords at Acoma consist of shaped and smoothed spruce saplings with foliage left at the top; Zuni swords are carved of juniper. In addition to these sticks, Parsons (1939:442) indicates that flat, painted boards are carried by women in sword swallowing performances. Women do not swallow sticks (though reportedly they did at one time in Zuni). White (1932a: 115) reports the use of these flat boards at Acoma, but he gives different Keresan names for the boards and the swallowing sticks. He describes the boards as carved and painted and notes that they are often referred to as dance wands.

It is not our intention to imply that sword swallowing was practiced in Chaco Canyon. The diameters of the Chetro Ketl ferrule sticks (1.1, 1.2 cm) and similar sticks from other archaeological sites suggest to us that these sticks may have been too large for swallowing. We do believe, however, that ferrule sticks should not automatically become labeled as prayersticks. In closing our comments on ferrule sticks we note that several older Navajo men present during the excavation of these items at Chetro Ketl quickly identified the ferrule sticks as medicine sticks. They indicated that they were used for placing medicine in a patient's mouth (more specifically, on his tongue) and that the lower portion was left unpainted as this was the "medicine area."

Plume Holders

A wooden cone and 35 rounded sticks split on one end were tentatively identified as plume holders. Smith (1952: 233) provides a good summary on cones in Pueblo ritual, but deals primarily with stone or temporary earthen cones used in altar arrangements. We noted references to wooden cones at Hopi (Stephen 1936: 169, Fig. 101; Voth 1912: Pl. V), where they were used in the Marau altar and in a dance during Powa′mû. In the latter instance the cones were carried on a tray and used by the Ta′chŭktĭ clowns.

Though split sticks for holding feathers probably are used in Pueblo ritual, we could find no references to them. Sticks unadorned except for small feathers tied to one end are frequently reported, however.

MISCELLANEOUS WOODEN AND VEGETAL OBJECTS

Our review of the Pueblo literature produced information on the use of cornhusk packets, reed cigarettes, carved cucurbita rind, and various kinds of sticks. Because these items are common in Pueblo ritual and relatively undiagnostic, we have not discussed them further, believing that their presence at Chetro Ketl merely confirms the Puebloan origin of the entire collection. For the same reason, we did not look for ethnographic analogues of other miscellaneous objects in Room 93 such as twig loops and yucca leaf paint brushes.

HISTORIC RITUAL WOOD

We believe that the presence of carved and painted wood at Chetro Ketl and other prehistoric sites in the Southwest establishes the presence of this ritual art form in the Mogollon and Anasazi culture areas by A.D. 1000. We further believe that its persistence in Puebloan lifeways is attested to by the frequent use of carved and painted wood in recent Puebloan ceremonies. In addition, there is some evidence from historic and proto-historic Puebloan sites for the employment of carved and painted wood. We have not documented all examples of carved and painted wood from historic sites, but instead have selected examples from several well known sites. The following summary provides only a synthesis of the data. In our opinion, most of the analogues in form are apparent.

Pecos

Kidder (1932: 293-4; Figs. 241-243) recovered a number of wooden implements from Pecos, some of which he identified as ceremonial paraphernalia. These included several flat zigzag lightning arrows, a small bow, a thin terraced slab of wood resembling part of a tablita, and a terraced paddle-like specimen of unknown use. In addition, a cache of ceremonial items from Room 30 contained two carved and painted sticks, one of which Kidder (1932: 293) described and illustrated. This stick was about 14 inches

long with a round handle, a terraced rectangular shaft, and a conical head. The tip of the stick was carved in flat facets. The entire object was painted blue-green. The second stick resembled the first but was badly decayed.

Kidder also discussed several unidentified wooden objects that included three narrow juniper slats perforated with two or more holes at various places on the slat. Each was well finished but unpainted. The general shape resembles a number of the Chetro Ketl slat specimens.

Hawikuh

Hodge's work at the historic Zuni town of Hawikuh produced a number of ritual items, including carved and painted wooden artifacts. Wooden objects associated with burials have been reported by Smith, Woodbury, and Woodbury (1966) and include prayersticks, plume sticks, reed cigarettes, and portions of shrines. Shrine objects were found in three graves. The most significant material was found with Burial 915.

Burial 915 was an adult female found in the northern cemetery in a supine and extended position. Numerous offerings were placed in the grave, but only the shrine objects are considered here. These included a flat, oval slab of wood perforated near the center and painted green on both sides. This specimen lay on the chest and was associated with several other smaller slabs which were badly decayed. Two other squared slabs were placed across the body at the pelvis (Smith and others 1966: 215). These were over a meter long and about four centimeters wide. A third shrine upright of similar proportions was found beneath the squared slabs. All of the sticks were painted.

The burial data from Hawikuh consist primarily of the field notes recorded by Hodge and his staff. The following is an excerpt from the field notes on Burial 915 (Smith and others 1966: 215).

> The body of Burial No. 915 was that of a medicine priestess and many of the medicines and the shrine poles buried with her were those used in the curative ceremonies for rattlesnake bite. The two long, squared poles were those used as part of the shrine and the long mass of fibrous wooden material (915-E-1) were stalks of the *Datura metaloides* which were placed in an upright position as part of the shrine . . . . The thin oval tablet (915-E) was a part of the shrine paraphernalia. It was fastened to a stick about eighteen inches high. In its entirety it represented the sun. The body color was blue. Encircling the outer edge were four colors in the order named, beginning at the edge—yellow, red, white, and black. Inside the circle formed by these colors a small bear was painted.

Fig. 4.11. Prayersticks from Sikyatki
(Fewkes 1898: Pl. CLXXIV).

Awatovi

The summary of data from the Hopi town of Awatovi is based on Smith's (1952) discussion of ritual items he identified in kiva murals at Awatovi and Kawaik-a. Reports on wood artifacts recovered from the site have not been published. Because kiva murals are ritual art forms, and the subject matter portrayed reflects much of Hopi ceremonialism, we have treated Smith's data and conclusions as a primary source on historic Hopi use of carved and painted wood. Objects portrayed in the kiva murals pertinent to our discussion include standards or altar-slats, headdresses, and prayersticks.

Smith found very few examples of standards or altar-slabs depicted in the murals. He reports that "although these slabs in actual practice take an almost infinite variety of forms, certain objects in one of the wall paintings are suggestive of them in a general way. In Test 5, Room 6, Front Wall Design 3 (Fig. 62 c) there appear in the spaces between some of the semicircular white areas in the lower band five black objects with long tapering stems and apparently elaborated upper portions that suggest the type of slats referred to" (Smith 1952: 133).

Most headdresses identified in the murals were formed "of feather devices, either singly or in some cases made up of complete wings or tails" (Smith 1952: 124). Two headdresses contained other elements, however. One consisted of a conical white "dunce cap" that was strongly reminiscent of the headgear worn by the Hopi War God in some ceremonies. The second headdress consisted of a mask with two curving white horns on the top of the head. In concluding his remarks on headdresses, Smith (1952: 124) wrote that "it is worthy to note that no example has been found in Group I suggesting the use of a painted board or *tableta* as a headdress, such as are frequently seen today in numerous Pueblo ceremonials, except in the peculiar case of the objects in Test 5, Room 2, Left Wall Design 6 (Fig. 67, *d*)."

Four types of prayersticks were identified in the murals: single long sticks with attached feathers, double prayersticks, ring or rectangular shapes with attached feathers, and slab or "board" prayersticks (Smith 1952: 131). The latter type included the flat, painted paddle-shaped slabs used by dancers in certain rituals. Two examples of this type depicted in the murals are not associated with anthropomorphic figures but are shown standing upright and dissociated from other elements in the design.

Sikyatki

Fewkes spent the months of July and August in 1895 at the Hopi site of Sikyatki making collections for the National Museum. He was assisted by Hodge in this work and most of the material was recovered from burials. Though few perishable items were found, Fewkes did collect a number of prayersticks from the graves (1898: Pls. CLXXIV, CLXXV). Several of these (Fig. 4.11 *e-f, n;* Fewkes 1898: Pl. CLXXV *t*) resemble ferrule sticks from Chetro Ketl and other Anasazi sites. Fewkes noted in reference to specimens *e* and *f* (Fig. 4.11) that they were unlike any modern prayersticks he had seen. The Sikyatki collection also included at least one example of a slab prayerstick (Fewkes 1898: Pl. CLXXV *u*).

5. CONCLUDING REMARKS

The painted and carved wood from Chetro Ketl is the largest and best preserved collection of its type yet reported from the Anasazi culture area. While the material significantly expands our perception of the structural and decorative attributes of this Chacoan art form, the condition of the artifacts and their contextual data place limitations on the functional interpretation of the collection. To more fully understand Chacoan culture, however, the collection should be considered in terms of context (however limited the data may be), its use, and its contribution to knowledge about Chacoan ritual. The following discussion takes into account some of the earlier interpretations proposed regarding the use and deposition of the wood. This has been done because we believe it is important to acknowledge the origin of some current thoughts about the collection and to place other interpretations in chronological order.

CONTEXTUAL RELATIONSHIPS

To reiterate briefly, Chetro Ketl is one of several large Chacoan towns located in the lower section of Chaco Canyon near a major break in the Chacra Mesa known as the Gap or the South Gap. The town's formal architectural plan is characteristic of many Chacoan towns, consisting of a long multistoried block of rooms with perpendicular room blocks at either end. A curved row of rooms joining the ends of the projecting room blocks created the typical D shape of these towns. Room 93 is an outside room at approximately the center of the primary (north) room block (Fig. 2.1).

Most of the carved and painted wood from Chetro Ketl was recovered from the second-story apartment of Room 93. We know of no similar artifacts from the first story of Room 93. If pieces of wood had dropped through the hatchway into this lower room they could have been picked up by anyone who entered it from the time of its abandonment to the recent historic period. Unlike most other rooms in this part of the pueblo, the lower room remained intact and could be entered through a hole in the outside wall. Inscriptions in the wall plaster dated 1880 and 1886 attest to visitors in the late nineteenth century and presumably other persons entered the room before and after this time.

Hewett excavated rooms bordering Room 93 on the east and west and recovered at least 13 pieces of carved and painted wood during the 1929-1934 seasons of work. These came from the north room block and because Room 101, bordering Room 93 on the east, was cleared during this period, we have presumed that the artifacts were from Room 101. Room 92 to the south of 93 also yielded two fragments of carved and painted wood and, like the Hewett pieces, they closely resembled certain specimens from Room 93. The items from Room 92 were found near the west wall on the floor of the first story, one room level below the collection in Room 93 (see Fig. 2.2).

In addition to the more than 200 pieces of wood from Room 93 (most of which were in fragmentary condition), the collection included scraps of cordage, pieces of twigs, some vegetal remains, faunal remains, and a few lithics. Almost all of this material was concentrated in two locations in the northeast quadrant of the room. There are no excavation notes giving specific vertical provenience of individual artifacts. Not all of the artifacts lay directly on the floor; many were mixed with silt and sand several centimeters above the floor. Horizontal placement of the majority of the specimens is shown on the floor plan reproduced as Figure 2.10.

During the excavation of the room Gordon Vivian postulated that the wood represented an altar that had been left assembled in the room and was crushed by the collapse of the roof. Much of the material was concentrated in one area of the room and the quantities of cordage mixed with the artifacts suggested to Vivian that some of the specimens, particularly the bird forms, had been suspended from the ceiling. The possibility that an intact altar had been left in place in the room was bolstered by some tentative evidence from the Mogollon area for in-place altars in caves. Cosgrove (1947:9), for example, had been told about a collection of painted wood that was found "set up in the dirt floor" of Greenwood cave, and Hough (1907:57), on the basis of hearsay, mentioned a cave in the upper Gila area that contained "bows, arrows, painted tablitas, and other objects," all of which were arranged along the walls.

Historic and recent accounts of the use of altars by Pueblo peoples suggested, on the other hand, that altars were erected for specific ceremonies and then dismantled at the conclusion of the ritual (see Stephen 1936:866-91 for an example of this process). This problem was resolved when analysis of the recovered material began, however. It was apparent during excavation that few whole specimens had survived intact, but subsequent study of the collection revealed that many of the forms were incomplete, and reconstruction effort over a period of years produced only a few whole items. Instead, the collection consisted of a number of partial artifacts represented by fragments and splinters mixed with an assortment of vegetal, faunal and lithic debris. The excavation also revealed that no roof timbers were present in the room, so that roof collapse on an intact altar was not a feasible solution to explaining the condition of the artifacts.

On the basis of this evidence Vivian conjectured that an intact altar had been vandalized in the room while the room was vacant and that parts of the paraphernalia had been removed. Morrison attempted to correlate classes of artifacts in the collection with their position in the room and particularly their placement in the two major concentrations of artifacts. He concluded that although the material may have been placed originally in the northeast part of the room, considerable scattering and mixing of fragments had taken place. He further determined that the distribution of the items as found did not reflect the original arrangement of the paraphernalia.

We suggest storage of ritual artifacts as an alternative to the intact altar hypothesis. Sacrosanct objects are often placed in back rooms of Pueblo villages when not in use (Parsons 1939: 427). Storage is usually temporary unless the items are no longer used, which may occur as a result of the loss of ceremonial knowledge or the death of the last person familiar with the ritual. In these cases they may be buried, sealed in walls or jars, sealed up in a room, or "put away in the hills" (Parsons 1939: 428). The collection of ritual gear discovered by Pepper (1920: 129-63) in Room 32 at Pueblo Bonito suggests such a procedure. It is also likely that material in many Mogollon cave shrines was stored rather than displayed. Photographs in the collections of the Arizona State Museum of a cave deposit near Silver City, New Mexico, show a number of wood items stacked against the cave wall. These items appear to have been placed in storage rather than arranged for ritual use.

If the Chetro Ketl artifacts were stored and forgotten or put away permanently, it still appears that the collection was vandalized after it was placed in the room. Prehistoric vandalism in Chaco Canyon has been documented by Judd (1954: 85, 335) at Pueblo Bonito, where burials had been robbed of jewelry. As was noted in Chapter 2, there is some evidence for the intentional destruction of a number of the specimens.

One of the ferrule sticks (Figs. 2.9, A.39 *b*) was severed with a cutting tool, and a horn (Fig. A.10 *b*) appears to have been twisted and broken by hand.

The lack of refuse in Rooms 92 and 93 suggests that this part of the town was occupied late in the history of Chetro Ketl and that rooms were left open on abandonment, or in some instances, sealed. The obsolete ritual gear could have been placed in a vacant room while limited occupation of Chetro Ketl continued. The room may have been sealed after the artifacts were left. Inasmuch as all artifacts in Room 93 were not found directly on the floor but in some instances slightly above the floor in a silt and sand level, we have conjectured that limited deposition of fine windblown or water deposited materials occurred in the room after it was abandoned and probably during the time the painted wood was stored in the room. Sometime after abandonment the stored ritual paraphernalia was vandalized. Vandalism may have occurred when roofing beams were removed from Room 93—possibly by late Mesa Verdian inhabitants of Chaco Canyon. At either this time or shortly thereafter parts of the artifacts were carried to nearby rooms by persons or possibly rodents. Destruction must have taken place in Room 93 because of the numerous small splinters of wood found throughout the room. It is unlikely that very small fragments would have been gathered up elsewhere and brought to Room 93. Only two small fragments of wood were found in Room 92.

Beam removal probably deposited additional sand over many of the artifacts. No vigas or savinos were found in the room and the roofing bark and adobe lay directly on the artifact zone. This action effectively sealed the artifactual deposit, providing the carved and painted wood some measure of protection from weathering and further vandalism.

CEREMONIAL USE

The archaeological context of the Chetro Ketl artifacts provides only limited information for interpreting the collection in a cultural context. Provenience data from Rooms 92 and 93 suggest that we are dealing with objects that had been removed from their primary cultural context and placed, by human or other agents, in a secondary context—in this case either storage or refuse. Presumed subsequent vandalism further disturbed the contextual relationships of the objects. We have no provenience data for the artifacts from Room 101 but have presumed a similar history of use and disposal for them. The Chetro Ketl collection is incomplete not only as a result of dispersion through several rooms of the town, but also as a result of seemingly intentional destruction of most of the items. This act further reduced the interpretive potential of the items singly and as a group. We should note that we have attempted not to assume that the collection represents parts of a single assemblage, although this might seem a logical conclusion to be drawn from the content and context of the collections. Inasmuch as contextual data are quite limited, it may be that the collection represents parts of several distinct assemblages. Although the major portion of the collection is known from Room 93, additional and possibly more complete items may be recovered in the future from nearby unexcavated rooms, thereby increasing the chances for determining how these objects were used.

Because we are not in a position to recover all of the archaeological data, we have proceeded on the basis that these data are limited, and that many of our statements regarding the function or use of the artifacts will be conjectural. We have approached functional interpretation of the Chetro Ketl artifacts on general and specific levels. On the general level our concern has been to identify the collection within a broad cultural framework—that is, we have asked how the artifacts served the community. On a more specific level our goal has been to identify more precisely the manner in which the objects were used.

We stated in Chapter 4 that we believed that the Chetro Ketl examples of carved and painted wood were non-utilitarian, and that they were used in ritual. We consider ritual to include the formal acts and procedures customary in religious *or other* rites. Our conclusions regarding the Chetro Ketl materials are tenuous and based only on analogy with recent Puebloan practices. Complete assemblages of carved and painted wood have not been found in good archaeological context in the Southwest (to our knowledge), so that there is little comparative data for postulating the use of such objects in a ritual milieu. In general, archaeologists working in the Southwest have assumed that the rare examples of painted wood that have been found, while not directly comparable to ethnographic examples, nevertheless comprised parts of ceremonial paraphernalia. These identifications often incorrectly viewed the fragment or object as intact and in its proper relation to other parts. The identification of "tablita" fragments, for instance, is assumed to imply a use analogous to that of a certain class of ethnographic Pueblo ceremonial headdress. By extension, when painted wooden objects are discovered archaeologically they are thought to be ceremonial in the sense of the ethnographice tablita—constructed for and used exclusively in religious and quasi-religious ritual.

While it is true that all non-utilitarian objects in a Puebloan society are not necessarily used in ritual,

there is ample evidence for the use of painted, flat, composite wooden objects among the ethnographic Pueblo in formal religious or sacred activities that may be classed broadly as ceremonial. Such objects commonly include altar parts, paraphernalia worn in dances, and flat, painted devices such as sticks or wands that are carried in ritual observances or placed on altars.

Chetro Ketl wooden objects are similar in form to a few of the ethnographic wooden objects used in ceremonies. Viewing the Chetro Ketl wood as a complete assemblage, we believe that it either represents a portion of a composite suite of artifacts such as an altar, or represents parts of ritual gear worn or carried in certain rites. Morrison observed that these rites may not have been totally religious in nature. While the Chetro Ketl wood can be said to be ritualistic in the sense that it is non-utilitarian, there is no evidence to show that the Chetro Ketl materials were ceremonial in the sense that much ethnographic painted wood is ceremonial. It does not seem unreasonable to suggest that the artifacts could have had a secular function, similar to that of the Hopi *mongkoho*, as paraphernalia used to indicate status roles. The fragments are not so large as to preclude attachment to the person and most could have been carried as badges of office or symbols of status.

We have speculated that the Chetro Ketl artifacts on a general level were utilized in some form of ritual observance. As was noted, ethnographic examples of flat, painted and carved wood can be broadly divided into those artifacts that are used in a more or less stationary position during the rite (normally an altar arrangement), and those artifacts that are carried or worn during the rite. It has also been noted that in some instances artifact function may shift, so that wands or sticks carried in dance or moving ceremony also may be placed on altars during kiva ritual or in shrines following a ceremony.

The archaeological evidence for use of wooden altars is virtually nonexistent. Smith (1952: 322) notes that "no certainly identifiable remains of wooden altars have been found in Pueblo ruins of any prehistoric period, even in cave ruins that have been protected from moisture and in which other perishable objects have been preserved." Although we found occasional references in the archaeological literature to altar pieces, for example, "altar fittings" at Aztec Ruin (Morris 1928: 313; 1939: Pl. 145), these identifications were not based on contextual information comparisons with ethnographic examples, or detailed study of the artifacts.

The morphological evidence for use of painted wood as altar paraphernalia is equally scanty. Though we did not expect the Chetro Ketl items to compare closely with recent altar forms, our general impression gained from study of the Chetro Ketl artifacts was that few of the items had the attributes necessary for altar use. In particular, most of the items were too small to have served effectively as altar slats, unless, as in some Hopi cases, numerous small items were tied to an upright framework. Evidence for inserting any of the slats or other objects into wooden frames or sand ridges to form altar backdrops was lacking, though holes present in many of the objects could have been used for tying the artifact to uprights. Morrison noted that most of the painted wood specimens, especially the slats, were decorated on both surfaces, suggesting that the complete objects were intended to be seen from both sides. Presumably this would not be a requirement for altar objects, which in most instances are positioned to be seen from only one side.

Morphological evidence also suggests that some of the flat fragments were intended to have formed parts of large, composite, three-dimensional constructions. Unfortunately, no union of components can be made from the fragments to support the postulated reconstruction of the three-dimensional forms, but enough examples of bird parts exist (at least 3 bodies, 3 heads, 4 wings, 2 bills, and 10 tails) to strongly suggest that this may have been the case. If so, this contrasts with usual morphology of the Pueblo slat altars.

In brief, we believe that Gordon Vivian's initial identification of the Room 93 material as altar parts was in error. It was an error that was compounded in later identifications, for in at least one instance a direct comparison was made between the Chetro Ketl artifacts and the Hopi Blue Flute altar. We believe that Smith's (1952: 322) speculation that "mural painting antedated the use of upright wooden altars as the focus for kiva ritual" is more correct, thus placing the development of upright wooden altars late in the history of Pueblo ritual.

Archaeological evidence for painted wooden artifacts used as hand-carried objects or items worn on the person during dance or other rites is essentially as tenuous as the data supporting the use of wood in altars. Many of the painted and carved wooden artifacts from the Mogollon area have been identified as "tablitas" or "wands," and similar "wands" have been reported from the general Anasazi area. In almost all instances, however, the basis for this identification is tentative or unsubstantiated. Essentially the only firm evidence we have for postulating the prehistoric or early historic use of hand-held objects or items worn on the body is depictions in kiva murals of humans carrying staffs, wands, bows and other ritual paraphernalia (Smith 1952; Vivian 1961; Hibben 1975). In most cases, however, this mural art postdates the wooden artifactual material under consideration.

Morphologically, some of the wooden items from Chetro Ketl are characterized by attributes that suggest that the object was carried or worn. The zoomorphic wands with reed wrapped handles and the oval form with handle probably represent the best examples of objects that may have been intended for carrying; however, other items such as the plaques could have been carried if handles on the objects were present. There is also ample ethnographic evidence for the use of ritual bows and arrows in dance and other ceremonies. The size of the Chetro Ketl objects correlates well with use as staff parts, wands and small images. In addition, as has been noted earlier, most of the artifacts from Chetro Ketl are decorated on both sides—an important aspect in moving ritual. Furthermore, attachment holes in many of the items, especially the horns and discs, suggest that some forms may have been attached to or suspended from perishable masks or other dance gear.

Tentatively, we are inclined to postulate that the Chetro Ketl artifacts were used primarily in ritual that involved what Parsons has termed "public dramatization." Parsons (1939: 478) notes that "the altar or esoteric ceremony is usually followed by a public dramatization or processional or dance or race." She continues, "Dramatization lends itself to greater variation than does kachina dance or altar ritual, yet there are certain stereotype features in the highly stylized drama complex; procession and parade of the fetishes; . . . finally, all those mimetic rites which consist in acting as you would have the Spirits act." Parsons (1939: 487) indicates that a large part of the ritual carried out in public dramatizations is based on sympathetic magic, "particularly on the concept that like causes like." Thus, "if you look like one with power, also if you act like him, you get his power" (Parsons 1939:489). This is particularly important in acts of sympathetic magic where ritual involves the practice of substituting an image or representation for the object or thing desired. Prayer-images and mask-images, as well as a number of other ceremonial objects, serve as representations of important aspects of Puebloan cosmology and myth. "Such representations are in varying degree forms of compulsive magic insuring the presence or imparting the power of the thing represented, and they are referred to by the very name of the things represented—lightning, clouds, rainbow, star" (Parsons 1939: 489).

The presence of identifiable bird and lightning forms, possible horned forms, and zoomorphic or anthropomorphic wands in the Chetro Ketl collection quite frankly has influenced our tentative identification of the artifacts as parts of images and other representations used in public ceremonies. We do not think that their use in this context precludes use in more stationary contexts (altar or esoteric ceremonies) but we doubt that this was their primary function. We would further postulate that the development of ritual art forms for public display was an important aspect of Chacoan ritual.

CHACOAN RITUAL

Chacoan ritual is a subject beyond the scope of this report and we do not intend to consider it in any detail. Rather, our purpose is to indicate how the Chetro Ketl artifacts may have figured in a generalized Chacoan ceremonial pattern.

Essentially all references to Chacoan religious organization (and there have been very few) have been based on interpretations drawn from architectural data. Basically, these have taken two approaches. On the one hand, some researchers have believed that Chacoan religious practices, as expressed through architecture, were essentially Puebloan (Vivian and Reiter 1960; Vivian 1959; Vivian and Mathews 1965). On the other hand, the theory that non-Puebloan forces may have influenced Anasazi religious practices, and those in Chaco Canyon in particular, has been expressed by Ferdon (1955) and others (Rohn and others 1968; DiPeso 1974). The architectural manifestations referred to include great houses, tower kivas, double-walled and tri-walled structures, rock-cut stairways, roads, masonry columns, and "platform mounds."

Though others have discussed the subject since, Ferdon was the first to elaborate upon the thesis of Mesoamerican influence in the religious development of Anasazi culture. He notes that between A.D. 1050 and 1330 at least five architectural similarities can be discerned among the high cultures of central Mexico and the Southwestern cultures, particularly the Anasazi, and he states, "Furthermore, these traits are found intimately associated with religious architecture in Mexico" (Ferdon 1955: 24). Although Ferdon considered that the impact of the cult of Quetzalcoatl on the Anasazi was great, he did state that "at the present state of our knowledge, the Mexican impact upon the San Juan Anasazi, as inferred from archaeological evidence, appears to have been insufficient to have drastically changed the latter's traditional social and religious organization" (Ferdon 1955: 25).

Vivian (1959) has suggested, however, that the changes noted in religious architecture in the Anasazi area, and particularly Chaco Canyon, not be attributed to the result of influence from high cultures in Mexico but instead to an evolutionary trend peculiar to this part of the Anasazi world. Vivian and Mathews (1965: 115) observe that "the developments in the

Chaco in the 11th and the early part of the 12th centuries were not in the direct line of the Northern Pueblo continuum . . . . The distinctive traits that we have so often emphasized—great kivas 50 to 60 feet in diameter, great kivas serving more than one community, tri-walled structures, tower kivas up to three stories in height, interpueblo water collecting systems —all imply a growing measure of specialization, social control, and interpueblo control." Vivian (1959: 85) conjectured that social control may have been invested in a "developing priestly class . . . concerned with ritual elaboration and its architecture, masks, wall paintings, and movable or slat altars." Vivian's hesitation in proposing an actual priestly ruling class in the Chaco prompted Peckham (1963: 71-2) to cite instances of "quasi-priestly-ruling-class" personages in modern Puebloan societies and to predict that such positions occurred prehistorically.

The question of whether changes in Chacoan religious patterns can be derived from the influence of external forces or represent internal shifts in a long-established system cannot be resolved through study of the Chetro Ketl artifacts. We do believe, however, that the artifacts suggest certain means for religious expression. In our opinion many of the architectural forms that are supposedly indicative of an elaboration of Chacoan ritual are more conducive to public display or dramatization than they are to more secretive and limited esoteric rites. In particular we would cite the rock-cut stairways, roads, great kivas, the colonnaded gallery at Chetro Ketl (if it was related to ritual practices), and large enclosed courtyards in towns as architectural manifestations suitable for public ceremonies. If social control was necessary it could be most effectively achieved through public dramatizations on roads, within great kivas, and in town plazas. To achieve more dramatic effect it is not inconceivable that elaborate paraphernalia would have been developed for processions, dances, and other public rites. In our view the Chetro Ketl artifacts would have served this purpose.

It is now generally accepted that during the period from at least A.D. 950 to approximately A.D. 1150 or slightly later two community types existed in Chaco Canyon. These have been identified as towns and villages, and differences between the two communities have been defined (Vivian 1970). One of the primary differences is the presence of the architectural forms discussed above in towns and not in villages. Obviously, ritual would have been carried out in villages, but the particular rites may not have been oriented necessarily toward public dramatization. In contrast, we believe that public dramatization may have been especially important in towns, not only for the occupants of towns but for village dwellers as well. A number of researchers have interpreted the presence of iso-lated great kivas in the vicinity of villages as an example of town-village integration. One means for increasing integration may have been the production of elaborate ceremonies by town priests for the inhabitants of villages.

We believe that this idea has merit, but the archaeological record may indicate otherwise. As was noted in Chapter 3, a number of carved and painted wood specimens closely resembling the Chetro Ketl artifacts were recovered from the village site of Bc 50 (Brand and others 1937) in Chaco Canyon. This suggests that similar ritual was practiced in both towns and villages or that the material at Bc 50 is out of context. While we are tempted to postulate that these items may represent loot vandalized from Room 93 at Chetro Ketl, we recognize the difficulty in proving this simple solution to a complex problem. Instead, we consider the presence of similar ritual artifacts in towns and villages as raising new questions regarding the relationships between Chacoan communities.

Appendix A

DESCRIPTION OF THE ARTIFACTS

Dulce N. Dodgen

FLAT CARVED FORMS

Birds

Head and Body Parts (Figs. A.1 *a-f*, 2.3). A parrot-like head with topknot is carved from a single thin piece of wood. Its flat surfaces and evenly rounded edges are smoothed. It is broken below the neck or breast; the side not illustrated is burned slightly on the upper half. Both sides are painted identically. The green (body paint) and the yellow (on the topknot, eye, and center of the beak) are lustrous and crackled; the brown paint in the center of the eye and on the beak is thick and lumpy. The broken topknot has lost the resin binder of the yellow band above and the brown resin paint below.

Maximum length, 16.9 cm; maximum width, 6.4 cm; average overall thickness, 0.4 cm.

The five fragments illustrated with the head may have been associated, for they are nearly identical in carving, thickness, and style and colors of paints, which also differ noticeably from other pieces in the collection. Fragments *b*, *d*, *e*, and *f* are 0.6 cm in central thickness; *c* is a splinter from one flat surface only. Paints are the same as those used on the head, and both sides of all pieces are painted identically. The surfaces not illustrated of *b*, *d*, and *f* and both flat surfaces of *e* appear to have lost the resinous paint base, leaving only the pale mineral green and yellow intact. Fragment *d* has two sinew bindings serving either to splice two small pieces into a large one or to repair a split that occurred during construction.

Head (Fig. A.2 *a*; reverse, Fig. 2.3). This specimen is constructed from two thin slabs. One side of the head and the bill are carved from one piece, while the opposing side of the head and neck are carved from another. These are held together by three sinew bindings. A split through the head from the corner of the mouth is repaired with two other bindings, one sinew and one hard (plant) fiber. This apparently occurred

during the carving of the bill since the stitches are painted over. Perforations are crudely drilled. Surfaces of both main elements are unevenly smoothed. The edges are cut squarely and smoothed.

Both sides are painted identically; the side not illustrated has lost most of the paint on the neck. The black paint is dull, flat, thick, and crackled; the white and yellow paints are similar. Thin green paint covers most of the neck over the black paint as though to simulate the iridescence of black feathers.

Length, bill to head, 13.8 cm; length, head to neck, 13.3 cm; average thickness of bill piece, 0.3 cm; size of neck piece, 0.4 cm thick at the base of neck, tapering to 0.2 cm at top of head.

Head (Figs. A.2 *b*, 2.3). This specimen is carved from a single thin section. Flat surfaces and rounded edges are smoothed; the upper edge is more sharply rounded; diagonal abrasions occur along the lower edge. It is broken through the approximate center of the head. The mouth is an incised line on both sides, 3 cm long from end of the snout and approximately 0.1 cm wide. A tiny nostril hole 4 cm from the end of the snout pierces the total thickness of the piece. A topknot is made of a narrow strip of tanned hide averaging 0.4 cm in thickness; it is 6.5 cm long and 1.2 cm wide at its base, tapering gradually to a rounded point. It is attached 8 cm from the end of the snout by a hard fiber thread sewn to the corners of the plume base and through a small hole 0.4 cm from the upper edge of the head.

The specimen is painted identically on both sides, and the paint is carried over the upper edge only. The blue on the head and topknot appears to have been applied first and later covered with a resin varnish which deepened the color slightly. Unevenly painted edges show flat or dull paint under the brownish varnish. The yellow of the beak is a thin watery application.

Maximum length, 9.7 cm; maximum width, 4.1 cm; central thickness, 0.7 cm.

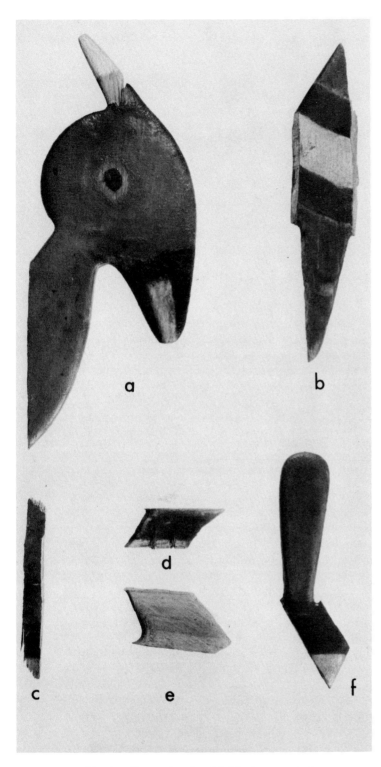

Fig. A.1. Parrot head, *a*; bird body parts, *b-f*.

Bill (Figs. A.2 *c*, 2.3). The bill is attached with three sinew bindings to a broken fragment to form a stationary joint. It is carved from a single piece with smoothed flat surfaces and rounded edges. The mouth is a slot 6.5 cm long. Perforations for the bindings are drilled, then punched. Edges and both flat surfaces show traces of thin yellow paint. The inside surface of the mouth is painted a dull black.

Maximum length, 10.3 cm; maximum width, 3.1 cm; thickness, 0.6 cm at center, 0.35 cm along edges.

Bill Fragment (Fig. A.2 *d*). This specimen is broken from the corner of the mouth to the central binding perforation. It is similar to one mandible of *c*; no binding or base piece is present. Traces of yellow paint show on both sides and edges. The inner mouth surface is dull black.

Maximum length, 9.5 cm; maximum width, 1.65 cm; maximum thickness, 0.5 cm.

Tail (Figs. A.3, 2.3). The wide, fan-like piece appears to have been carved from a single thinned slab, although a narrow section is now missing. Surfaces are well smoothed; edges of the straight sides are cut square and smoothed. The scalloped edge is especially well carved; scallops are nearly equal and are evenly thinned and rounded on both sides. A slot 5.5 cm long and 0.6 cm wide receives the handle-like appendage. This second element is split longitudinally and broken across the distal end. The two elements are held together with three sinew bindings, and a fourth is further down the handle (see Fig. B.1 *a-b*). A hole and small notch beyond the last binding indicate the former location of a fifth tie. All are approximately 2 cm apart. Both sides are painted identically; the thick, gritty white along the scalloped edge was applied first; the black on the remainder of the tail is dull, and the green on the handle is chalky and fugitive.

Tail: length of unbroken straight side, 14.8 cm; approximate original width, 21.0 cm; thickness, 0.5 cm, tapering abruptly to 0.2 cm at the scalloped edge.

Handle: length, 11.5 cm; width below tail, 1.5 cm; width inside tail-slot tapers from 0.9 to 0.7 cm; thickness, 0.6 cm.

Tails (Fig. A.4 *a-b*). Each of these tails is carved from a single thin section. The flat surfaces of *a* are smoothed, though coarsely grained. The scalloped edge is slightly thinned and rounded; other edges are squarely cut. The lower half of the illustrated side is concave (the area measures 3 cm vertically by 5.8 cm horizontally—the full width of the object—just above the scalloped edge). Two carefully drilled holes at the top are broken out to the edge. The object was originally painted in the same manner on both sides. The illustrated side is a flat green on the upper two-thirds

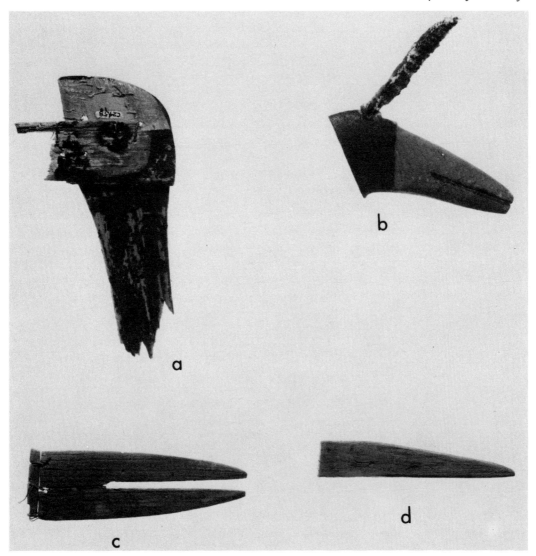

Fig. A.2. Bird heads, *a-b;* bills, *c-d.*

and a pale resinous brown below. The side not shown indicates the green was once mixed with a resin base and the area below it was painted a dark resinous brown.

The flat surfaces of specimen *b* are unevenly smoothed and the edges are irregularly squared. A piece is broken out between three triangularly placed perforations at the top; a fragment along one side is missing. On the side not illustrated is an unpainted area at the top of the specimen. It is slightly concave and appears to have been overlapped by a second, attached element before the object was painted. This element could have been another shaped piece of wood or possibly a flexible material such as cloth or hide joining the wing to a body to produce a moveable joint. The specimen is painted generally the same on both sides; the upper band is green, the central

band is black, and the lower band is yellow. All three colors are thick and flat or dull; a white layer appears to underlie the green only.

a: maximum length, 7.9 cm; maximum width, 5.8 cm; thickness, 0.6 cm, 0.4 cm at center of concavity.

b: maximum length, 9.9 cm; maximum width, 6.0 cm; average thickness, 3.5 cm.

Tail Fragment (Fig. A.4 *c*). This fragment is nearly identical to approximately half of 4 *d* except for having large scallops. Surfaces and edges are well smoothed. Only traces of white remain on the lower band. The middle band is black and the upper band is yellow; both are thin and dull.

Length, 9.4 cm; maximum width, 4.2 cm; thickness, 0.4 cm to 0.2 cm at scalloped edge.

Fig. A.3. Bird tail.

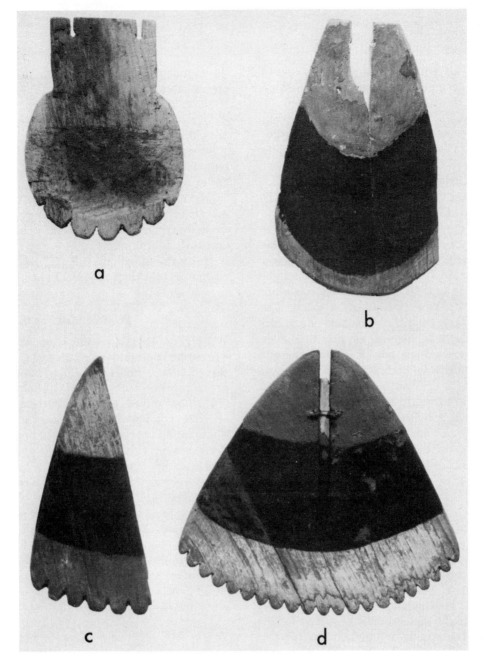

Fig. A.4. Bird tails.

Tail (Fig. A.4 *d*). Carved from a single thin section, this specimen has flat surfaces and well-smoothed, rounded edges. Its scalloped edge is carefully and evenly carved and is slightly thinned. A slot 6.4 cm deep holds a fragment of a narrow projection that appears to taper or decrease in width (perpendicular to that of the tail piece) toward the opening of the slot. The two elements are held fast with two sinew bindings which pass through perforations in the tang-piece (rather than passing over as on the large black and white specimen just described in Fig. A.3), then through two holes in the tail. The white paint on the lower band is thick, dull, and chalky. The black on the middle band is very thick, crackled, lustrous, and

was applied from the base of the tail to the edge of the white band. The yellow above is thick, crackled, lustrous, and is applied over the black. Both sides are identically painted with paint carried over the edges.

Tail: maximum length, 9.5 cm; maximum width, 10.2 cm; thickness, 0.45 cm at base, tapering to 0.2 cm along scalloped edge.

Tang: length, 5.4 cm; width, 1.2 cm at center, tapering to approximately 0.7 cm at inserted end.

Tail Fragments (Fig. A.5). The four similarly shaped and painted fragments *a-d* appear to have come from at least three, or possibly four, separately carved objects when outlines and painted bands are extended.

The proportions of the painted stripes are too divergent for the fragments to have fit in the same object.

The flat surfaces of specimen *a*, which is carved from a single thin section, are smoothed over rather rough wood grain. The edges are slightly rounded; the zigzag edge is roughly shaped. The object is broken along the two parallel sides and at the base. Both sides are painted identically with bands of thick, slightly lustrous black and dark resinous brown. There is a trace of green on the upper broken edge.

Specimen *b* is carved from two thin, flat sections spliced together with one sinew binding. The wood grain is slightly different on each piece and the adjacent edges had been smoothed before the pieces were joined; therefore, the binding is clearly a splice. The object is broken along the parallel outside edges and irregularly along the base. Surfaces are smoothed over coarse grain; the zigzag lower edge is crudely carved. It is painted identically on both sides; the paints are the same as on *a*. A large area of resin-base green remains at the top of the left section.

In item *c*, which is carved from a single thin section, the flat surfaces are smoothed, with slightly rounded edges. It is somewhat more carefully worked than the other three similar fragments. The painting is identical on both sides, as on the specimens described above.

Specimen *d* also is carved from a single thin section. The flat surfaces are smoothed over coarse grain and the edges are slightly rounded. It is broken along one edge. The opposite, parallel edge is finished or smoothed and a broken sinew binding is placed similarly to that on *b*. This piece was, therefore, also previously spliced. It is painted identically on both sides; the paints are the same as those described for *a*.

Flat smooth surfaces also are found on specimens *e* and *f*, both of which were carved from single thin sections.

The surfaces of *e* have slightly rounded edges. It is broken along the two parallel sides. The object is painted the same on both sides; the yellow along the scalloped edge is thin and matte; the remainder of the piece is painted in a green that is thick, crackled, chipped, and covered over with an untinted coat of resin that overlaps slightly onto the longest broken edge.

Specimen *f* is thinly convex in cross section with the lower, straight edge tapered and more sharply rounded than the upper concave edge. The lower unpainted end is a carefully shaped tang or flange; the parallel sides are square-cut and smoothed. The notches appear to have been drilled holes, and the parallel sides above the notches are the only broken edges. Both sides are painted alike, a chalky light green.

a: maximum length, 13 cm; maximum width, 5 cm; average thickness, 0.3 cm.

b: maximum length, 13.9 cm; maximum width, 6.7 cm; thickness, 0.4 cm along base, tapering to 0.25 cm along upper edge.

c: maximum length, 8.2 cm; maximum width, 2.6 cm; thickness, 0.45 cm at lower end, tapering to 0.15 cm at upper edge.

d: maximum length, 11.9 cm; maximum width, 4.7 cm; average thickness, 0.3 cm.

e: maximum length, 8.4 cm; maximum width, 2.5 cm; thickness, 0.3 cm.

f: maximum length, 3.9 cm; maximum width, 1.8 cm; maximum thickness, 0.45 cm.

Possible Bird Forms

Wings (Fig. A.6 *a-d*). These three fragments represent a presumed pair of naturalistically shaped wings, each carved from a single thin, flat element. The surfaces are smoothed and edges slightly rounded. The scalloped edges are particularly well carved. Specimens *a* and *b* were joined together with two sinew bindings; the lower one is broken (a mere tuft remaining); the upper is 2-ply Z-twisted, then S-twisted. Specimen *c* seems to be a section of the opposite wing analogous to *a*. Each piece is broken along the longest side. Black and white paints are flat and dull; white is very fugitive. Figure 6 *d* shows the reverse side of all three fragments. The unpainted oval-shaped areas that indicate the former presence of some sort of backing at each wing joint, possibly cloth or leather, are visible. From the loose and broken bindings of *a* and *b*, it is difficult to tell whether this was a moveable or fixed joint.

	a	*b*	*c*
Max. length	13.0 cm	10.2 cm	12.7 cm
Max. width	5.0 cm	1.9 cm	2.5 cm
Avg. thickness	0.35 cm	0.2 cm	0.25 cm

Tail (Fig. A.6 *e*). The flat surfaces of this piece, carved from a single thin section, are smoothed over rather rough grain; edges are irregularly rounded. There is a fragment of one sinew binding 1.4 cm below the short straight edge. Both sides have traces of black and white paint; the side illustrated appears to have two black chevrons on a white background; a 1.5 cm wide band along the upper short, straight edge on both sides is covered irregularly with thick resin. Traces of white paint form a very even line below the resin area suggesting that the straight edge *may* have been inserted *into* another wooden piece and the resin used as a glue.

Length, 7.9 cm; maximum width, 3.7 cm; average thickness, 0.2 cm.

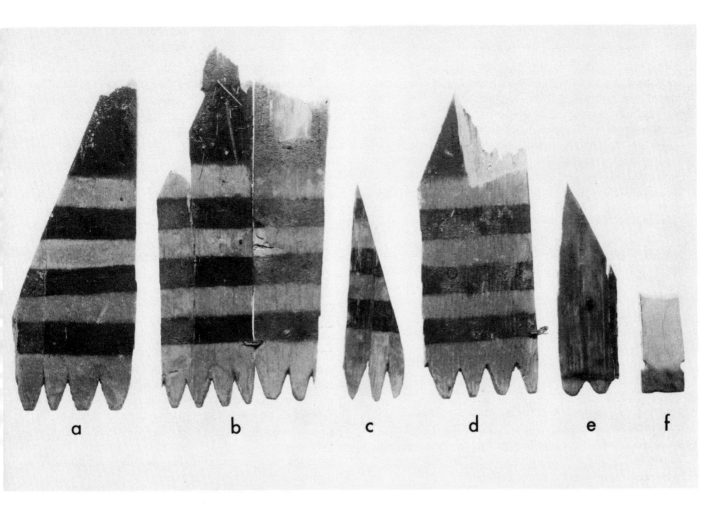

Fig. A.5. Bird tail fragments.

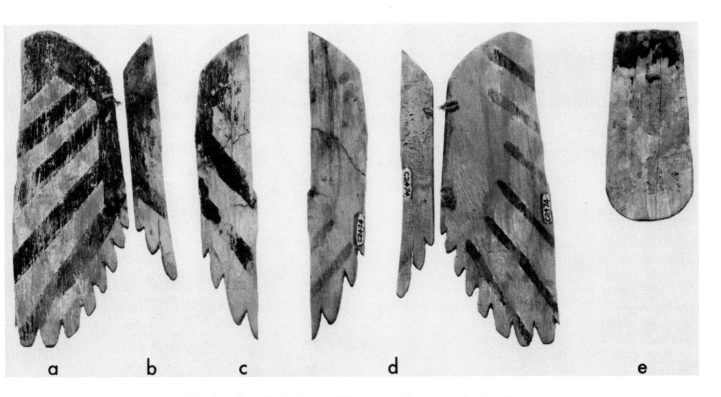

Fig. A.6. Possible bird parts. Wings, *a-c*, (*d*, reverse of *a-c*); tail, *e*.

Tail Fragment (Fig. A.7 *a*). This piece is carved from a single thin, flat section. The surfaces are smoothed and the edges rounded. The scalloped edge is slightly thinned and rounded in cross section. The yellow paint on the scalloped edge is lustrous and slightly crackled. The brown paint above is thick and rather lumpy. The reverse side is identical.

Maximum length, 2.3 cm; maximum width, 3.5 cm; thickness, 0.45 cm, thinned along scalloped edge to 0.2 cm.

Curved Fragment (Fig. A.7 *b*). The surfaces of this fragment, carved from a single thin, flat section, are smoothed. The edges are cut square and smoothed. Both sides and the right edge (above the break) show traces of pale green pigment. The outer, curved edge has traces of a reddish pigment. The piece is slightly scorched at the tip.

Maximum length, 13.6 cm; maximum width, 2.5 cm; average thickness, 0.55 cm.

Curved Fragment (Fig. A.7 *c*). The surfaces of this fragment, carved from a single thin, flat section, are smoothed. Abrasion marks run diagonally across the wood grain; the edges are rounded. There are no indications of pigment on any surface.

Maximum length, 11.6 cm; width of broken base, 6.8 cm; average thickness, 0.45 cm.

Shaped Fragment (Fig. A.7 *d-e*). Carved from a single thin section, this fragment has smoothed surfaces. What was apparently intended to be the visible surface is shown in *d*; the reverse side is *e*. The object is broken at the narrow end and through the two drilled, then punched, perforations. Side *e* is carved in two planes; the step between them is parallel with the diagonal lower edge, suggesting that a second parallel-sided piece was fitted into the thinner, unpainted area and secured through the two holes producing an immoveable elbow joint. The area above the step is painted alike on both sides; the lower band is a flat, dull yellow; the upper band is green and appears to have been mixed with a resinous base.

Maximum length, 6.4 cm; maximum width, 1.3 cm; thickness at wide end, 0.45 cm; thickness at narrow end, 0.6 cm.

Slotted Fragment (Fig. A.7 *f*). Carved from a single thin slab, this fragment has flat surfaces and smoothed, rounded edges. One outer edge and slot are the only remaining finished edges. There is no evidence of any perforation along the slot. Most of the piece is yellow; the stripe at the lower end is blue. Both colors are fairly thick and appear to have originally been covered with resinous varnish. The opposite side is a resinous green.

Maximum length, 10.7 cm; maximum width, 3.0 cm; average thickness, 0.45 cm.

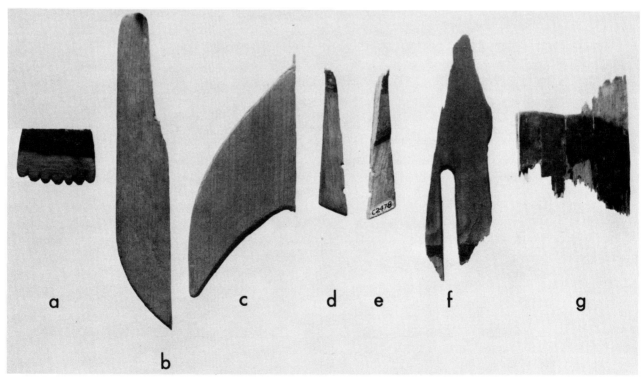

Fig. A.7. Possible bird parts. Tail, *a*; various fragments, *b-g*.

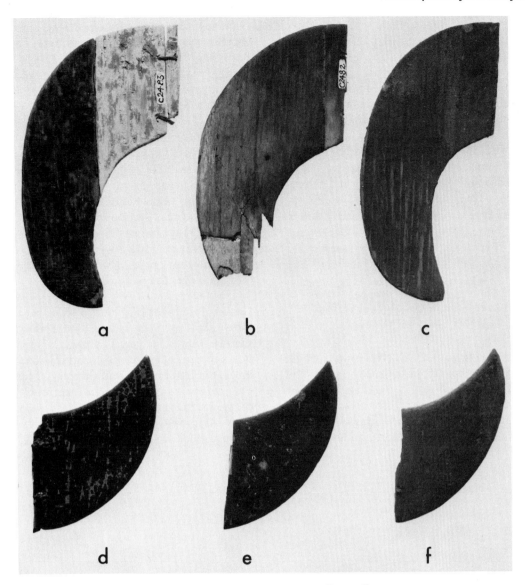

Fig. A.8. Curved fragments or "horns."

Fragment (Fig. A.7 *g*). This irregular fragment is carved from a single flat section. It has smoothed surfaces and a single finished, unbroken well-rounded edge. The yellow paint (above) is thick and lustrous; the brown (below) is thick and crackled and may be pure resin. Only one-half of the brown area is intact on the reverse side.

Maximum length, 6.2 cm; maximum width, 5.7 cm; thickness of unsplit area, 0.55 cm.

Horns

Curved Fragments (Fig. A.8 *a-c*). Three specimens are similarly shaped and painted horn-like objects. Each is carved from a single thin, flat section. Specimen *a* has

a small fragment attached at its base with two sinew bindings. The joint is fixed and immoveable. Specimen *b* is broken through two similarly placed perforations; a wider splinter is split from the base of *c*, apparently just to the side of any holes for binding. The surfaces on all three appear to have been painted identically on both sides with dark resinous green. One piece of *a* has lost the gum base from both surfaces; the right section of *a* is now a pale, flat green.

	a	*b*	*c*
Max. length	12.2 cm	10.8 cm	11.9 cm
Width at horn base	4.5 cm	4.8 cm	4.6 cm
Avg. thickness of all fragments	0.25 cm		

Curved Fragments (Fig. A.8 *d-f*). Each of these three small, similarly shaped and painted pieces is carved from a thin, flat section. The surfaces are well smoothed with rounded edges. A small narrow fragment is joined to the base of *d* by two sinew bindings. Fragment *e* is broken through two similarly placed holes, and *f* is broken through one of these perforations. Both sides of all three are painted with dark resinous green. Both surfaces of *d* and one surface of *e* are highly lustrous, crackled, and missing several small chips of crackled paint. Both surfaces of *f* and the reverse side of *e* have thin, dull green brushed over a surface texture similar to *d*. The unbroken perforation in *f* is filled with paint.

	d	*e*	*f*
Max. length	8.50 cm	8.20 cm	8.3 cm
Width at horn base	4.70 cm	4.50 cm	4.6 cm
Avg. thickness	0.25 cm	0.25 cm	0.3 cm

Curved Fragment (Fig. A.9 *a*). Carved from a single flat section, this piece has flat smoothed surfaces. The edges are slightly rounded and somewhat flatter on the outer curve. The object is tightly attached to a narrow fragment by three sinew bindings. This immoveable joint may be a splice rather than an attachment to a second, separately shaped element since the carved ends of the fragment continue the curvature of both sides of the horn-like piece. The specimen is painted identically on both sides, a chalky light green.

Maximum length, 9.7 cm; width at base, 4.6 cm; average thickness, 0.5 cm.

Curved Fragment (Fig. A.9 *b*). Carved from a single thin, flat section, this piece is coarse-grained with smoothed surfaces. The edges are rounded with the outer curve more sharply rounded than the inner. It is broken along the wide base. The yellow on the left is slightly lustrous; the brown on the right is thick and grainy, perhaps indicating pure resin. The reverse side is identically painted.

Maximum length, 13.8 cm; width along broken edge, 6.9 cm; thickness, 0.6 cm.

Curved Fragment (Fig. A.9 *c*). Carved from a single thin slab, this piece has smoothed flat surfaces and slightly rounded edges. The piece is broken along one side and through three perforations. The yellow paint at the top and bottom and the central black stripe are both slightly lustrous. The side not illustrated is completely covered with dark brown resin.

Maximum length, 8 cm; maximum width, 3.5 cm; average thickness, 0.35 cm.

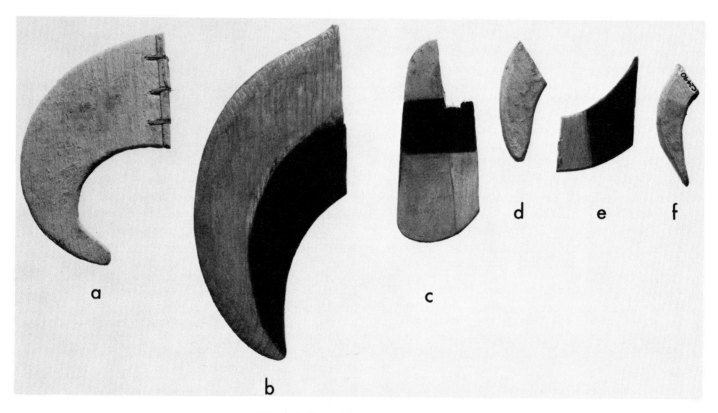

Fig. A.9. Curved fragments or "horns."

Curved Fragment (Fig. A.9 *d*). Specimen *d* is carved from a single thin section. It has smoothed flat surfaces and rounded edges. It is covered with a thick, dull yellow paint. The reverse side is identical.

Maximum length, 4.9 cm; maximum width, 2.1 cm; thickness, 0.55 cm.

Curved Fragment (Fig. A.9 *e*). Carved from a single thin section, the flat surfaces of this piece are smoothed with slightly rounded edges. The narrow end is broken through a small perforation; 0.1 cm from the perforation is a small round concavity (0.2 cm in diameter) drilled into the center of this edge. Under magnification it appears to be filled with amber resin or a similar material. Its function is not apparent. Resin does not occur anywhere else along the edge. The yellow paint to the left is thick and slightly lustrous. The brown to the right is thick, crackled, and lustrous and appears to be pure plant resin. The reverse side is identical.

Maximum length, 5.9 cm; maximum width, 3.6 cm; thickness, 0.45 cm.

Curved Fragment (Fig. A.9 *f*). Carved from a single thin section, this fragment has smoothed flat surfaces and well-rounded edges. It is broken along the slightly flared base. All surfaces are painted a thick golden yellow.

Maximum length, 5.0 cm; width at base, 0.6 cm; thickness, 0.55 cm.

Long, Curved Fragments (Fig. A.10 *a-b*). Each of these pieces is carved from a single thin section and has smoothed flat surfaces and well-rounded edges. The thickness diminishes slightly from the outer to the inner curve. Specimen *a* is painted identically on both sides. The brown on the left is thick, crackled, and lustrous; the right is covered with resin only. Both sides of *b* were originally painted identically. The tip retains the brownish color of *a*, having broken off before the rest of the object lost its paint. In shape and color, *b* is nearly identical to *a*.

Maximum length: *a*, 29.2 cm; *b*, 25.5 cm; width 14 cm from tip: *a*, 4.1 cm; *b*, 4.1 cm; average thickness: *a*, 0.6 cm; *b*, 0.6 cm.

Curved Fragment (Fig. A.11 *a*). Carved from a single thin section, this piece has smoothed flat surfaces. The curved edge is slightly rounded and the straight edge is squarely cut. Two broken sinew bindings remain. Both sides are painted identically with brown paint that is thick and resin-like. The reverse side is burned along the outer curve.

Maximum length, 15.3 cm; width at base, 4.9 cm; average thickness, 0.5 cm.

a b

Fig. A.10. Curved fragments or "horns."

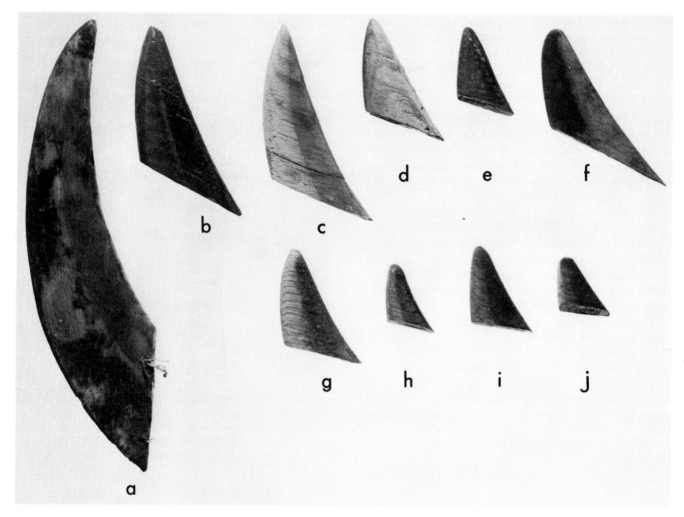

Fig. A.11. Curved fragments or "horns."

Curved Fragments (Fig. A.11 *b-j*). Nine small, broken curved fragments are similar in color and proportion to those shown in Fig. A.10 *a* and *b*. All are carved from thin flat sections and have smoothed surfaces and well-rounded edges. Specimen *f* is thinner and not as sharply pointed. The inner longitudinal half of each piece is (or has evidence of having been) painted with brown resin, as on Fig. A.10 *a*. Specimens *b-f* are painted resinous green along the outer longitudinal half; the analogous areas on *g* through *j* are unpainted. Both sides of *c* and the illustrated side of *d* have lost the resinous coat and base. On each specimen, both sides are painted identically.

Maximum length of *c*, 7.1 cm; average central thickness of *d-g* and *i-j*, 0.6 cm; range of the above, 0.55-0.65 cm; central thickness of *h*, 0.4 cm.

Oval Form With Handle

Fig. A.12 is an oval-shaped artifact with a broken handle-like appendage attached perpendicularly at its center. The flat oval is constructed from four thin slats that were carved separately then joined together with sinew at two points between each slat. The surfaces are irregular, with abrasions diagonal to the wood grain. The edges are unevenly squared and craftsmanship is generally crude. A small perforation occurs at the center and near the edge of each long side; a broken sinew binding remains in one. At the right end (as illustrated), one central slat has a small hole near the edge; at the opposite end another small hole pierces the edge of the second central slat and contains a broken sinew binding. Four large holes, averaging 0.65 cm in diameter, are located around the center of

Fig. A.12. Oval form with handle.

the oval (approximately 3 cm and 1.5 cm apart). Through these pass the cords which fix the handle to the large piece. Two smaller holes, one on either side of the handle, approximately 0.4 cm in diameter and 1.5 cm apart, are likewise utilized. Two larger holes, approximately 0.5 cm in diameter, are placed near the center of the two outer slats, 2 cm in from the edges. The handle is made from a single flat piece with squared edges; the free, broken end appears to have been cut, then broken off. It is attached to the oval form by a rather complicated use of split twigs and yucca cordage which pass through 11 holes averaging 0.3 cm in diameter; the various tying methods are illustrated in Figure B.1 *d-g*. The composite object was decorated after construction and the unillustrated side of the oval was left unpainted. The checkerboard pattern was produced by applying irregular squares of black over a background of white. The black is slightly oily and the white is fugitive. The handle is all black except in the area of the binding.

Oval section: maximum length, 23.9 cm; central width, 12.0 cm; average thickness, 0.3 cm.

Handle section: length, 12.5 cm; width, 4.2 cm; average thickness, 0.35 cm.

Hoop Fragments

These four pieces (Fig. A.13) appear to have come from the same curved object. It was constructed from two thin slats of soft wood, bent and sewn together with sinew and yucca cords. The coarse-grained surfaces are only slightly smoothed and the edges are

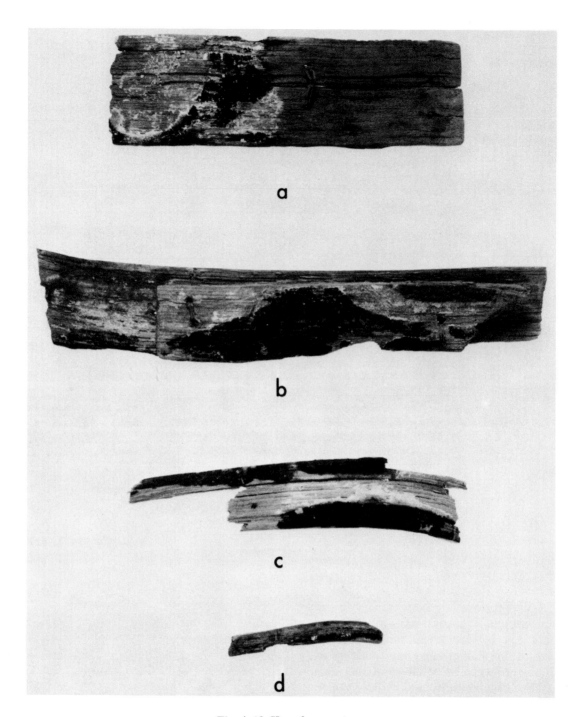

Fig. A.13. Hoop fragments.

generally squared. Specimen *a* appears to be of the original width while *b*, *c*, and *d* have split off along the grain. The right end of *a*, which was overlapped by another piece before being painted, is cut off squarely and smoothed; the opposite end was sawed slightly across the inside surface, then broken off. One sinew stitch apparently joined an overlapping piece to *a*. Specimen *b* is two fragments sewn together. One end of each piece is cut off squarely, though unsmoothed. The opposite ends are broken, the wider one first having been cut or sawed before breaking. A sinew stitch analogous to that on *a* is tied through two perforations in each fragment. The yucca cord fragment pierces both pieces but is broken on the inside hoop surface. Four other small holes and impressions of cordage in the paint indicated other former bindings. Fragment *c* has three small holes, two located in the unpainted, once overlapped area. Specimen *d* is a small fragment; one long edge is cut off squarely and smoothed; the other is broken. Paints are dull oily black and dark brown resin applied over fugitive white on the outer surface only. The inner surface of *a* has traces of a reddish-purple stain.

	a	*b*	*c*
Max. length	14.00 cm	19.3 cm	10.30 cm
Max. width	3.60 cm	3.2 cm	2.50 cm
Avg. thickness	0.25 cm	0.3 cm	0.25 cm

Miscellaneous Forms

Abstract Form with Multiple Appendages (Fig. A.14 *a*). Carved from a single thin section, this piece has smoothed flat surfaces. The edges are well rounded and smoothed. It is split longitudinally; three narrow appendages are broken off. None of the small shaped pieces in the collection approached the particular proportions of the supposed projections on this piece. The left edge of the lower appendage broke through a vertical perforation. A small concavity (0.2 cm in diameter) drilled out just below the perforation is approximately 0.2 cm deep, and under magnification was found to contain a resin-like material. This is identical to the same feature described on the fragment illustrated in Fig. A.9 *e*. Here also its function is unknown. Traces of pale green pigment are evident on the side illustrated, especially on the broadly-curved edge and on the reverse side. The reverse side also shows slight scorching on the upper area.

Maximum length, 20.2 cm; maximum width, 5.9 cm; average thickness, 0.65 cm.

Paddle-Shaped Fragment (Fig. A.14 *b*). Carved from a single thin section, this piece has smoothed flat surfaces. The edges are rounded and are thinner along the upper part of the curved border. The object is split

lengthwise and broken across the narrow end. Traces of pale green pigment occur on both sides and the carved edge; traces of pale reddish pigment are visible on the upper portion of the reverse side.

Maximum length, 26.5 cm; maximum width, 3.0 cm; average thickness, 0.5 cm.

Slat-Pointer (?) (Fig. A.14 *c*). This specimen is carved from a single thin section. The flat, coarse-grained surfaces are smoothed, the edges are cut square. The parallel sides of the shaft on the side not pictured are rounded slightly by rough, uneven gouging or pecking. Other edges are more or less smoothed. Parallel sides of the base are broken, indicating that this section was wider. Red traces are visible on the arrowhead, with pale green traces below. Both sides are painted identically, except that the side illustrated has three faint red dots along the center of the shaft and base. Edges from the shoulder of the base to the tip of the head are red.

Maximum length, 21.7 cm; maximum width, 4.0 cm; average thickness, 0.7 cm.

Squared Fragment (Fig. A. 14 *d*). This thin, flat piece is broken along its two longest sides. It appears to have the same wood grain as *c*. Both sides and square-cut edges are pale green. Thickness is the same as *c*, and although *d* does not fit directly onto *c*, it does seem to be a part of an extension of the squared end.

"Ears" (Fig. A.15 *a-b*). These two similar pieces are each carved from a single thin section. The surfaces of both are slightly convex and smoothed over coarse grain; the curved edges are rounded and the straight edges are squared. Each has two small perforations along the longest straight edge. The upper hole of *b* contains a yucca cord fragment. Paints used on both sides of both pieces are identical and consist of a brown resin around the outside and a white curvilinear strip outlining a blue strip. A yellow stain covers the entire surface. The side not illustrated has a striped design rather than the curvilinear design shown. The two pieces seem not to have been used as a pair since they do not mirror one another exactly in shape or painted surface.

Maximum length: *a* 4.2 cm; *b*, 5.2 cm; maximum width: *a*, 3.6 cm; *b*, 2.8 cm; average thickness: *a*, 0.3 cm; *b*, 0.25 cm.

Elongated Curved Fragments (Fig. A.15 *c-d*). These two similar pieces are each carved from a single thin section. The flat surfaces are smoothed and the edges slightly rounded. On each the split runs lengthwise through two small perforations, approximately 1 cm apart, and near one end. Four narrow horizontal bands of black on an unpainted background decorate

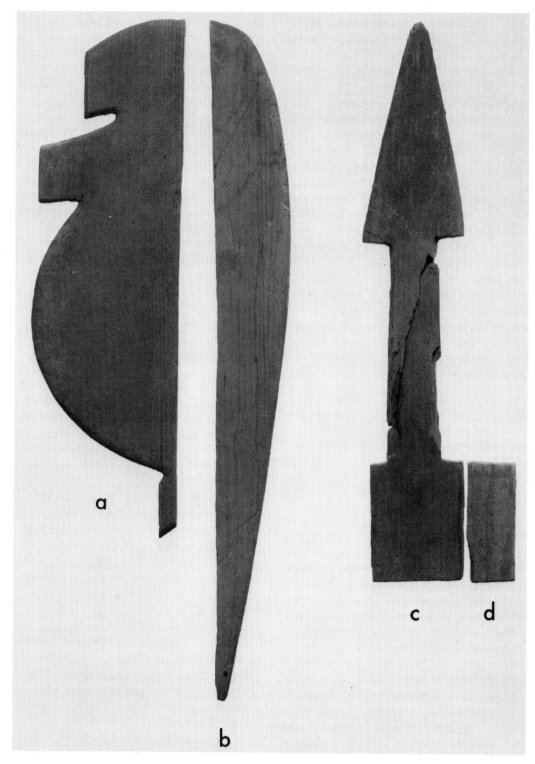

Fig. A.14. Abstract form with multiple appendages, *a*; paddle-shaped fragment, *b*; slat-pointer (?), *c*; squared fragment, *d*.

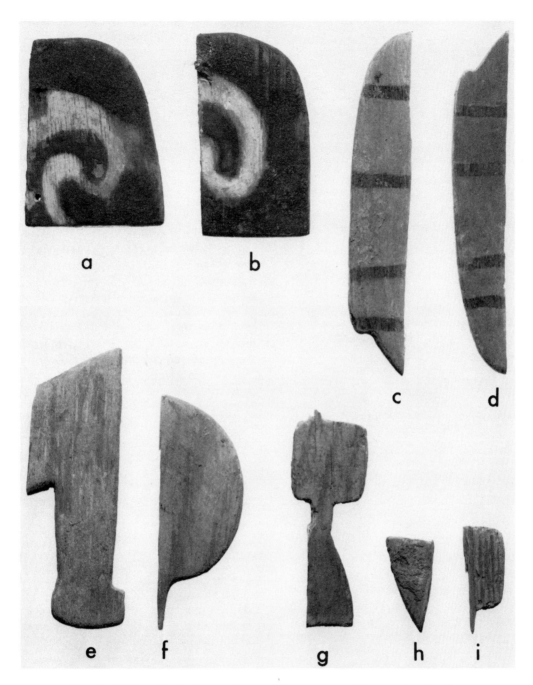

Fig. A.15. "Ears," *a-b*; elongated curved fragments, *c-d*; fragments of anthropomorphic form (?), *e-f*; small carved form, *g*; small carved fragments, *h-i*.

both sides of each specimen. Each appears to be approximately half of the original shape. The two pieces may represent analogous sections of a pair of similar objects—they differ too greatly in wood grain and color and in placement of the painted stripes to have been parts of the same object.

Maximum length: c, 9 cm; d, 9 cm; maximum width: c, 1.6 cm; d, 1.4 cm; average thickness: c, 0.3 cm; d, 0.35 cm.

Fragments of Anthropomorphic Form (?) (Fig. A.15 *e-f*). Both of these pieces are carved from thin flat sections; the wood grain is identical. Surfaces are smoothed, the edges rounded and well carved. There are no traces of pigment on either piece.

Maximum length: e, 6.1 cm; f, 7.2 cm; maximum width: e, 2.2 cm; f, 2.4 cm; average thickness: e, 0.35 cm; f, 0.3 cm.

Small Carved Form (Fig. A.15 *g*). This piece is carved from a single thin section. It has smoothed flat surfaces and edges cut square and crudely whittled. A small broken projection remains at one end. Both sides have traces of pale green pigment. The diagonally curved edge is painted red.

Maximum length, 5.5 cm; maximum width, 2.0 cm; thickness, 0.45 cm.

Small Carved Fragments (Fig. A.15 *h-i*). These two thin, flat pieces appear to be parts of a carved object similar to *g*. There are traces of pale green on both sides of *h* and traces of red pigment on the edges of both. Edges are crudely whittled and their average thickness is 0.45 cm.

Rectangles

Rectangular Fragment (Fig. A.16 *h*). This piece is carved from two thin, flat sections held together with two sinew bindings. The surfaces are smoothed and are irregular in thickness. The edges are square-cut and slightly smoothed. The piece is broken through the two binding perforations and along the long, outside edge of the larger piece. It is painted identically on both sides. The lower part of the object is a chalky, pale green; the upper part is unpainted.

Maximum length, 6.0 cm; maximum width, 3.6 cm; average thickness, 0.25 cm.

Rectangular Fragments (Fig. A.16 *i-l*). Carved from single thin, flat sections, fragments *i*, *k*, and *l* are split along one side; specimen *j* is whole. Edges are irregularly square-cut. Short pieces of hard fiber cordage remain on *j*, *k*, and *l*, indicating that the four rectangular pieces were sewn together in a method closely

similar to, if not identical to, the Holbein stitch described by Wasley (1962: 388); a diagram of this type of binding is given in Figure B.1 *h*. Painted after construction, both sides are painted with thick, grainy white with dull black designs.

	i	*j*	*k*	*l*
Max. length	4.20 cm	4.3 cm	4.4 cm	4.6 cm
Max. width	0.45 cm	2.8 cm	2.2 cm	1.0 cm
Avg. thickness	0.25 cm	0.2 cm	0.3 cm	0.2 cm

Discs

Disc Fragments (Fig. A.16 *a-d*). These four fragments are carved from single thin, flat sections of similarly grained wood. The surfaces are smoothed; the edges are irregularly whittled and smoothed and slightly rounded. Proportions and painted areas are too divergent for any two of *a*, *b*, or *c* to belong to the same object; *d* could be from the opposite side of *b*, being of the same thickness. All of the specimens may have had a projection like that on Figure A.15 *h* at their lower edge. Specimen *a* has a small hole near the center of the curved outer edge; *c* and *d* are split through a similarly placed perforation. Only *c* is painted identically on both sides with bright blue paint; *a* and *b* have some blue areas on the illustrated side only. Specimens *a*, *b*, and *d* each have small areas of brown resin on the most sharply curved section of the edge.

	a	*b*	*c*	*d*
Max. thickness	5.50 cm	4.90 cm	5.3 cm	4.70 cm
Max. width	1.75 cm	1.50 cm	1.5 cm	1.70 cm
Avg. thickness	0.45 cm	0.35 cm	0.4 cm	0.25 cm

Disc Fragments (Fig. A.16 *e-g*). Fragment *e* is carved from a single thin, flat section. The surfaces are smoothed and the edges are slightly rounded. Both sides are painted alike with a dull black border.

Carved from a single thin, flat section, fragment *f* has smoothed surfaces and unevenly rounded edges. Both sides are covered with irregular thicknesses of pale green, chalky pigment.

Also carved from a single thin, flat section, fragment *g* has smooth surfaces and slightly rounded edges. It is broken through four small perforations. It is painted on the illustrated side only with a dull, fugitive black paint.

	a	*b*	*c*
Max. length	3.2 cm	4.70 cm	2.6 cm
Max. width	1.7 cm	1.70 cm	0.7 cm
Thickness	0.2 cm	0.35 cm	0.3 cm

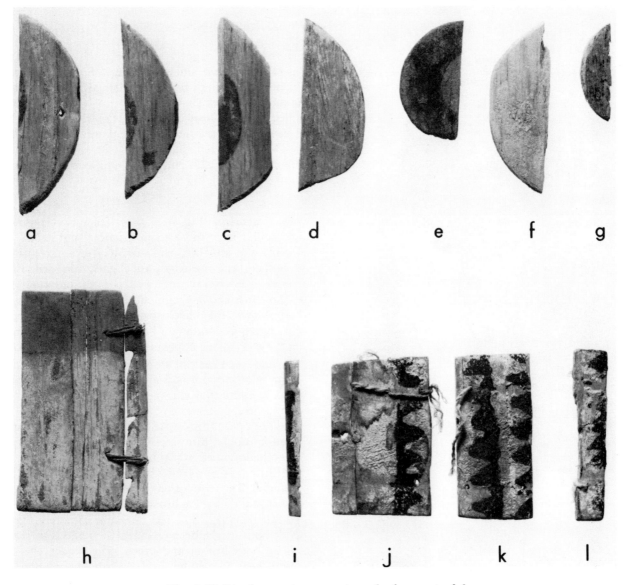

Fig. A.16. Disc fragments, *a-g*; rectangular fragments, *h-l*.

Disc (Fig. A.17 *a*). This piece is carved from a single thin section; surfaces are smoothed and are slightly thinner toward the square-cut edge. There is a long oval-shaped, shallow concavity at the center of the side not illustrated, possibly to facilitate the drilling of the two central holes or to better fit the disc to a narrow vertical mount, such as a round stick. There are six hard fiber cord bindings consisting of the central tie, broken on the back concave side; two tight bindings to mend the crack probably made while drilling one of the center holes; and three fragments of unevenly spaced ties that may have joined this disc to other elements. One small perforation also occurs at

bottom center near the edge. The side illustrated is painted with thick resinous brown; the center area appears to be stained yellowish, possibly from surrounding resin. The opposite side is not painted.

Maximum length, 7.0 cm; maximum width, 5.7 cm; thickness, 0.4 cm, tapering to 0.2 cm at edge.

Discs, Appended (Fig. A.17 *b-c*). These two closely similar pieces are bound to narrow fragments which seem to fit together, although the association is not conclusive. By extending the broken ends of the fragments, the pieces appear to have been attached along one side of a slat or similar shape. Both are unevenly carved from thin, flat sections; coarse-grained surfaces are smoothed and the edges are cut square. Each curved piece is tightly attached to the narrow fragments with two sinew bindings. Both are painted identically on both sides. The strip around the outside is stained yellowish; the inner area is painted with a thick, resinous brown. A thick, crackled, and slightly lustrous green is painted on the pointed, broken ends.

Maximum length: *b*, 6.75 cm; *c*, 6.7 cm; maximum width: *b*, 2.9 cm; *c*, 3.1 cm; average thickness: *b*, 0.5 cm; *c*, 0.45 cm.

Disc Fragments (Fig. A.17 *d-e*). These two fragments are similar to *b* and *c* in proportions and color. The woods are similar, the surfaces are irregularly smoothed, and the edges are slightly rounded. Fragment *e* is broken through two perforations analogous to those in *b* and *c*. Fragment *d* is painted the same on both sides with a thick lustrous resin; fragment *e* probably was also painted on both sides although the resin on the reverse side appears to have been dissolved off.

Maximum length: *d*, 7.3 cm; *e*, 7.35 cm; maximum width: *d*, 1.4 cm; *e*, 3.3 cm; average thickness: *d*, 0.35 cm; *e*, 0.4 cm.

Scalloped Disc (Figs. A.18 *a*, 2.5). This piece is carved from a single thin section. The flat surfaces are smoothed and slightly thinner toward the edges. The scalloped edge is carefully carved and slightly rounded. The straight edge is cut square. Two perforations at the base are broken out. Both sides are painted identically; a dull red line approximately 0.2 cm wide outlines the brown central area and is surrounded by both brown and green. The object was split apart near its center, and the smaller portion was apparently exposed to harsher weathering, having lost most of the resin, particularly from the green paint. The green and brown on the larger piece are thick, crackled, and lustrous on both sides.

Maximum length, 5.4 cm; maximum width, 5.5 cm; average thickness, 0.35 cm.

Scalloped Disc (Figs. A.18 *b*, 2.5). This piece is carved from a single thin section. The flat surfaces are smoothed and slightly thinner toward the edges. The scalloped edge is slightly rounded. The scallops are less even and less defined than on *a*. The specimen is broken along the base through two perforations. It is identically painted on both sides. The green around the outside is thick and chalky, the purplish center is dull. The central area on both sides has been outlined with a thin line of dull red paint.

Maximum length, 4.5 cm; maximum width, 5.6 cm; average thickness, 0.35 cm.

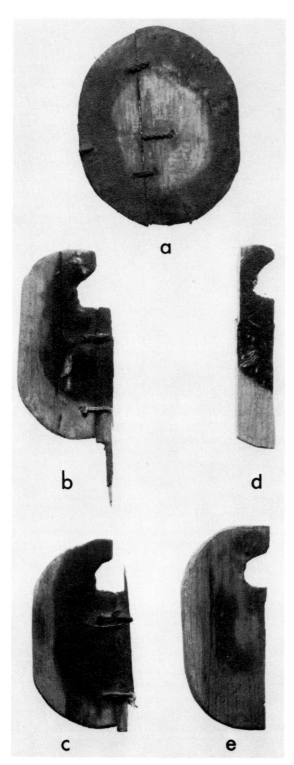

Fig. A.17. Disc, *a*; appended discs, *b-c*; disc fragments, *d-e*.

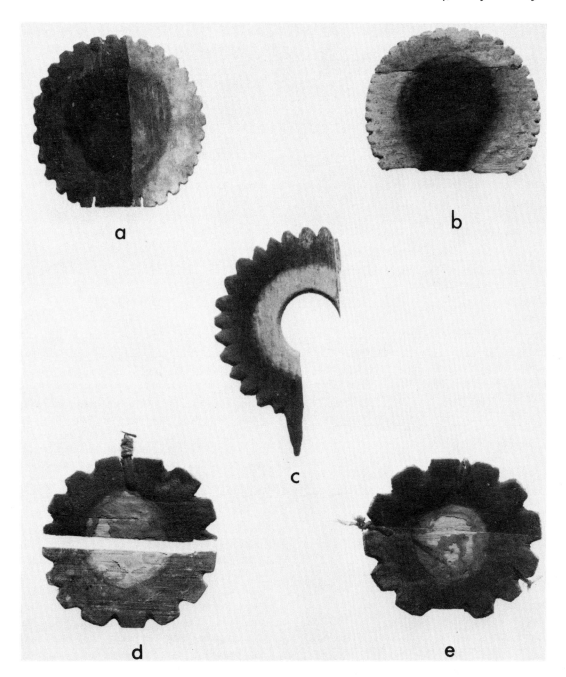

Fig. A.18. Scalloped discs.

Fragmentary Disc with Scalloped Edges (Figs. A.18 *c*, 2.5). This fragment is carved from a single thin section. The flat surfaces are smoothed and the scalloped edge is thinned and very carefully carved. The inner, circular edge is well rounded. Approximately one-half of the original shape is missing. The projection at the bottom would have been about 1.8 cm wide if the missing portion were as symmetrical as the recovered piece. This specimen appears to have been painted identically on both sides although the side not illustrated retains only a chalky, golden yellow around the hole. The yellow on the illustrated side is thick and lustrous, the brown around it is thick and slightly shiny. The blue on the projection has a slight sheen.

Maximum length, 7.0 cm; average radial width of circle, 2.0 cm; average thickness, 0.6 cm.

Scalloped Disc (Figs. A.18 *d*, 2.5) Carved from a single thin section, this specimen has smoothed, flat surfaces; the edges are slightly rounded in the notches of the scallops and are cut square on the flat outer edges. Four perforations occur near the edges; the uppermost is pierced with a tie of narrow doubled split twig which is wrapped with sinews; a fragment of sinew binding remains in the lower hole. The green center is thick and chalky, the brown border is thick and resinous but dulled. On the opposite side the round center is a dull black with thin, brownish resin in the border around it.

Maximum length, 5.2 cm; maximum width, 5.5 cm; average thickness, 0.35 cm.

Scalloped Disc (Figs. A.18 *e*, 2.5). On this specimen, carved from a single thin section, the flat surfaces are smoothed and the edges are shaped as on *d*. There are three perforations: the uppermost is pierced by a broken, doubled split twig binding; the other two have broken sinew bindings. The scallop opposite the twig binding is broken off. The paints are similar to those on *d*; the brown on the upper part of the illustrated surface is less weathered and lustrous. The reverse side is colored the same as *d*.

Maximum length, 4.9 cm; maximum width, 5.8 cm; average thickness, 0.45 cm.

Scalloped Semicircular Fragments (Figs. A.19 *a-b*, 2.5). Each of the specimens is carved from a single thin section. The flat surfaces are smoothed with scallops averaging 1 cm in width. Specimen *a* has slightly rounded edges; *b* has squarely cut edges. The crackled paint on the illustrated side of *a* has been overpainted with brush strokes of thin dull green. The reverse side is covered with a thick coat of crackled lustrous green.

Specimen *b* is slightly larger in original radius than *a*. Both sides of *b* are covered with a thick, lustrous, slightly crackled green; judging from the scalloped edges, light matte green was applied first and then was covered with a resinous varnish which darkened the color. Seven scallops have small irregular dots of dark black-brown resin near their centers on the illustrated side only.

Maximum length: *a*, 9.7 cm; *b*, 11.9 cm; average width: *a*, 2.4 cm; *b*, 3.2 cm; average thickness: *a*, 0.3 cm; *b*, 0.2 cm.

Scalloped Circular Fragment (Figs. A.19 *c*, 2.5). Carved from a single thin section, this specimen has smoothed flat surfaces. The scallops, averaging 1.2 cm in width, have squarely cut edges. The specimen has broken through six perforations—a pair near each side and a pair near the center. Both sides are painted similarly; the green around the outside is thick,

crackled and chalky; the center is unpainted. The unpainted area of the reverse side is smaller and off-center.

Maximum length, 12.2 cm; maximum width, 6.1 cm; average thickness, 0.2 cm.

Semicircular Fragment (Figs. A. 19 *d*, 2.5). This piece is carved from a single thin section. The slightly irregular surfaces are smoothed with abrasions diagonal to the wood grain. Slightly over half of one side has been painted in a green and black checkerboard design. The green is somewhat chalky with distinct short, dabbing brush strokes; the black is dull and flat. The reverse side is covered completely with a thick, dull, grainy black.

Maximum length, 14.6 cm; maximum width, 3.9 cm; average thickness, 0.25 cm.

Ovates

Ovate Disc Fragments (Figs. A.20, 2.6). This specimen consists of two pieces of a disc or plaque that was originally oval-shaped and was carved from four thin slats spliced together with sinew. Fragment *a* is approximately one-half of the original form; the two halves were held together by two bindings and the elements composing each half were joined by two more bindings. Approximately 0.5 cm is split from the straight side of *a* through two perforations. Fragment *b* is a single element broken along its longest side through two holes; a single sinew binding on the opposite side holds a splinter of the missing fourth element. Broken perforations on the longest sides of *a* and *b* directly coincide with one another. Surfaces are smoothed and edges are slightly rounded. Paints are the same on both sides; the illustrated surface of *b* is the least altered, and furnishes the best evidence of the original condition of the paints. The interior green line is thick and dull; the bordering white line is thick and chalky, underlying the green. The rest of the piece is a very thick and lustrous dark brown. One wide line (right of the upper green line) on both sides of *b* is unpainted and is stained yellowish. The design layout shown on *a* and *b* continues across the central splice, in contrast to the reverse side (*c*), where the same design elements are used on each half, but the placement is different and apparently independent on either half.

Maximum length: *a*, 17.2 cm; *b*, 17.1 cm; maximum width: *a*, 6.4 cm; *b*, 4.7 cm; average thickness: *a*, 0.25 cm; *b*, 0.3 cm.

Ovate Disc Fragments (Figs. A.21, 2.6). This object was originally an oval formed by two elongated semicircles attached together along their straight edges by three bindings. Carved from two thin sections, the

Fig. A.19. Scalloped disc fragments, *a-c*; semicircular fragment, *d*.

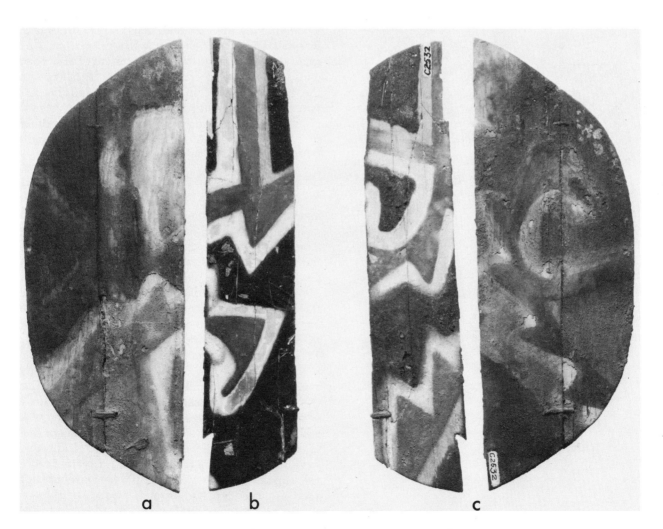

Fig. A.20. Ovate disc fragments, *a-b* (*c*, reverse of *a-b*).

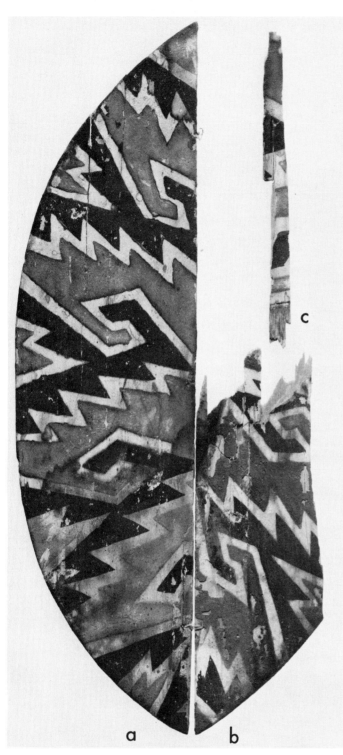

Fig. A.21. Ovate disc fragments.

piece has smoothed flat surfaces and square-cut edges. Approximately one-third of *b* is intact. One complete sinew binding lashes *a* to *b*; one broken sinew tie remains in the perforation at the opposite end of *a*, and a sinew thread remains in the central hole. Specimen *c* is a small fragment perhaps broken from one of the edges of *b*. Nearly one-half of the left edge of the fragment (as illustrated) is painted; it is broken through two perforations. All three pieces are painted similarly on both sides. Thick, chalky white was applied first over all surfaces, then the fret motif in dull green and thick, non-resinous brown was painted in. The combination fret and jagged line motif is quite similar to that found on Flagstaff Black-on-white ceramics. The two halves were painted separately before being sewn together. A feature of interest is a long, narrow oval of thick resin at the center of the plaque on both sides; resinous material does not appear elsewhere on the pieces. This area is mainly on the fragmented half, *b*, and is approximately 6 cm long and at least 1 cm wide (it is more clearly visible on the side not illustrated). Approximately 1 cm below the central perforation on *a* is a groove in *b* (on the side not illustrated) which indicates the possible location of another binding. This feature suggests the former attachment of a handle-like projection. Three small notches occur along the outer curve of *a* which may have served in construction; one is 11 cm from the upper end (straight line measure), and the other two are close together 11.5 cm from the lower end.

Maximum length: *a*, 26.4 cm; *b*, 14 cm; maximum width: *a*, 6.8 cm; *b*, 5 cm; average thickness: *a* and *b*, 0.3 cm.

Plaques

Four fragments (Fig. A.22) are similarly shaped and painted. They do not appear to be from one specimen, but seem to be pieces from the same side of four separate, related objects. Each is carved from a single thin slab (the sinew ties on *b* mend a split rather than serving to splice two pieces together); the surfaces and the even, well-rounded edges are smoothed. Each retains the broken base of a small, tapering projection on the upper, curved edge; *c* and *d* may have had a wide neck-like projection at their bases like that on *a*. Fragments of two flat pieces are attached to either side of the upper edge of *a*; each is split through three perforations through which pass the sinew bindings. Each piece tapers in thickness from 0.5 to a 0.1-cm rounded edge and is bound tightly in such a way that, when whole, each would project away from the major piece at a 45-degree angle. Specimens *c* and *d* appear to have had similarly attached pieces, as evidenced by the unpainted areas and multiple perforations along their upper edges. On all four objects, the sides not illustrated are painted identically to those illustrated.

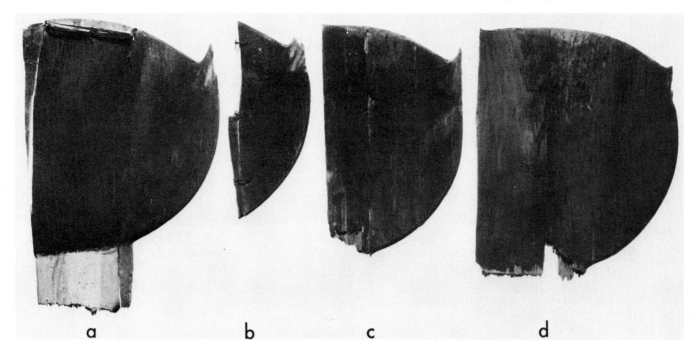

Fig. A.22. Plaque fragments.

The objects are covered with a thin dull black. A vertical stripe of thick powdery yellow is painted on the lower projection of *a*. The small projections on *a* and *b* have narrow unpainted areas on each side that may have resulted from being overlapped by thin slotted appendages rather than from being left unpainted as part of the decoration of the objects; the small projections of *b*, *c*, and *d* all show traces of yellow.

	a	*b*	*c*	*d*
Max. length	16.50 cm	11.0 cm	14.0 cm	12.8 cm
Max. width	11.00 cm	4.8 cm	12.1 cm	8.3 cm
Avg. thickness	0.35 cm	0.5 cm	0.5 cm	0.5 cm

Zoomorphic Wands

Parts of three similar wands are illustrated in Figures A.23 and A.24. Figure A.23 (*a* and *b*) shows both sides of one nearly complete wand with a snake-like head at the distal end, horizontal crosspieces, and a handle wrapped with a bulrush leaf. Figure A.24 shows the distal end of a second wand (*a*); a long, split section of a third wand staff (*b*); and 12 whole and fragmented crosspieces (*c-j*), possibly belonging to the second and third wands since they do not fit anywhere along the first. Six of these are still bound together in two groups of three. Figure A.24 *k* is a single unattached object similar to those projecting from the upper ends of Figures A.23 and A.24 *a*. The staff of

the first wand (Fig. A.23) was found broken in three places and has been repaired; the neck and adjacent crosspiece were burned, as were the ends of one side of two crosspieces in Figure A.24 *f*. Judging from the nearly complete wand, the staff was carved from a single long, thin slat, wider at the handle end and tapering slightly to the head. Surfaces are irregularly smoothed and edges slightly rounded. Each crosspiece is carved from a single thin section. Each has irregularly smoothed surfaces and edges slightly rounded. Craftsmanship is generally crude. Crosspieces (apparently about 10 to a wand) were sewn together with two sinew stitches placed just inside the shoulders of each piece. These were attached to the first wand with four additional sinew stitches, one at each end of the line of crosspieces and two others in between. On the underside of three unattached crosspieces, resin appears to have been used as an adhesive, further securing these to the staff. The handle of the complete staff was finished with a long, narrow leaf wrapped clockwise, with the upper, narrow end tucked under the wraps and the wide, lower end secured at the base of the wand with a hard fiber cord.

Figure A.23*b* shows features on the reverse side of the wand head. Three sinew stitches are visible, two holding small, thin fragments of wood. The larger piece (on the left) is painted with a black eye motif on a band of green like the opposing side of the head and it is believed to have projected at an angle from the head, as shown in the illustration. As shown, much of

a   b

Fig. A.23. Zoomorphic wand, *a* (*b*, reverse of *a*).

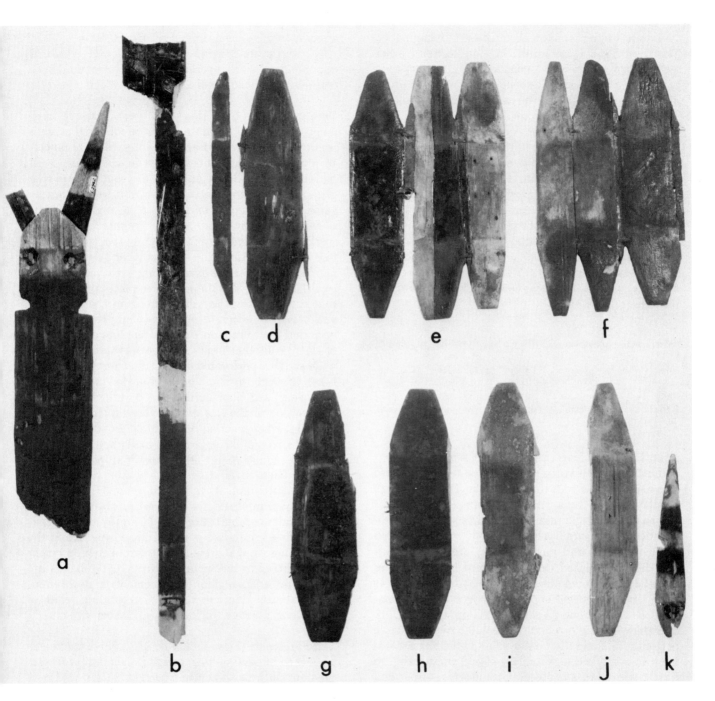

Fig. A.24. Zoomorphic wands. Distal end, *a*; split section of
a staff, *b*; crosspieces, *c-j*.

this side of the head is unpainted; apparently it was once overlapped by larger pieces than those now held by the stitches.

Paints are the same on all of the wand fragments. The wand itself is unpainted in some sections; other sections are a flat light green, a thick, lustrous resin brown, or a flat black. The center sections of the crosspieces are resin brown overpainted with flat black. The tapering side sections are dark resinous green and flat light green, sometimes overpainted with flat black. The staff fragment in Figure A.24 *b* is too different in wood grain and size to belong to the staff head in Figure A.24 *a*. Below the green band near the bottom of the staff are imprints of wide wrappings such as those forming the handle of the first wand.

Figure A.23: Length of staff, 57 cm; width of staff at handle base, 4.3 cm; width of staff at shoulder, 3.9 cm; thickness of staff, 0.5 cm at head, 0.8 cm at handle base; average length of crosspieces, 15.1 cm; average width of crosspieces, 3.5 cm; average thickness of crosspieces, 0.4 cm.

	a	*b*	*c-j*	*k*
Max. length	25.0 cm	37.3 cm	*e*, center slat: 15.7 cm	11.2 cm
Max. width	5.0 cm	4.0 cm	*f*, right slat: 4.4 cm	2.0 cm
Avg. thickness	0.4 cm	0.3 cm	0.4 cm	0.25 cm

Slats

Thin, Elongated Slats (Fig. A.25 *a-f*). One whole long, painted slat and two fragments (*a*), one painted base fragment (*b*), and four unpainted base fragments (*c-f*) possibly belong to a single grouping. Each slat is carved from a single thin section; surfaces and slightly rounded edges are well smoothed. All unpainted bases, of whole and partial pieces, are very smooth and slightly polished as though from handling. The three largest painted pieces (*a*) were bound together at two points along their continuous edges, one approximately 3 cm and one 23 cm from the upper end. Only four sinew bindings remain. The outer two slats have perforations along their outer edges indicating attachment to other, perhaps similar, pieces, presumably to form a wider fan-like object. On the wide, upper end of the two painted slats at the left, an unpainted area suggests a small, overlapping piece was once held in place by the hard fiber cordage fragments. These are wrapped around two adjacent sinew bindings and pass through a perforation near the end of each slat.

Both sides of the decorated pieces appear to have been painted initially a dull red-orange over the area now covered with the black-on-white design. After the red was either washed or worn off (only thin traces remain), thick chalky white was applied on one side

only, followed by the dull black design bands. The lower, narrow end of *b* appears to have been dipped in green paint. One of the unpainted fragments (*e*) appears to have been dipped in brown resin.

a: maximum length, 48.2 cm; average width of upper ends, 2.4 cm; average width of lower end, 0.75 cm; average thickness of all pieces, 0.25 cm.

Thin, Elongated Slats (Fig. A.25 *g-n*). Multiple fragments of a second set of slats (*g-n*) sewn together with sinew probably formed another long, fan-like object. By placing the fragments together in accordance with perforations, bindings, and similarly painted areas, a general idea of the original form and its size can be gained. Each piece is carved from a single thin slat; surfaces are smoothed, edges irregularly squared, workmanship generally crude. Only five sinew bindings are intact. Along the outer edge of *g*, which has a notched area near the narrow end, are two hard fiber cord fragments; the shape of the piece and the fact that these bindings are different from the inner ties and placed in different positions along the edge suggests that their function was to attach the complete set of slats to another object. Three fragments from the wide ends are perforated 0.5-0.3 cm from the edge (*h*, *i*, *n*). Through the small holes in *n* (the longest piece), a broken hard fiber cord is laced, attaching to the reverse side of the slat two small, thin fragments of tanned leather (each approximately 1 x 0.5 cm) suggesting a fringe-like edging originally across the wide end of the whole object. Both sides of all pieces appear to have been covered first with a thin coat of light green paint; upon its fading or removal, thin, dull black and white paints were applied on one surface. On the sides not illustrated of *g*, *h*, and *k*, long, irregular bands of resin-like material are visible along the edges. These may represent some sort of reinforcement once adhered to the wood with pitch; the bands are too uneven and irregular to be elements in decoration.

Maximum length of *k*, 52 cm; maximum width of *n*, 3.5 cm; average thickness of all pieces, 0.2 cm.

Slat Fragments (Figs. A.26 *a-d*, 2.7). Three fragments appear to be parts of long tapering slats similar in proportions to those shown in Figure A.25 *g-n* and may also have formed a fan-like object. Carved from single thin sections, the fragments have smoothed flat surfaces and squared edges. At the wide end of *a*, a small rectangular area is broken out between four perforations; the pairs of holes are located 0.5 and 1.3 cm from the edge. A fifth perforation is 7 cm from the wide end near one lateral edge. Fragment *b* is a section split from a slat painted similarly to *a*; the break passes through two small holes placed like those on *a*. Fragment *c* appears to be a piece of the narrow

Fig. A.25. Elongated slats (two possible fan-shaped groupings, *a-f* and *g-n*).

end of a tapering slat; the narrow projection at the lower end is cut off squarely and smoothed at the end. Also at the lower end *c* is broken through a central perforation 2 cm from the end. Another small hole is located at the center, 7.5 cm above the first. Just across from the latter perforation and 2 cm below the broken end is a shallow, 0.2 cm notch. Both surfaces and the shortest side of *c* are clearly smoothed and darkened from handling. Since the longest, unbroken edge is clean, its corners sharp and unworn, and the paint on the upper part uneven, this piece probably was bound to another slat, grouped like those in Fig. A.25. Specimen *d* is a small fragment that appears to have come from a slat similar to *a* in thickness; its tapered width is nearly identical to the central area of fragment *a*. Each piece is painted identically on both sides, except for *a* and *b* where the areas under the design that are stained with thin yellow are uncolored on the reverse surfaces. The paint on the lower two-thirds of *a* and *b* is a crackled resin green (the binder is weathered from the lower fragment of *a*). The upper one-third is a thin yellowish stain. The design is a band of thick white outlined in a clear, flat blue. The area above the design is a reddish-brown resin. Specimen *c* is dark green above and is unpainted below except for remnants of a brown resin. Specimen *d* is a solid green.

Maximum length of *a*, 15.5 cm; maximum width of *a*, 3.5 cm; average thickness of *a* and *d*, 0.2 cm; average thickness of *b* and *c*, 0.3 cm.

Slat Fragment (Figs. A.26 *e*, 2.7). This long fragment is carved from a single thin section; the surfaces are smoothed and taper in thickness to the narrow, slightly rounded left lateral edge. The object is split longitudinally through two perforations, one 1 cm from the upper, slanted edge and one 4 cm below it, and is broken across the lower end. A small fragment is missing along the upper end and one side. Two small holes, 0.5 cm apart, are located near the thinned edge. On the surface not illustrated is an unpainted area around the upper three perforations suggesting an overlapped, appended piece. The green on the upper one-fourth of the side illustrated overlaps a coat of white. The lower three-fourths is striped with black stain and a thin yellow stain. The stripes on the opposing side are identical; however, no green occurs.

Maximum length, 18.3 cm; maximum width, 1.0 cm; thickness, 0.3 cm, tapering to 0.1 at the finished edge.

Slat Fragments (Fig. A.26 *f-h*). These three fragments are split longitudinally. They are similarly shaped and painted, each having been carved from a single thin section. Surfaces are smoothed, tapering in thickness

from the broken edge to thin, narrow, rounded edges. Each is broken through four small perforations placed in pairs within unpainted bands. All three are apparently split from the same side of similar pieces; no two seem to have belonged together. The thin yellow stain on the unpainted areas appears to have been applied to the missing overlapped pieces and is therefore incidental to these fragments. The painted areas are a flat green, overlying a coat of white; the surfaces not illustrated are the same overall green.

Maximum length of *g*, 13.7 cm; maximum width of *g*, 0.7 cm; average thickness of all pieces, 0.3 cm, tapering to 0.1 cm.

Slats (Fig. A.27 *a-b*). Two similar pieces are each carved from a single thin section. Surfaces are smoothed and edges squared. Each has a small perforation near one edge; on *a* it is 2.2 cm from the upper edge; on *b* it is 2.5 cm. A splinter is broken from the right edge of *b*. Both sides of *a* and *b* are painted identically with a chalky white below a flat black; only traces of white remain on *a*. One long edge of both slats is painted black with traces of light green.

Maximum length: *a*, 20.4 cm; *b*, 20.1 cm; maximum width: *a*, 1.8 cm; *b*, 1.4 cm; average thickness: *a*, 0.3 cm; *b*, 0.25 cm.

Slat Fragments (Fig. A.27 *c*). These two small fragments are held together with a single sinew binding. The remaining portion of the lower end of the largest piece is a finished edge, cut off and smoothed. From the lack of paint approximately 0.5 cm along the edge on the reverse side and to some extent on the side illustrated, it seems possible that this piece may have been thrust into a slot in another piece. The surfaces appear to have been painted alike with thick white applied overall, followed by dull black stripes; paints on the side not illustrated are worn and fugitive.

Maximum length, 4.7 cm; width of larger piece, 1.2 cm; average thickness, 0.15 cm.

Slats (Fig. A.27 *d*). This group consists of five related pieces, four of which (at the right) could have been sewn together in the sequence illustrated, although all perforations and painted bands do not quite coincide. The piece at the left appears to be an outer element and could have formed part of another similar slat group. Surfaces are smoothed and edges squared. The upper edges of the three inner pieces clearly show the method of shaping, which was cutting or sawing from both sides, then breaking. Three pieces have small notches cut across one edge near the narrow, lower end; the remaining two are broken off at the base. On both sides paints are faded or present only in thin

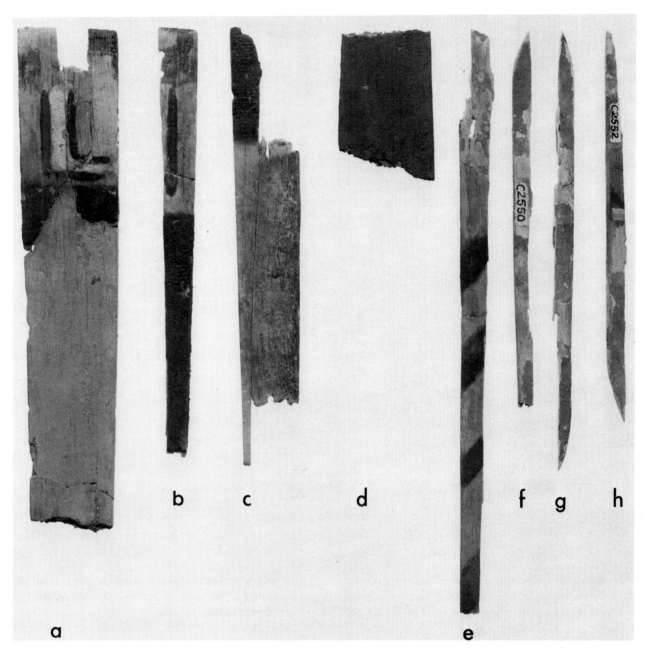

Fig. A.26. Slat fragments.

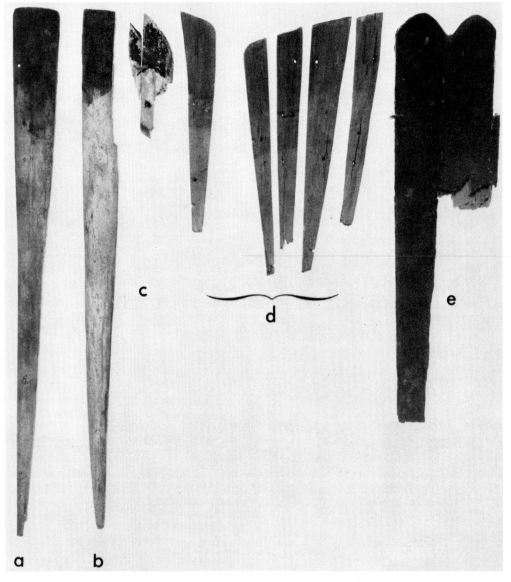

Fig. A.27. Slat fragments.

traces; bands of color are generally comparable on both sides except for an additional narrow, black stripe between the brown and green bands on the side not illustrated.

Maximum length, 10 cm; maximum width, 1.4 cm; average thickness of all pieces, 0.35 cm.

Slat Fragment (Fig. A.27 *e*). This double slat form is carved from a single thin section. The surfaces are smoothed; the straight edges are squared and the upper scalloped edge is slightly rounded. The object is broken across the base and approximately half of one of the slats is missing. Considering the sinew binding along one edge and the broken perforation across from it (both 4 cm from the upper edge), the piece may have been joined to other similar forms to compose a large fan-like object. Also, the unbroken, straight edges appear to have been connected tightly to the

other edges before the pieces were painted. Both sides are painted identically, a bright resin green partially covered with shiny black.

Maximum length, 15.9 cm; maximum unbroken width, 4.1 cm; average thickness, 0.3 cm.

Tapering Slats with Pointed Ends (Fig. A.28 *a-f*). Six similar pieces are possibly fragments of feathers or flower petals, each carved from a single thin section. The flat surfaces are smoothed and the edges are cut square. Two sinew bindings join together two slats and a splinter of a third (*a*) approximately 3 cm from the upper edge and just below the widest point of each piece. Single or double perforations in the same location on *b-f* indicate they were probably joined to other similar pieces to form a fan or possibly a circular flower form. A portion of the lower end is broken from all pieces; the two connected slats of *a* are broken

[96]

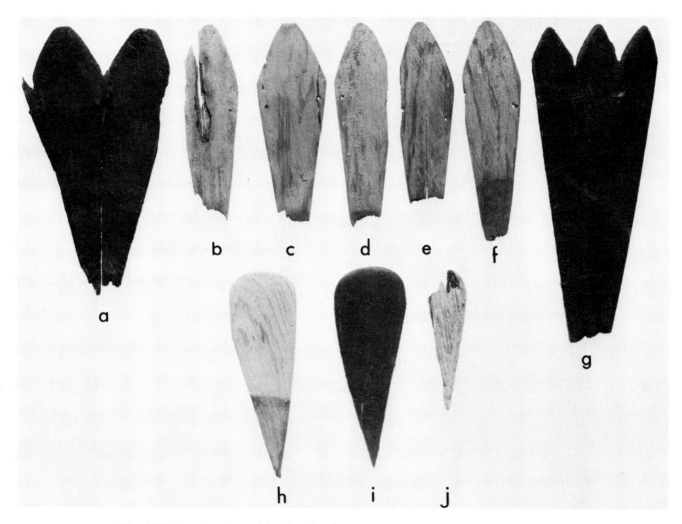

Fig. A.28. Tapering slats with pointed ends, *a-g*; tapering slats with rounded ends, *h-j*.

through central perforations at the base of each. Both sides of all pieces are painted identically; the two nearly whole sections of *a* retain dark, crackled green and resin brown paints; others are weathered, retaining only pale, powdery green pigment. On both sides of the connected slats, the green appears to have been repainted; thick irregular brush strokes of the same paint cover the crackled, worn first coat.

a: maximum length, 10 cm; maximum width of center slat, 2.7 cm; average thickness of both slats and fragment, 0.2 cm.

Tapering Slats with Pointed Ends (Figs. A.28 *g*, 2.7). These three narrow forms are sewn tightly together with sinew; each is carved from a single thin section. The flat surfaces are smoothed and the edges generally squared. The bindings are placed 2.5 cm from the upper and 2 cm from the lower edge on each slat. Evi-

dence of an upper perforation and a lower binding fragment on the outer edge of the longest slat indicates former attachment to another piece. The right edge of the shortest slat has no perforations and, therefore, appears to be the outer edge of the originally complete object. Both sides are painted identically with lustrous green and thick resin brown. They appear to have been renewed with the same paints, covering chipped or worn areas as well as the binding and perforation on the longest side, perhaps indicating reuse in the broken state.

Maximum length, 11.3 cm; maximum width of single slat, 1.6 cm; average thickness of all pieces, 0.2 cm.

Tapering Slats with Rounded Ends (Fig. A.28 *h-j*). Two large feather or petal forms (*h-i*) and one small one (*j*) are each carved from a single thin section. The flat surfaces are well smoothed and the edges evenly rounded. The thickness of each piece decreases gradually from the lower to the upper end. The two large pieces are broken on one tapering side and across the base along the diagonal wood grain. The smaller piece is split more nearly through the center with part of the rounded end missing. Both sides of each are painted identically in green; *h* and *j* have lost the resin binder of the green paint; traces of brown pitch remain on the unbroken edge of the base of *h*.

	h	*i*	*j*
Max. length	7.7 cm	7.5 cm	5.1 cm
Max. width	2.5 cm	2.8 cm	1.4 cm
Thickness	0.45-0.3 cm	0.4-0.2 cm	0.4-0.2 cm

Slats with Squared Ends (Figs. A.29 *a-f*, 2.7). These six related pieces could have belonged to the same object, judging from the placement of paints and the cord bindings. Each was carved from a single thin section; the flat surfaces are smoothed over somewhat coarse grain; the edges are rounded and slightly thinned. Perforations are located 1.3 to 2.4 cm from the upper ends, near each lateral edge, and sewn through them are broken lengths of hard fiber cordage, originally holding several pieces together. Holbein stitching is employed (see Fig. A.16 *i-l*). About 0.8 cm from the lower end of each piece is a central perforation; a broken plant fiber cord binding remains in the basal perforation of *f*. With the excep-

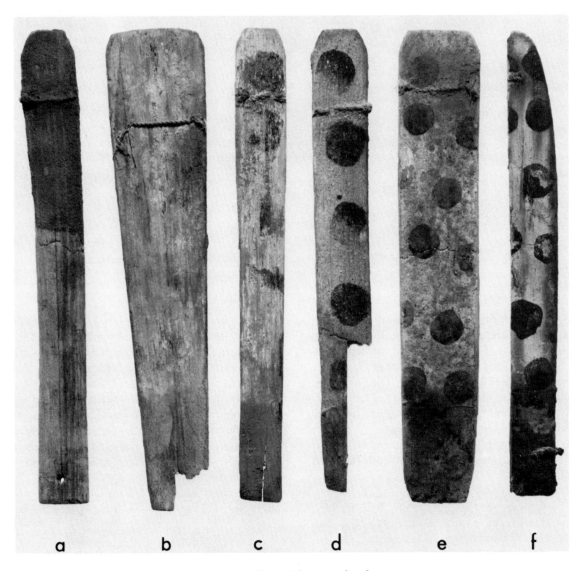

a   b   c   d   e   f

Fig. A.29. Slats with squared ends.

tion of *a*, the surfaces shown are painted a grainy white with black polka dots approximately 2 cm from the base of each piece to the upper ends. Below this area on *d, e,* and *f* are traces of brown resin. On the illustrated side, specimen *a* has traces of black and white in the area above the base section but is over-painted with dull green 4.8 cm from the upper end. Specimens *b* and *c* have traces of green around the upper cord fragments. Judging from *f,* the least altered piece, the reverse sides of all pieces were painted with dark resin green on the upper half with resin brown below.

Maximum length: *a,* 12.4 cm; *e,* 12.4 cm; maximum width: *a,* 1.4 cm; *e,* 2.2 cm; average thickness of all pieces: 0.25 cm.

Slat Fragments with Rounded Ends (Figs. A.30 *a-c,* 2.7). This group represents the upper ends of three similar forms, each carved from a single thin section. The flat surfaces are smoothed and the edges rounded. No perforations are evident. Each is broken near the edge of a second lower band or area of green; the lower end of *a,* the shortest piece, was first scored or sawed diagonally, across the surface illustrated, then broken off. Both sides of all three are painted iden-

tically, originally with a stripe of resin-based green above a stripe of thin resin brown, now weathered.

Maximum length of *c,* 12.1 cm; maximum width of *c,* 1.9 cm; average thickness of all pieces, 0.15 cm.

Slat Fragments (Fig. A.30 *d-g*). These four fragments appear to be from related pieces. Each is carved from a single thin section. The flat surfaces are smoothed over relatively coarse grain; the edges are cut square. The lower end of *e* (as illustrated), the second largest piece, was first scored across one side, then broken. Specimens *d, f,* and *g* each have a central perforation near the center of a wide green band at the rounded end. In an additional perforation on *d* is a short length of plant fiber cordage tied on either side in an overhand knot. Within the green band on the unillustrated side of *d* and *e* is a diagonal unpainted area bordered by ridges of green paint where a second element, a narrow slat, was affixed presumably as a crosspiece. Aside from these overlap areas, reverse surfaces of all pieces were painted as those illustrated, using stripes of resin brown and flat green over a thin yellow stain.

Maximum length of *d,* 12.4 cm; maximum width of *e,* 2.0 cm; average thickness of all pieces, 0.15 cm.

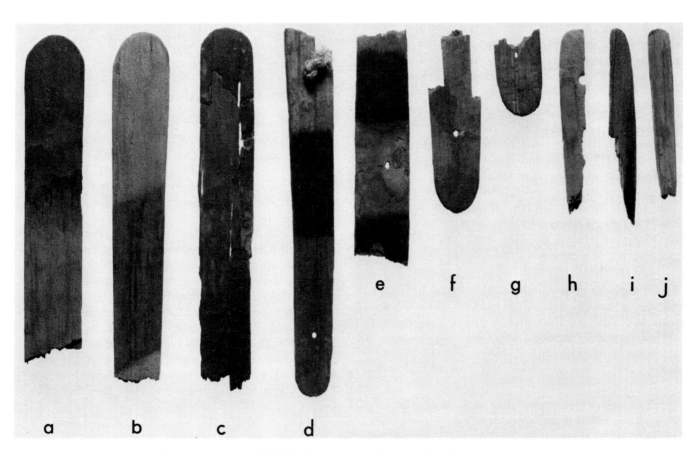

Fig. A.30. Slat fragments with rounded ends.

Slat Fragments (Fig. A.30 *h-i*). Two small, longitudinally split forms are each carved from a single section. The biconvex surfaces are smoothed and the edges rounded. Specimen *h* is broken through a large (0.25 cm diameter), smoothed, drilled perforation located in the center 1.5 cm from the upper edge. Both sides of *h* are unpainted. Specimen *i* is a dull, flat black below and has a thin yellow stain above on the illustrated side; the opposite side is yellow all over.

Maximum length: *h*, 6.2 cm; *i*, 6.8 cm; maximum width: *h*, 0.9 cm; *i*, 0.8 cm; average thickness: *h*, 0.45 cm; *i*, 0.3 cm.

Slat Fragment (Fig. A.30 *j*). A small narrow plume or petal form, carved from a single thin section, is broken at one end through a single central perforation. The surfaces are well smoothed, the lateral edges are squared, and the edge of the unbroken end is rounded. Both sides are painted with a pale, chalky green; the broken end is unpainted for approximately 1 cm on one side.

Maximum length, 5.7 cm; maximum width, 0.8 cm; average thickness, 0.25 cm.

Slat Fragment (Fig. A.31 *a*). This small fragment may be from the upper end of a slat form. The edges are rounded and it is painted identically with a pale chalky green on both sides. It appears to have been cut, then broken off at the lower end.

Maximum length, 2 cm; average thickness, 0.25 cm.

Slat Fragment (Fig. A.31 *b*). This small narrow form is broken at the lower end through a single central perforation. Carved from a single thin section, it has well-smoothed surfaces. The lateral edges are squared and the upper edge rounded. Both sides are covered with a pale chalky green. On the side not illustrated the lower end is unpainted for approximately 1 cm.

Maximum length, 5.7 cm; maximum width, 0.8 cm; average thickness, 0.25 cm.

Slat Fragment (Fig. A.31 *c*). This piece has been broken at both the top and the bottom. The edges are rounded. The side illustrated is green; the opposite surface is painted an orange-yellow.

Maximum length, 5.5 cm; average thickness, 0.5 cm.

Slat or "Plume" Fragments (Fig. A.31 *d-i*). The left edge of specimen *d* is slightly rounded; the opposite edge is split off along the grain down to 2 cm from the lower end. The lower end is slightly thinned and rounded and is covered unevenly with black pigment.

Otherwise the fragment is unpainted. The upper end has been scored across on one surface then broken off.

Specimens *e* and *f* are biconvex with similarly rounded edges. Both are painted a pale green on all surfaces and could have belonged to the same object. Specimen *f* is broken through one perforation; a hard plant fiber cord fragment remains in a second perforation. The upper end of *e* is broken through two perforations; the lower end is carved slightly concave.

The flat surfaces of specimen *g* are very smooth. It is broken at both ends and along both long edges except for one diagonal, square-cut area 6 cm long on the lower left edge. The left edge is broken through a perforation near the upper end. Only the unbroken edge is painted, with resin brown and pale green; the rest is unpainted.

The flat surfaces of *h* are very smooth. The long edges are cut square; the lower end is unevenly cut off and the upper end broken. A shallow notch 0.9 cm long is located near the lower end. The fragment is unpainted except for a gray stain on the notched edge.

Both long edges of *i* are slightly rounded, the unnotched side less than the notched side. The lower end is rounded; the upper end irregularly burned. A shallow notch 0.5 cm wide is located 2 cm from the lower end of one edge. All surfaces are unpainted.

	d	*e*	*g*	*h*	*i*
Max. length	19.3 cm	11.0 cm	11.7 cm	9.40 cm	11.40 cm
Max. width	1.4 cm				1.70 cm
Avg. thickness	0.4 cm	0.4 cm	0.45 cm	0.35 cm	0.45 cm

Slat or "Plume" Fragments (Fig. A.31 *j-m*). The long edges of *j* are cut square. The fragment is broken at the lower end through two large perforations. The upper end was first scored then broken off. Two other perforations are 5 cm from the upper edge. Both surfaces and edges are covered with dull green stains of resin green paint.

The long left edge of *k* is slightly rounded; the lower end is cut square; the other edges are broken. Both sides are painted identically with thick, crackled resin and a single stripe of dull resin green; the unbroken edges are also painted.

The three unbroken edges of *l* are rounded; both surfaces and edges are painted with thick resin green.

The long left edge of *m* is rounded; the upper end is cut square. The fragment is broken along the long side and at the narrow base. Both surfaces and unbroken edges are painted with thick, crackled resin green.

	j	*k*	*l*	*m*
Max. length	14.0 cm	13.0 cm	9.2 cm	12.8 cm
Avg. thickness	0.25 cm	0.3 cm	0.5 cm	0.4 cm

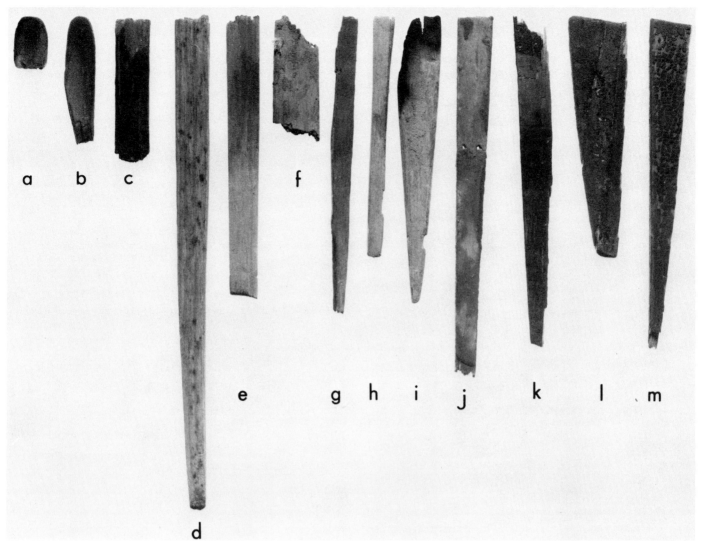

Fig. A.31. Slat fragments.

"Plume-Circle" (Figs. A.32 *a-c*, 2.8). The seven incomplete sections of this large, flat, formerly circular object are composed of 20 whole and 4 fragmentary plume-shaped elements joined together with sinew. The circular form is a conjecture based upon a reconstruction of the black and white design layout on the side shown in Figure A.32 *b*. In Figure A.32 *c*, lines forming the fret motifs were extended within the circular band drawn by using the radii which most closely duplicate the inner and outer curvature of the plume sections. The layout illustrated was found to be the only plausible placement of the fret elements within the circular space. It is entirely possible that the plumes formed two semicircular forms rather than one complete hoop; however, they all appear to lack an outer finished edge, and instead have bindings or perforations indicating attachment to other similar pieces. Individual plumes are joined together with sinew bindings at two places along their lateral edges,

averaging 2.2 cm from the upper and lower end. Two plumes have broken sinew stitches at the center of the lower or inner edge. If the reconstruction is correct, these two bindings directly oppose one another on the hoop form and could have held a central disc or other piece. One plume has a broken split twig binding (1.5 cm long) at the center of the upper or outer edge. In the reconstruction, opposite this plume is another which is broken through two perforations 2.5 cm from the top or outer edge. Each piece is carved from a single thin section; flat surfaces are smoothed, edges squared. Both sides of all pieces were painted with an undercoat of white. On *a* the central rectangles are black, outlined with brown bands and on the edges by resinous green bands (see Fig. 2.8). On the opposite side (*b*) is a negative design in flat organic black.

Average length of plumes, 8.95 cm; average maximum width of plumes, 2.6 cm; average thickness of plumes, 0.2 cm.

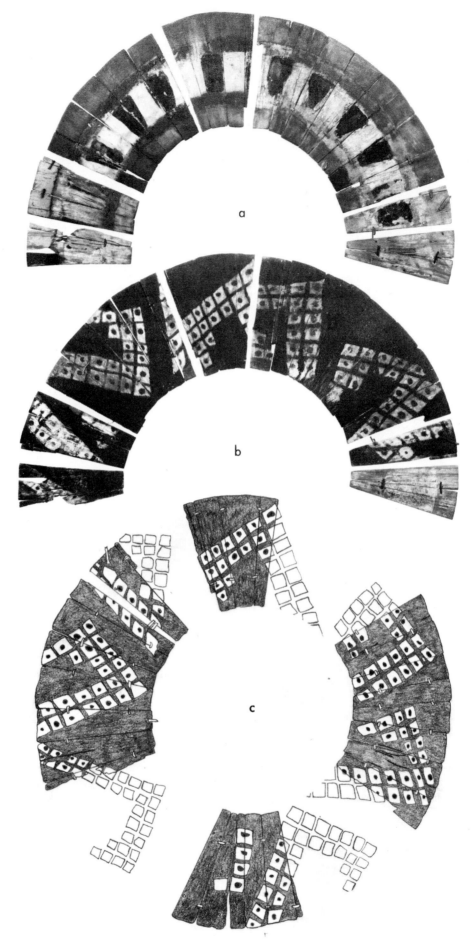

Fig. A.32. "Plume circle," *a*; reverse, *b*; *c*, reconstruction of design layout on *b*.

Fig. A.33. Slats and slat fragments.

Slats (Fig. A.33 *a-c*). These three similar slat pieces are each carved from a single thin section; the flat surfaces are smoothed and the edges slightly rounded. The upper end of each is beveled on one surface, decreasing in thickness at approximately 1 cm from the end to a thin edge approximately 0.2 cm thick. Three perforations occur in this area on each; all are broken out to the edge. The lower end of each slat is cut at an angle across the wood grain. Near this end are two pairs of perforations, one above the other; two broken sinew bindings remain in *a*, one fragment in *b*, and one whole sinew binding in *c*. On the beveled edge of each slat is a narrow, unpainted area around the perforations, and at the opposite end of each, on the surface opposite from that on which the bevel occurs, another unpainted area surrounds the lower perforations. Both indicate once-overlapped pieces, a narrow element

above and a wider one below. Specimen *c* differs from *a* and *b* in that the bevel is on the opposite side of the slat from the bevels on *a* and *b*; that is, specimen *c* mirrors, rather than matches, *a* and *b* in form. All are painted identically on both sides, *a* with heavy, crackled resin green under very heavy organic black resin paints; *b* and *c* retain only the pale green pigment at each end, but traces along the edges of both indicate that the paint was originally the dark resin green.

Maximum length of *a*, 21.1 cm; maximum width of *a*, 2.8 cm; average thickness of all pieces, 0.6 cm.

Slat (Fig. A.33 *d*). This slat piece is possibly similar to *a-c* in original form. It is carved from a single thin section; the surfaces are smoothed and biconvex in cross section; the upper edge is cut square; the others are rounded. Like *a-c*, it has the upper end beveled on one surface, beginning about 1 cm from the edge; four perforations occur in pairs at this end, one retaining a plant fiber cord fragment. At the opposite end are six perforations, placed in pairs; fragments of the same cordage remain in all six. Both sides and all edges are covered completely with a weathered coat of brown resin.

Maximum length, 19.2 cm; maximum width, 2.7 cm; average thickness, 0.5 cm.

Slat Fragments (Figs. A.33 *e-f*, 2.7). These two similarly painted pieces could have been parts of the same object. Each is carved from a single thin section; the flat surfaces are smoothed and the edges cut square. Both ends of *e* are finished; it is split lengthwise near one lateral edge. On the illustrated surface four paired perforations are within a rectangular unpainted area; on the reverse side around the lower three perforations is a similar unpainted area. The placement and shape of both suggest that two other slat-like pieces, about 3 cm wide, were attached to *e* by sinew bindings (four remain), and that both projected from *e* in the same direction beyond the unbroken edge. Both sides of *e* are painted similarly. A thin yellow stain underlies a zigzag design in a clear flat blue and a brown resin. On the side illustrated the brown resin overlies an earlier coat of dull red. On the opposite side resin is present only in traces, leaving more red in view. The small fragment *f* is painted only on one side with the same paints as *e* and could have been part of the overlapping piece, although the two perforations do not match those in *e* directly. The longest side and upper end of *f* are unbroken, finished edges.

Maximum length of *e*, 18.4 cm; maximum width of *e*, 2.4 cm; average thickness of *e*, 0.35 cm; average thickness of *f*, 0.3 cm.

Slat (Fig. A.33 *g*). This slat form is carved from a single thin section, with the flat surfaces smoothed over rather coarse grain and the edges cut square. Each end decreases slightly in thickness, more pronouncedly at the upper end. The slat is split lengthwise through four large, evenly spaced perforations; the holes average 0.25 cm in diameter and are smoothly drilled. A pair of similar perforations are placed approximately 2 cm from each end, and in each pair are fragments of doubled, split twigs. The object is unpainted except for irregular traces of white and orange on the surface illustrated.

Maximum length, 19.2 cm; maximum width, 2.7 cm; average thickness, 0.55 cm.

Thin Tabular Fragment (Fig. A.34 *a*). This specimen is a splintered section possibly from a flat carved plume form. The edges are cut square and it is painted green on both sides except for about 3 cm at the wide end where it is unpainted. It is broken at the narrow end and lengthwise through a hole 2 cm from the wide end. There is a second, unbroken hole 0.5 cm from the same end.

Maximum length, 8.5 cm; maximum width, 0.9 cm; average thickness, 0.35 cm.

Thin Tabular Fragment (Fig. A.34 *b*). This long, flat carved wooden piece is split along both lateral edges. It perhaps belonged to a semicircular form. Each narrow end is a finished edge, is rounded, and is painted green, as are the flat surfaces.

Maximum length, 13.7 cm; maximum width, 1.1 cm; average thickness, 0.7 cm.

Slat Fragment (Fig. A.34 *c*). This specimen, carved from a single thin section, has flat surfaces that are irregularly smoothed, somewhat whittled, decreasing in thickness from the center to each end; edges are squared. The object is broken across the wide end, and a narrow splinter 5.5 cm long is split from the upper half of one lateral edge. A perforation 0.25 cm in diameter is 4 cm from the narrow end and 1.5 cm from the long, straight side; a notch measuring 0.2 x 0.3 cm is located 2.2 cm from the narrow end on the same straight edge. Both sides and edges are stained as though from handling. Traces of brown resin are visible on the side illustrated.

Maximum length, 11.2 cm; maximum width, 3.0 cm; average thickness, 0.25 cm.

Slat Fragment (Fig. A.34 *d*). This fragment is a section of a slightly tapered, flat, carved wooden slat. The edges are squared; the object is broken at both ends. Two small perforations are visible; each is near a lateral edge 2.4 cm from the narrow end. The specimen is unpainted.

Maximum length, 11.0 cm; maximum width, 1.7 cm; average thickness, 0.35 cm.

Handle (Fig. A.34 *e*). This long, handle-like piece is carved from a single thin section. The flat surfaces are smoothed with many deep diagonal and vertical striations evident. The long edges are slightly rounded and the base is cut square. One perforation is placed at the center, 2.2 cm from the wide end. The other end is irregularly broken through two large (0.3 cm diameter) perforations placed in the center only 0.3 cm apart. Both sides and edges, particularly in the central area, are smoothed and stained dark as though from handling, although the dark areas appear resinous under magnification. On both sides the broken end has traces of resin green paint.

Maximum length, 33.0 cm; maximum width, 3.5 cm; average thickness, 0.5 cm.

Fig. A.34. Slat fragments, *a-g*; "snake-lightning" fragments, *h-j*.

Flat Tapering Fragments (Fig. A.34 *f-g*). These two pieces are similarly carved and the wood grain suggests that they could have belonged to the same object. The lateral edges are cut more across-grain than any of the other pieces in the collection. All surfaces are smoothed, the edges and tapered ends are well rounded. All surfaces are without pigment. Each has a small burned area near one edge.

Maximum length of *f*, 14.8 cm; maximum width of *f*, 2.1 cm; average thickness of *f* and *g*, 0.7 cm.

"Snake-lightning" Fragments (Fig. A.34 *h-j*). These three pieces are closely similar in paints and wood grain and presumably were part of the same object. All are carved from single thin sections. The flat surfaces are smoothed and the edges are rounded. Both sides of *i* and *j* are painted identically in green and brown stripes. The "head" (*h*) is green. The green paint is thick, crackled, and lustrous on *h* and *i*. On *j* the green appears to have been repainted; the surface is dull, showing brush strokes over the crackled first coat. The brown is thick resin. The opposite sides of *h* and *i* have lost the resinous binder, with only pale green and a yellowish stain remaining.

Maximum length of *h*, 5.7 cm; maximum width of *h*, 2.9 cm; average thickness of all pieces, 0.4 cm.

ROUND CARVED FORMS

Bows and Arrows

Non-functional Arrowshafts (Figs. A.35, 2.9). Fragments of the proximal half of four similar non-functional arrows are shown in Figure A.35 *a-d*. Specimens *a-c* have wooden fletching; *d* is just the arrowshaft. Shafts are decorticated branches, and in two cases (*a* and *b*) are well smoothed. All four are crooked and unsuitable as functional arrows. A nock is carved in the proximal end of *a*, *b*, and *c* averaging 0.25 cm in depth and width. Approximately 0.6 cm from the proximal end of *a* and *c*, just below the nock, is a shallow groove around the entire circumference of the shaft, suggesting an imitation of the tight binding placed in this location on functional arrows to secure solid wood nockplugs in the reed mainshafts. Specimen *b* represents perhaps one-half of the original length of the arrows; it is broken off 37.5 cm from the proximal end. The distal end of *d* has been scored then broken and a splinter 8 cm long split from the shaft; approximately 5.5 cm from this end, reddish-brown bark remains. Fletching elements are each cut from single thin wooden slats with flat surfaces generally smoothed and edges cut square. Overall workmanship is crude. Fletching is attached to the shafts by sinew and plant fiber cordage; the sinew passes

through a single perforation in each element about 1.5 cm from its proximal end and a plant fiber cord is lashed around the narrowed distal ends of the wooden feathers. Only *a* retains the complete three-element fletching; the method of tying used at the proximal end is illustrated in Figure B.1 *c*. Specimens *b* and *c* each have two fletching elements attached. All of the fletching elements are painted with resin, dulled and opaqued with much fine sand. The upper and lower band on each shaft is a dull green, and the band between an organic black; *d* has traces of green underlying the long area of black. The fragments shown in *e* represent the proximal ends of four additional fletching elements.

Maximum length of shafts: *a*, 25.5 cm; *b*, 37.5 cm; *c*, 24.0 cm; *d*, 35.2 cm; average diameter of all shafts, 0.65 cm; average outside length of fletching on *a*, 20.0 cm; average maximum width of fletching on *a*, 2.3 cm; average thickness of all fletching elements, 0.25 cm.

Non-functional Bows (Fig. A.36). These objects represent broken segments of five similar bows, each shaped from a split section of a soft wood branch. All are too fragile to have been functional. The bows are similar in cross section, with both wide surfaces (outer and belly) parallel and flat with evenly rounded edges. Width and thickness vary little, with only slight tapering toward one end of *b* and both ends of *c*. Only *b* appears to have an unbroken nock end; it is slightly thinned and cut off squarely with slightly rounded corners; a central split 1 cm long at one end could have received the knotted end of a bowstring. The bark has been removed and the surfaces smoothed. Specimen *a* retains fairly symmetrical double curves; *b* is slightly curved along its center. All retain evidence of once having an overall covering of closely placed wrappings of a red-brown, bast-like cordage that was coated with a thick dark pitch or resin. On all pieces one surface is weathered more than the other, but cordage impressions are visible (2-ply?; Z-twist; average 2 mm diameter). On the opposite surface, cord fragments are held within the thick resin coat. Along the central area of all pieces, except *e*, are traces of colored pigment—on *a*, red; on *b*, red, yellow, and a purple stain; on *c*, red and yellow; and on *d*, green. The resin coating may have been darkened beyond its natural color, possibly with an organic black.

Maximum length of *a*, 67.0 cm; average maximum width of all pieces, 1.3 cm, tapering very slightly toward ends; average thickness of all pieces, 0.65 cm.

Wooden Arrow Fragment (Non-functional?) (Fig. A.37 *a-b*). These two pieces of decorticated, smoothed twigs resemble the shafts of the wood-fletched non-functional arrows. Both are broken off at each end.

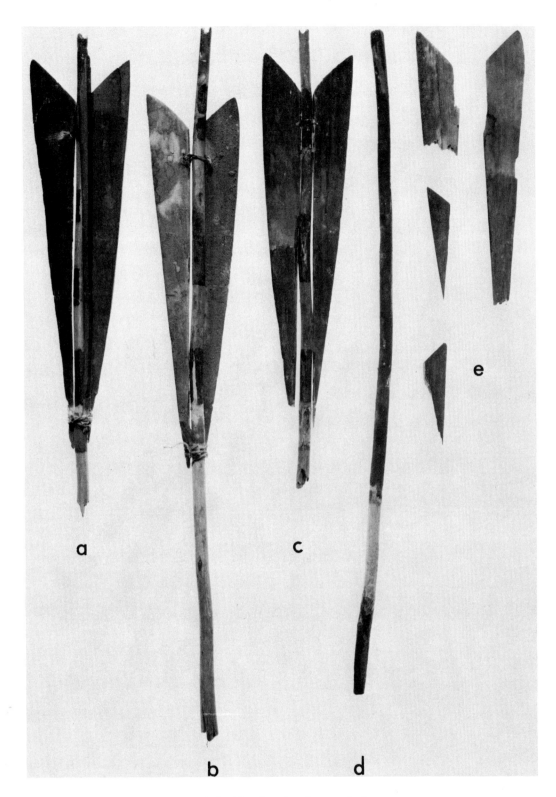

Fig. A.35. Non-functional arrowshafts.

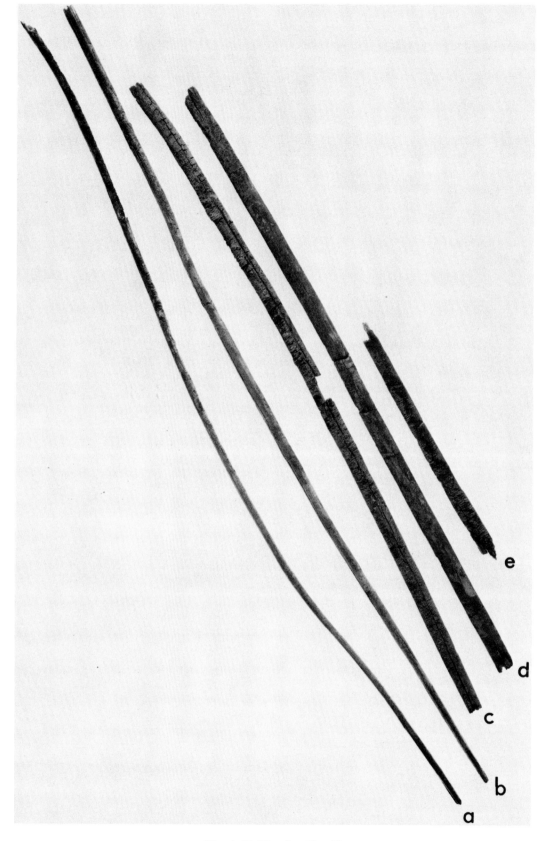

Fig. A.36. Non-functional bows.

The longer piece (a) has a deep groove sawed perpendicular to its length, 3.5 cm from one end; there are no other alterations and it may be raw material for an arrow shaft. The shorter piece (b) retains traces of green and brown resin paints.

Maximum length of a, 49.8 cm; average diameter: a, 0.75 cm; b, 0.65 cm.

Reed Mainshaft Fragments (Fig. A.37 c-e). These specimens represent five fragments of functional arrow mainshafts. All are made from reeds (*Phragmites*). All specimens except the center and lower fragments in e are nock ends. Specimen c has a deep V-shaped nock cut into the reed and a wooden plug (0.45 cm wide and deep); 4 and 14 cm from the nock end are two wide sinew wrappings, both retaining the fragments of three split quills. A black band 1.7 cm wide occurs just below the upper binding and a 0.1 cm wide black band is placed just above the lower binding; the distal end of c is burned off. Specimen d has a shallow (0.1 cm) U-shaped nock cut into a reed node; the end is bound tightly with sinew 0.2 cm down the shaft; 3 and 8.2 cm from the nock end are two sinew bindings each retaining three fragments of split quill fletching. Two specular black bands (0.5 cm wide, 0.1 cm apart) are placed 0.3 cm below the upper binding and traces of a third black band, 0.2 cm wide, occur immediately below the lower binding; the distal end is crushed. The top fragment in e has remnants of a nock end and binding. It is covered with a reddish-purple stain that occurs on the other two fragments in e as well; the upper and lower fragments in e also have traces of pale green. The middle fragment in e is a reed shaft fragment, perhaps from the fletch area. The lower fragment in e is a broken fragment of a possible shaft.

Maximum length of c, 37.3 cm; average diameter: c, 0.85 cm; d, 0.7 cm; e, upper fragment, 0.6 cm.

Wooden Foreshafts (Fig. A.37 f-g). These two specimens represent one nearly whole and one broken foreshaft shaped from evenly tapered branches; both are smoothed over natural bark surfaces. The more complete specimen (f) retains a smoothly tapered tang (6.2 cm long) covered with traces of a resin adhesive. Specimen g is broken off at the shoulder or base of the tang. Traces of several painted green dots are visible near the tang end of g. The distal ends of both are broken off and are worn or smoothed by use.

Maximum length: f, 23.0 cm; g, 17.0 cm; diameter at shoulder: f, 0.85 cm; g, 0.9 cm.

Reeds with Sinew Wrappings (Fig. A.37 h-i). Specimen h is a long section of reed (*Phragmites*) broken at both ends, with a wide sinew binding at one end; no quill fragments are evident nor is the node

Fig. A.37. Arrow fragments: non-functional (?), a-b; reed mainshaft fragments, c-e; wooden foreshafts, f-g; reeds with sinew wrappings, h-i.

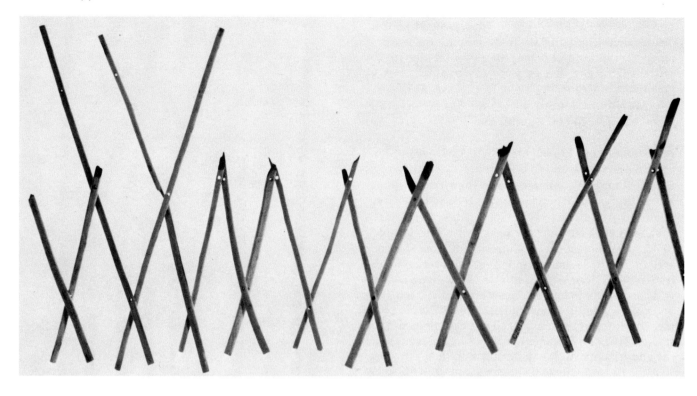

Fig. A.38. Lightning lattice.

near the wrapped end pierced (to receive a foreshaft tang). Specimen *i* is a long, thin, tapering reed section cut off at each end; the only other alteration is a small wrapping or sinew near the widest (upper) end.

Maximum length of *i*, 62.6 cm; diameter: *h*, 0.8 cm; *i*, maximum 0.7 cm.

Lightning Lattice

Two complete and 25 incomplete, similarly shaped sticks (Fig. A.38) look as if they may once have formed a lightning lattice or frame. All diameters vary. Each was fashioned from a round decorticated and smoothed twig which was then shaved or sanded flat on two opposing surfaces, leaving the narrower edges rounded. Ends are cut off squarely. The two whole, unbroken sticks each have three perforations drilled through from one flat surface to the other, one at the center and one approximately 5 cm from each end. Of the remaining, similarly drilled sticks, 19 are burned off at varying lengths between one end and the central hole, three are burned off just to one side of the center hole, two are broken off through the center perforation, and one is broken through one end hole. There is no evidence of painted decoration or of a method of attachment, and it is probable that the bieces were unassembled at the time they were burned and broken.

Maximum lengths of whole sticks, 26.1 cm and 26.2 cm; average width of all sticks, 0.5 cm; average thickness of all sticks, 0.4 cm.

Prayersticks

Carved Prayersticks (Figs. A.39 *a-b*, 2.9). This is a nearly identical pair of carved prayersticks. Specimen *a* is slightly warped or bent. Specimen *b* was cut or slashed diagonally near the center with a sharp tool, then broken in two (it is shown as repaired). The upper end of both sticks is carefully carved into a spherical shape, slightly wider in one dimension than in that perpendicular to it. Approximately 5.3 cm below the base of the lobed end on both sticks is a straight-sided lobe or ferrule ringing the shaft; the portion between the lobes on both is slightly barrel-shaped. The diameter of the shafts below the second lobe decreases gradually toward the rounded, lower ends. Both lobes on *a* are a pure, pale, chalky green, while those on *b* have black paint applied over the pale green paint. The shafts of both sticks, between the lobes and down to approximately 6.7 cm from the lower ends, are covered with black specularite paint.

Maximum length: *a*, 34.6 cm; *b*, 35.5 cm; upper lobe diameters: *a*, 1.6 and 1.25 cm; *b*, 1.85 and 1.4 cm; lower lobe diameter: *a*, 1.5 cm; *b*, 1.7 cm; average shaft diameter: *a*, 1.1 cm; *b*, 1.2 cm.

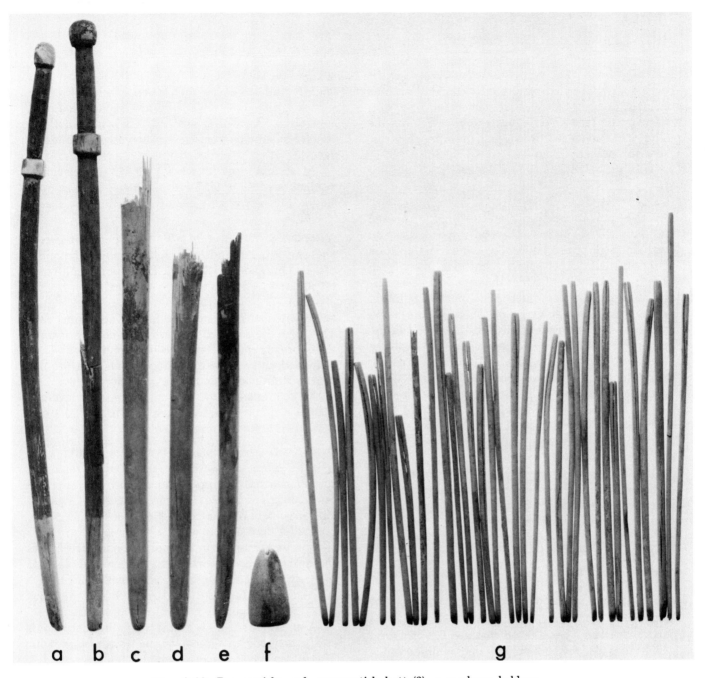

Fig. A.39. Prayersticks, *a-b*; prayerstick butts(?), *c-e*; plume holders: carved cone, *f*; round sticks, *g*.

Prayerstick Butts (?) (Fig. A.39 *c-e*). All three of these large round sticks decrease in diameter from one broken, splintered end to a blunt, rounded point. The bark is removed from all three, and *c* and *d* are well smoothed and slightly polished. Specimen *e* is of softer wood with a less smooth surface; on one-half of its lower third are deep spiral striations; the lower tip is slightly flattened. Traces of resin and, on *e*, of a purple stain appear to be only incidental smudges.

Maximum length of *c*, 27.2 cm; maximum diameter: *c*, 1.6 cm; *d*, 1.5 cm; *e*, 1.3 cm.

Plume Holders

Carved Cone (Figs. A.39 *f*, 2.9). This small cone is carved from the soft stalk of the yucca or agave plant. All sides are convex, tapering to a rounded apex in which is carved a notch 0.4 cm deep, 0.4 cm wide, and 1.1 cm long. A cone approximately 1.5 cm deep and 1.7 cm in basal diameter is carved into the base of the object. A hole approximately 0.2 cm in diameter penetrates the center of the wooden cone from the upper notch to the basal concavity. Through this hole is a strand (single?) of sinew, knotted at the apex of the concavity and broken off 0.4 cm beyond the notch opening. Surfaces are generally smoothed over soft, coarse grain. Pale green appears to have colored the inside of the notch and brown resin the outer cone surface; only traces remain.

Height, 4.3 cm; maximum diameter, 2.5 cm.

Round Sticks (Fig. A.39 *g*). Thirty-five sticks are well smoothed and rounded and all are slightly tapered and flattened at one end. This end is split for several centimeters along each stick. The edges of the split on about one-half of the sticks are smoothed for 2-3 cm from the end, indicating that this may have been the original length of the crack, with natural splitting accounting for the various greater lengths of the cracks among the sticks. Feather barbules were found in the split ends of two sticks, suggesting their use as plume holders; no pigment is evident. All 35 were burned to various lengths on the non-split end.

Longest stick: length, 24.0 cm; average diameter, 0.41 cm.

MISCELLANEOUS OBJECTS

In addition to the specimens discussed below, the collection includes numerous scraps of painted wood, yucca leaves, and yucca braid and cordage that are neither described nor illustrated.

Wooden and Vegetal Objects

Assorted Sticks (Fig. A.40 *a-d*). Specimen *a* is a large, crudely finished stick with red-brown bark intact. It is irregularly cut off at each end and is slightly curved or bent, with a large notch 3.5 cm from each end on the outward-curved side. The notches are 0.3 cm deep and 1 cm wide; they are very crudely whittled out.

Specimens *b* and *c* are round curved sticks which have been irregularly smoothed and rounded and smoothed at each end. Specimen *b* has a band of fugitive black paint 4.5 cm wide encircling its center, while *c* has no evidence of paint or other alteration.

Three rows of short (0.3 cm), parallel, diagonally incised lines cover all but the outer curved surface of specimen *d*. This very smooth polished and curved stick has one slightly tapered, rounded end and one end broken off.

	a	*b*	*c*	*d*
Max. length	23.2 cm	19.5 cm	17.00 cm	16.50 cm
Avg. diameter	1.3 cm	0.6 cm	0.35 cm	0.35 cm

Assorted Sticks (Fig. A.40 *e*). One whole stick and three fragments of similar sticks are represented in this group. The sticks have two flat, parallel surfaces and slightly rounded edges; each tapers in width from the center to the ends, which are also slightly rounded. One piece is burned at one end. The whole stick and one fragment have smudges of resin green on one surface.

Maximum length of whole stick, 25.0 cm; average maximum width of all pieces, 0.65 cm; average maximum thickness of all pieces, 0.35 cm.

Assorted Sticks (Fig. A.40 *f-g*). Specimen *f* is a well-smoothed round stick split through the pithy center. One end is broken off; the opposite end is cut off squarely. There is no trace of paint.

Specimen *g* is a flat, course-grained stick split lengthwise along one side and broken across one end. The edges are rounded, tapering in thickness toward the unbroken end. A large hole, 0.3 cm in diameter, is burned through from both sides 1 cm from the unbroken end. There is no trace of paint.

Maximum length: *f*, 19.7 cm; *g*, 14.0 cm; average diameter of *f*, 1.1 cm; average thickness of *g*, 0.4 cm.

Paint Brushes and Applicator Sticks (Fig. A.40 *h-k*). A strip of yucca leaf with the sharp edges removed, specimen *h* has its upper end cut off squarely; the lower, brush end is cut or worn diagonally with 0.4 cm long fibers freed of leaf-skin. Black paint covers both sides for 3.5 cm from the bristle end.

Specimen *i* is a strip of sotol leaf and, like *h*, has the spiny edges removed, the upper end cut off squarely, and the lower end worn slightly diagonally. It is shredded for approximately 0.2 cm. Resinous green paint irregularly coats the lower 6 cm.

A smoothed stick, *j* is split through the central pith and is generally plano-convex in transverse section. The upper end is cut off squarely; the lower end is tapered for 2 cm to a thin edge which has been worn or sanded to a round-diagonal. Diagonal striations are evident on the smoothed, tapered area of this end. Dull red paint irregularly covers the lower 3 cm.

Specimen *k*, a thin split section of wood, has flat surfaces and squared lateral edges. The ends are cut off squarely and are smoothly thinned. The central area of the stick appears to have been stained from handling. Diagonal striations are visible on both flat surfaces. Each end is irregularly stained for approximately 2 cm with dull black paint. A trace of red occurs under the black on one end.

	h	*i*	*j*	*k*
Max. length	12.20 cm	18.50 cm	11.9 cm	13.00 cm
Max. width	1.40 cm	0.90 cm	1.0 cm	0.80 cm
Avg. thickness	0.15 cm	0.15 cm	0.5 cm	0.25 cm

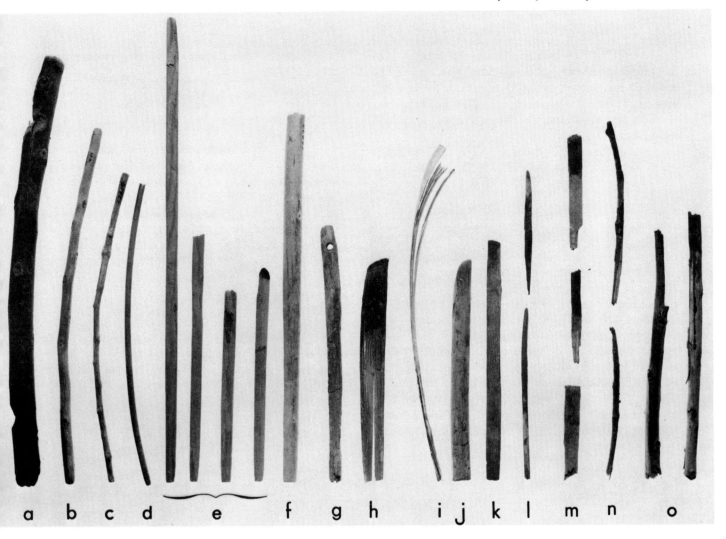

Fig. A.40. Assorted sticks, *a-g*; paint brushes and applicator sticks, *h-o*.

Paint Applicator Sticks (Fig. A.40 *l-o*). All of these sticks and twigs seem to have been used to stir or apply paint. Two narrow split twigs (*l*) are tapered to a thin edge at one end, which in both cases is worn diagonally. The opposing ends are broken off. The worn ends are irregularly covered with green paint for approximately 3 cm on each stick.

Three thin, flat sections of split wood (*m*) are slightly smoothed on each side. There is no other shaping except for the end used to stir or apply paint; on two, this is cut off squarely. All three have resinous green paint covering approximately 2 cm of the lower end.

In *n*, two small twigs are split off at one end to produce a thinned point; both are irregularly covered with resinous green paint on 3-4 cm of the lower end.

The two split sticks in *o* appear to have been broken from the same twig. The bark is partially removed; there is no other alteration save the use of one end to mix or apply resinous green paint.

Dimensions of longest piece:

	l	*m*	*n*	*o*
Max. length	9.4 cm	6.5 cm	10.0 cm	13.1 cm
Max. width	0.4 cm	0.9 cm	0.4 cm	0.7 cm
Avg. thickness	0.2 cm	0.6 cm	0.3 cm	0.5 cm

Curved, Wrapped Fragments (Fig. A.41 *a*). Five broken pieces of round twig are bent or curved. Probably all were once U-shaped like the specimen at the extreme left. Multiple sinew wrapping along the straight length of each fragment holds in a splice a length of split twig. The spliced pieces suggest an original hoop form composed of two half-circles of bent twigs. All twigs are slightly smoothed over natural, vertical ribbing. Small dents occur along the inside of each curve, probably as part of the bending process. Traces of white occur along the inside surface of each fragment and the outer surface is stained red-orange.

Straightened length of *a*, 15.5 cm; average diameter of all pieces, 0.45 cm.

Paired Sticks (Fig. A.41 *b-d*). These pieces represent one fragment and two pairs of round sticks, bound together in the same way. Specimen *c* may be the complete form; its base is cut off diagonally, then broken; *b* is simply broken across the base, and *d* is a fragment broken out of the center of a stick similar to the longer of the two elements composing *b* and *c*. All elements are small, round hardwood twigs. Both prongs of *b* are tapered to a rounded point; the longest prong of *c* tapers to a sharper rounded point; its short element is cut off squarely. Both prongs of *b* and *c* are curved toward the ends. In both cases, the shortest element is diagonally cut off for approximately 4 cm along the lower end. This tapered lower end is bound tightly to the long twig by means of multiple wraps of

sinew. Except for the lower 2 cm of *c*, which is unpainted, the twigs are painted an overall flat black.

Straightened length of *c*, 15.7 cm; average diameter of all pieces, 0.3 cm.

Twig Hoops (Fig. A.41 *e-f*). These specimens represent one complete and one broken split twig hoop or ring. Each is a very narrow split stem bent to form a circle with ends overlapped and tied together with plant fiber cordage. Specimen *e* has two other broken fiber wrappings opposing each other on the hoop and two broken sinew bindings similarly placed; *f* has one of each binding type. One sinew tie on *e* appears to have held two small sticks, or perhaps feather quills, onto the hoop; a tuft of white material (possibly cotton) is held in the knot of the sinew tie on *f*. No pigments are visible.

Average diameter of *e*, 3.0 cm; average width of split twigs, 0.15 cm.

Twig Loop (Fig. A.41 *g*). This small object is composed of three concentric loops of split twigs held together with several wraps of knotted plant fiber cordage. The free ends are cut off irregularly; no pigments are visible.

Maximum length: 2.4 cm; average width of twigs, 0.2 cm.

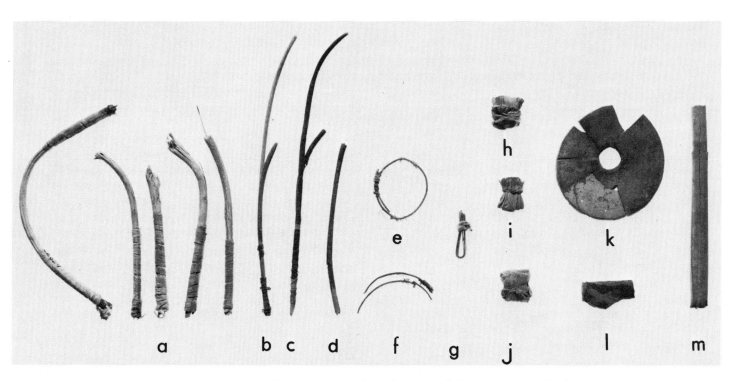

Fig. A.41. Miscellaneous items. Curved, wrapped fragments, *a*; paired sticks, *b-d*; twig hoops, *e-f*; twig loop, *g*; cornhusk packets, *h-j*; cucurbita rind fragments, *k-l*; reed cigarette, *m*.

Cornhusk Packets (Fig. A.41 *h-j*). Three small bundles or packets are each composed of a wide strip of cornhusk folded several times to form a small flat rectangle and tied around the center with plant fiber cordage. Only one packet was unfolded, revealing no contents. All three bear traces of resin green paint.

Dimensions of *h*, 1.7 x 1.5 x 0.6 cm.

Cucurbita Rind Fragments (Fig. A.41 *k-l*). Specimen *k* is a disc cut from the center base of a cucurbita rind. The smooth outer surface is concave, the inner surface convex with irregular ridges fanning out from the center. An opening 1 cm in diameter is cut out of the center. Inner and outer edges are sanded smooth. Three pairs of tiny perforations are placed triangularly around the center hole, approximately 0.7 cm from its edge. The outer rind surface and the inside of the center hole are painted a dull red; the reverse is unpainted. An additional feature is a small (0.1 cm wide and deep) groove, 1.2 cm long, radiating from just above and to one side of one pair of perforations to the rind edge.

Specimen *l* is a small piece of rind, cut straight along two adjacent edges and broken on the other two; the outer rind surface is convex. Both surfaces are painted a dull red, with a black negative design applied over the red on the outer curved surface.

Diameter of *k*, 6.0 cm; average thickness of *k*, 0.3 cm; average thickness of *l*, 0.25 cm.

Reed Cigarette (Fig. A.41 *m*). A length of reed (*Phragmites*) has one end burned and one end cut off squarely 2.5 cm above the single node. The node septum has been carved out; the reed was found to contain what appeared to be several small, irregularly cut pieces of a thick leaf or stem.

Maximum length, 10.5 cm; average diameter, 0.8 cm.

Sticks (Fig. A.42 *a-b*). The writer may well have erred in grouping these forked twigs (*a*) with artifacts. However, they were found on the floor of Room 93 among the other objects and their form suggests use as supports or props. One (second from left) is worn at the lower, tapered end as if from being stuck in the ground. Other ends are broken off irregularly except for the lower ends of two, which are burned. One stick is also broken off at each end, but at three intervals along the stem are split perforations.

Specimen *b* is a long, thin twig that is unaltered on the surface. It has been pierced at three places along its length with round holes that taper at each end. The twig has been broken at the top and cut squarely at the bottom. It is unpainted.

Longest *a* specimen (second from left): maximum length, 22.0 cm; maximum width, 0.6 cm; average

thickness of *a* specimens, 0.4 cm; length of *b*, 24.0 cm; average diameter of *b*, 0.3 cm.

Sticks Spliced with Yucca Leaf (Fig. 42 *c-h*, *k*). Six fragments of split-stick construction were recovered. Each consists of two broken pieces of the same material spliced together with strips of yucca leaf.

Three examples (*c*, *f*, *k*) consist of split-twig pieces with both ends of the split-leaf wrapping secured under all wraps. On one example (*e*), one end of the wrapping material is secured under all wraps and the other end is tied in an overhand knot around two of the outer wraps. On two more fragmentary pieces, one end of the splicing material is held under one wrap (*d*), or under all wraps (*g*). In *h*, two flat split twigs are secured together with several wraps of split leaf; one end is tied with a square knot, the other with an overhand. All ends of the spliced twigs are broken off except on *f*, which is burned at the spliced end.

Maximum length of *e*, 18.6 cm; maximum width of *e*, 1.3 cm; straightened length of *k*, 26.8 cm; maximum width of *k*, 0.8 cm.

Split-Twig Bindings (Fig. A.42 *i-j*). The collection includes several examples of split twigs used as binding material. Two split-stick pieces are spliced together with a narrow split twig, wrapped several times with no knots (*i*) or tucked ends. There are four isolated square knots of split twig (*j*). Three coils of split twigs suggest raw material for construction purposes. Material ranges in width from 0.3 cm to 1.0 cm.

Yucca-Leaf Loops (Fig. A.42 *l-o*). The largest number of loops, bindings, and ties were made from split leaves of yucca. Especially interesting are 13 loops of narrow split leaves—two are illustrated in *l*—all very similar in the shape they assumed upon use and subsequent drying. All except one are tied with square knots. Similarly shaped are 26 smaller loops of split yucca—two are illustrated in *m*—looped once and knotted in a simple square knot. Loop length ranges from 2 to 6 cm. The only example of a yucca loop attached to something else is one loop 7 cm long (*n*) tied in a square knot with one end shaped around an unworked stick, broken at each end. There are fifty-one strips of split yucca leaf of various shapes and widths—two are illustrated in *o*; each is tied with a square knot to form a loop. Most are broken and suggest no special use. One fragment is tied only in an overhand knot.

	l (right)	*m (top)*	*n*	*o (right)*
Max. length	14.00 cm	4.0 cm	7.0 cm	16.0 cm
Max. width	0.25 cm	0.3 cm	0.3 cm	0.8 cm
Avg. thickness	0.20 cm	0.1 cm	0.2 cm	0.2 cm

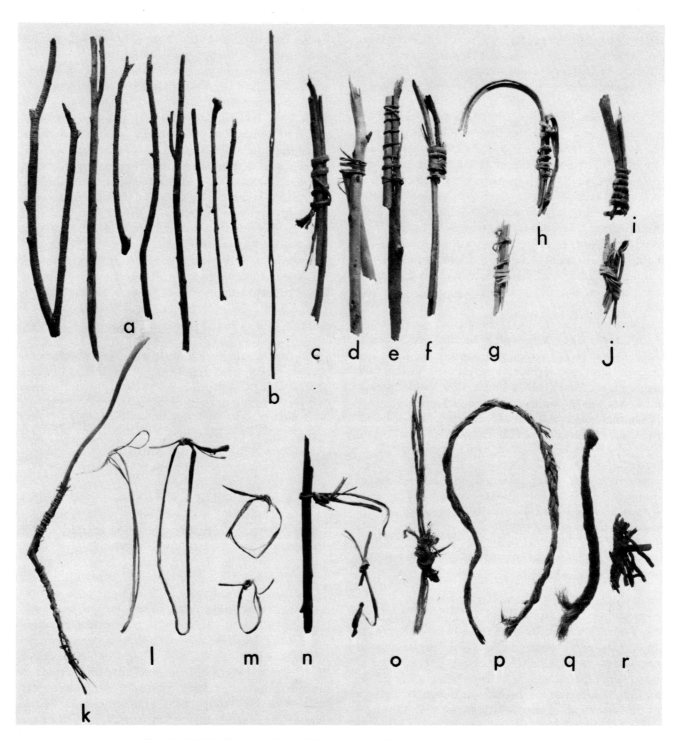

Fig. A.42. Miscellaneous items. Sticks, *a-b*; sticks spliced with yucca leaf,
c-h, *k*; split-twig bindings, *i-j*; yucca-leaf loops, *l-o*; yucca-leaf braid, *p*;
yucca-fiber braid, *q*; matting fragment, *r*.

Yucca-Leaf Braid (Fig. A.42 *p*). Four pieces of simple, three-element flat braid are made of partially shredded leaf strips. Total length of all four pieces, approximately 112 cm.

Yucca-Fiber Braid (Fig. A.42 *q*). A section of flattened, three-element braid is probably made from yucca fiber. At one end the elements are loose; at the other the braid is finished with a flat knot.

Maximum length, 16 cm; maximum width, 0.9 cm; average thickness, 0.5 cm.

Matting Fragment (Fig. A.42 *r*). One small piece from the selvage edge of simple over-two, under-two (?) twilled matting was recovered from Room 93.

Maximum length, 5.5 cm; maximum width, 2.5 cm; width of single element (perhaps split leaf yucca), 0.5 cm.

Reed Loops (Fig. A.43 *a*). Three long loops of reed leaf and fragments of two others were recovered. They are doubled and tied at one end with yucca cordage, and the ends are cut off uniformly just below the cord bindings. Of the two loops illustrated, one is double and is burned at one end, and the other is single.

Specimen at right (double loop): maximum length, 18.0 cm; maximum width, 0.9 cm; average thickness, 0.7 cm.

Yucca-Leaf Ties (Fig. A.43 *b*). Three specimens (two of which are illustrated), each composed of two lengths of split yucca leaves, are tied with square knots to form a doubled suspension loop or wrapping.

Piece at right: maximum length, 10.0 cm; maximum width, 0.6 cm; average thickness, 0.2 cm.

Cordage

Cotton Cordage (Fig. A.43 *c*). There are seven lengths of cotton cordage in the collection (one is illustrated). One is light blue; the others are white. Six are single-ply, Z-spun; one is 3-ply, Z-spun, S-plied.

Maximum length, 9.2 cm; maximum width, 0.1 cm.

Bast Fragments, Cordage (?) (Fig. A.43 *d*). These fragments of bast appear to be reddish juniper bark. Several strands are loosely Z-spun single-ply. The remainder is a bundle of short lengths and shredded bark.

Maximum length, too fragmentary to measure; maximum width of a fragment, 0.5 cm; average thickness, 0.2 cm.

Hard Plant Fiber Cordage (Fig. A.43 *e*; 148 specimens, 3 illustrated).

5 pieces of single-ply, S-spun

128 pieces of 2-ply
    84: S,Z
    42: Z,S
     1: loosely S
     1: loosely Z

1 piece of 3-ply: 2 pieces (Z,S) and 1 (S-spun) Z-replied

13 pieces of 4-ply
    4: 2(2-ply; Z,S) Z-replied
    3: 2(2-ply; S,Z) S-replied
    2: 2(2-ply; unspun, S) Z-replied
    1: 2(2-ply; Z,S) Z-replied with 2(2-ply; unspun, S-plied)
    1: 4 (S-spun) Z-replied

1 piece of 5-ply: S-spun, Z-plied

Hard Plant Fiber Composites (Fig. A.43 *f-g*). One length of brown cordage (*f*) is composed of one 2-ply (Z,S) cord looped around two supporting parallel cords in a method identical to that illustrated in Kidder and Guernsey (1919: 115, Fig. 43). The two foundation cords are 2-ply (S,Z). One cord contains two split quills. A second white cordage composite (*g*) is virtually identical to *f* except that a third cord is sewn through and around the completed composite.

Maximum length: *f*, 8.0 cm; *g*, 9.0 cm; maximum width: *f*, 0.35 cm; *g*, 3.0 cm; average thickness: *f*, 0.2 cm; *g*, 1.5 cm.

Cornhusk with Cordage (Fig. A.43 *h*). A length of cornhusk is cut off at each end, slightly twisted, and wrapped around the center with a length of 2-ply (Z,S) hard fiber cordage. There are no knots.

Maximum length, 8.5 cm; maximum width, 2.2 cm; average thickness, 0.6 cm.

Vegetal Remains

Also found in association with the carved wood were a few vegetal remains (Fig. A.44 *a-e*). These include 20 whole and fragmentary flint corn cobs, several corn husks, and seven pieces of corn tassels (*a*), as well as six lengths of corn stalks (not illustrated), four of them squarely cut off at one end. In addition there were one cucurbit stem (*b*), one fragment of pumpkin rind (*c*), pumpkin seeds (not illustrated), a common kidney bean (not illustrated), two pinyon nut shells (not illustrated), three cockleburs (*d*), four pieces of sotol leaf (not illustrated), and numerous lengths of small-diameter *Phragmites* stem (*e*), some burned on one end.

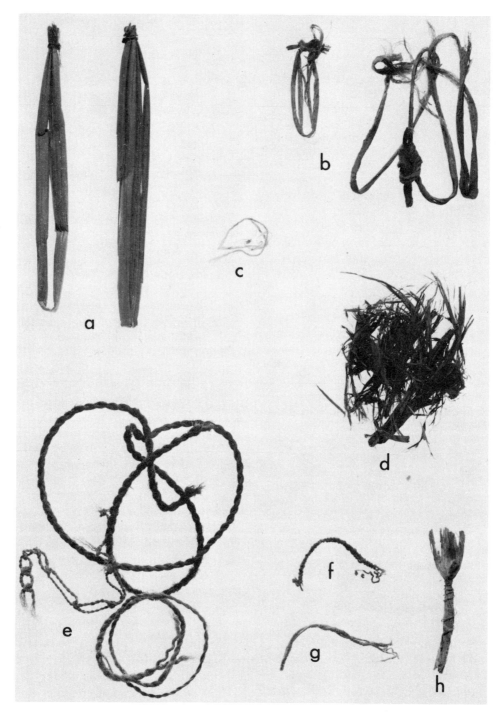

Fig. A.43. Reed loops, *a*; yucca-leaf ties, *b*; cotton cordage, *c*; bast fragments, *d*; hard plant fiber cordage (3 specimens), *e*; hard plant fiber composites, *f-g*; cornhusk with cordage, *h*.

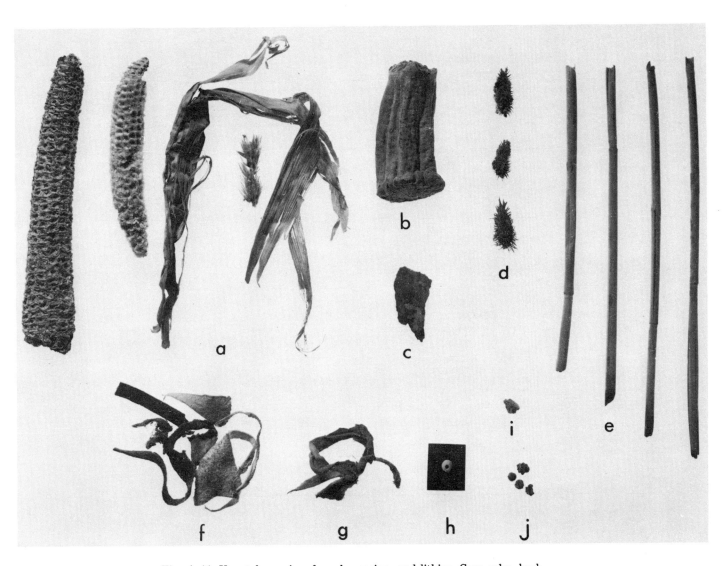

Fig. A.44. Vegetal remains, faunal remains, and lithics. Corn cobs, husk, tassel, *a*; cucurbit stem, *b*; fragment of pumpkin rind, *c*; cockleburs, *d*; *Phragmites* stems, *e*; scraps of tanned hide, *f*; scraps of rawhide, *g*; white shell disc bead, *h*; nodule of chrysocholla, *i*; nodules of azurite, *j*.

Faunal Remains

The faunal material (Fig. A.44 *f-h*) found among the artifacts includes six pieces of tanned hide (*f*). All appear to be scraps; three are painted black on the fleshy surface and white on the reverse surface. One retains some short hair and is painted green. The largest piece is 9.5 x 1.7 cm. Two scraps of rawhide (*g*) were also recovered; the longest measures approximately 15 cm; both are unpainted. One small white shell disc bead (*h*), 0.7 cm in diameter, also came from Room 93.

Unaltered animal remains consist of two feather quill fragments and one small wad of downy feathers. The few animal bones found in the room were a med-ial splinter of deer metapodial (*Odocoileus* spp.); a distal condyle of deer metapodial (*Odocoileus* spp.), possibly grooved for splitting; a lumbar vertebra of a cottontail rabbit (*Sylvilagus* spp.); a right mummified forearm of *Sylvilagus* spp.; and a right ulna and radius of a pack rat (*Neotoma* spp.).

Lithics

Minerals recovered (Fig. A.44 *i-j*) consist of one nodule of chrysocholla (*i*) and four nodules of azurite (*j*). The tools recovered were one broken chalcedony saw, two thin chalcedony scrapers, and one round, flat, quartzite stone perhaps used for polishing (not illustrated).

Appendix B

TECHNICAL ANALYSES

Dulce N. Dodgen

PAINTS

Painting is by far the most important embellishment technique used on the Chetro Ketl wooden objects, and the retention of several bright, clear colors on these relatively well-preserved eleventh-century artifacts is especially striking. Only two other forms of decorative surface alteration are evident. The sole example of incising is found on the small, well-smoothed stick shown in Figure A.40 *d*, which is covered with short, parallel, shallowly inscribed hatch marks. The close wrappings of reddish bast cordage that appear to have covered the entire length of all five non-functional bow fragments (Fig. A.36) and over which a thick coating of resinous material was applied, could be considered a third decorative technique.

Approximately 12 percent of the pieces in the collection have no decoration or surface alteration beyond sanding or smoothing, and may simply represent a stage of incomplete construction. Examples are the flat carved fragments shown in Figures A.7c, A.15e-f, and A.34f-g. All other pieces are painted with at least one color; two pieces have five colors. Brush work varies from the rather crude band encircling the small disc (Fig. A.17a) to the extremely well-controlled painting on the plaque (Fig. A.21). In decreasing order of frequency, colors are green, brown, black, yellow, white, blue, red, and a magenta or reddish-purple. Both paints and stains were used, the latter probably organic, the former, and the largest group, generally inorganic.

Organic substances can be identified only with great difficulty in this dry state. However, after careful examination and comparison with practices among historic Pueblo Indian peoples, we assume that the majority of pigment binders or vehicles, varnishes, and very possibly at least two colorants (yellow and purple) are organic in nature. Microscopic examination showed crushed charcoal to be the color source in the majority of black paints, but other forms of carbon such as soot may also have been used. The extensive use of tree gum or resin as a paint vehicle, as a varnish,

and either in its natural state or tinted, as a paint, is a particularly interesting characteristic of the Chetro Ketl wood. Probably other plant gums were used also, but the dark brown color of resin and its odor when moist suggest its presence in the majority of lustrous paints and varnishes.

Fifteen key samples of paint were submitted to the Pacific Spectrochemical Laboratory in Los Angeles for semiquantitative spectrographic analysis, a method particularly suitable for assaying the inorganic content of very small quantities (Harrison, Lord, and Loofbourow 1949: 425; Shepard 1961: 144). Because removal of a large number of paint flakes from these already rather fragile objects seemed out of the question, specific samples were selected that would represent each color or paint type and variant. Results are given in Table B.1, an adaptation of a form used by Gettens (1962a: 562, Table 2), and are discussed below.

Although the spectrographic method was the best for our purposes, its disadvantages and limitations should be kept in mind. Sensitivity of detection varies somewhat from element to element, and analysis is ordinarily restricted to the metallic elements and some of the metalloids (Harrison, Lord, and Loofbourow 1949: 425-6; Shepard 1961: 144; Waring and Annell 1953:1175). The inability to detect the presence of chlorine and sulfur, for example, hampers the specific identification of certain ore pigments. Furthermore, Shepard (1961: 144) states that it "cannot be used for quantitative determination of elements that occur in concentrations greater than 10 percent." However, the data obtained from the selected samples, coupled with microscopic examination, and, in some instances, simple chemical tests, do permit making reasonably accurate estimates of the composition of the majority of paints.

All paints were viewed microscopically. As a result, charcoal (a major source for black and presumably also a darkening agent in other paints) was found, as well as other significant inclusions.

TABLE B.1

Spectrographic Analyses of Key Paint Samples

Sample	More Than 10%	5-10%	1-5%	0.5-1%	0.1-0.5%	0.05-0.1%	0.01-0.05%	0.005-0.01%	0.001-0.005%	0.0005-0.001%	Percent Inorganic Content
I green	Cu Si	Al		Fe	Ca Mg Zn Ti		Sr Zr Mo	Cr Mn	V Ag		54.8
II green	Cu Si	Al		Fe Ca Mg	Na	Ti	Sr Mo	Zr	Mn V Cr	Ag	47.9
III brown	Si	Al	Fe Mg K Ca	Na	Cu Ti		Zr Sr	Mn	Cr V Bo Ni		47.5
IV black			Ca Al Na	Si Mg		Mn Fe	Pb Zr V	Ti	Bo		6.9
V black	Si		Al Ca Fe Mg	Na	Ti	Cu Mn	Pb Sr Zr		Bo V Cr Ni		36.9
VI black	Fe Si		Al Mg Ca	Na	Cu	Ti Mn	Zr V	Cr Sr	Ni		51.7
VII black	Fe	Si	Ca Al	Cu	Na Mg	Ti	Sr	Mn Bo	V Cr		30.9
VIII yellow	Si	Al		As Ca Mg	Fe Ti Cu		Zr		Bo Mn		33.4
IX yellow	Si		Al Ca	Mg	As Fe Na Ti	Cu	Zr Sr	Mn	Bo Cr		24.2
X white	Ca	Si	Al	Fe	Mg Na Sr	Ti		Mn Zr	Bo		20.7
XI white	Ca		Si	Mg	Sr Cu Al	Na Fe	Bo Ti	Mn			29.9
XII blue	Cu Si		Al	Fe Mg	Ca Na		Ti Pb Yb	Sr Zr Mn	Bo V Ag Cr		44.3
XIII blue	Si Cu		Al Fe	Mg	Ca Na Ti		Zr Pb	Sr Mn	Cr Ag V Bo		46.4
XIV red	Si Fe	Al	Ca	Mg Na	Ti Cu	Pb	Mn Sb Mo Sr Zr	Bo V Cr			52.2
XV purple	Si		Al Ca Mg	Fe Na	Cu Ti		Zr Sr Mn Bo		Cr		44.8

Sand, crushed quartz, and other similar particles were found in all paints and to some extent in the stains. Most of these inclusions are probably unavoidable impurities such as matrix, in the case of mineral pigments, and material picked up from stone surfaces on which pigments were ground and mixed. However, on the effigy arrows shown in Figure A.35, fine sand appears to have been intentionally mixed, heavily and evenly, into reddish-brown resin to produce an opaque, matte brown paint. Both intentional and unintentional sand, clay, and dirt probably account for the relatively large amount of silicon (more than 10 percent in 11 samples, from 5 to 10 percent in 20 others) as well as most of the aluminum reported in all tested samples (from 5 to 10 percent in five samples, from 1 to 5 percent in nine others).

Green

Green is the most frequently used color, occurring in 29 percent of the painted objects and showing the greatest range of tints and shades. It ranges from a light chalky lime (approximated in Maerz and Paul 1950: Pl. 26A5) to a dark forest green (Pl. 24A12). Sixty-eight percent of the green paints fall into the latter group of dark shades and appear to be mixed with a resin base or vehicle that tends to impart varying degrees of luster. Twenty-two percent either had a watery base originally or have lost a water-soluble binder, such as resin, through exposure to moisture; these are powdery, fugitive, and of the lightest color. Several pieces with resinous green on one side show loss of the dark, lustrous binder on the opposing surface with only the light green pigment remaining. The object shown in Figure A.8 *a* was originally covered completely with this green paint, but, as illustrated, one fragment was exposed to less favorable conditions, and on both sides there is loss of the resinous component with only the pale mineral pigment intact. This condition was duplicated by placing splinters covered with resin green on a damp blotter for a short time, then allowing the surface to dry thoroughly. The resultant pale color and powdery texture were identical to that of the weathered green pieces.

Ten percent of the greens have a matte finish and a coloring midway between the first two groups, suggesting the use of a different binder. All but one example are applied over a coat of white that could have absorbed the vehicle, leaving the paint dull and flat.

All green paints are similar microscopically, being generally composed of finely crushed, apple-green crystals mixed with varying amounts of white, blue, and more or less colorless particles. Two samples were submitted for analysis (Table B.1, Samples I and II), a

light and a dark shade. As expected, copper is the chromogenic element, making up a reported 27 percent of the first sample and 21 percent of the second.

From the frequent occurrences of the green copper carbonate mineral malachite in Chaco ruins (Brand and others 1973: 60; Judd 1954: 285; Pepper 1920: 373), its occurrence in paints on other archaeological wooden objects (Cosgrove 1947: 139-40; Hough 1914: 100; Wasley 1962: 383), and its widely reported use as a colorant among historic Pueblo Indians (Smith 1952: 25-32), its presence in the Chetro Ketl paints is not unexpected. However, four samples of green pigment from the collection, plus the small green mineral nodule found in the same room, were subjected to a simple chemical test (reaction in hydrochloric acid [Pough 1953: 170]) and found to be negative for the presence of a carbonate. It is still possible, however, that malachite was used as a color source for some of the large number of greens.

Both of the spectrographic samples were 19 percent silicon, suggesting the possibility of the green copper silicate, chrysocolla. Although no record of the use of this mineral as a pigment was found in Southwestern literature, Gettens (1962b: 563) reports its occasional use for bright green paints in ancient Old World paintings. Two impurities found in chrysocolla are alumina and an iron oxide (Dana 1964: 686); both green paint samples contained more than 5 percent aluminum and just under 1 percent iron. Since chrysocolla accompanies other copper ores and occurs at least as close as eastern Arizona (Dana 1964: 686), its use in Chaco Canyon is plausible.

Other possible sources for the green pigments are the two closely similar copper sulfate minerals, brochantite and antlerite. Two of the four samples tested chemically definitely contained a sulfate (reaction with calcite in an acid solution [Pough 1953: 190]). These are also found together with other copper ores and occur as close as eastern Arizona (Dana 1964: 756). Though these two minerals and chrysocolla may not have been as easily obtained as malachite (see Brand and others 1937: 55-6, 60, for probable sources of azurite and malachite), preferred pigment colors may have been traded from distant sources as they have been in recent times. This is especially true in the case of green, which along with blue, is a highly valued color among most Pueblo groups (Bunzel 1932: 861; Dutton 1963: 138-9; Roediger 1961: 94-6; Stephen 1936: 1191). There are several references to Hopi use of "a copper ore," not specifically identified, as the source of green and blue (Parsons 1939: 274, 341; Stephen 1936: 232, 470).

Pinyon gum is frequently recorded as being mixed with copper ore pigments as a binder by the Hopi (Bourke 1884: 120; Hough 1902: 469; Parsons 1939:

341; Stephen 1936: 232, 470). The copper ore paint traded by Santo Domingo to Zuni is ground with water, then mixed with pinyon gum (Bunzel 1932: 861); the practice is the same at Acoma (White 1932a: 131). Smith (1952: 30) lists many instances of mixing ground pigments with saliva generated by chewing various seeds containing characteristic oils. The method of preparing green copper ore paint for masks by using squash seeds with resin green is described in detail by Stephen (1936: 470). For preparing an altar paint (Stephen 1936: 470) muskmelon seeds are chewed, and the resultant saliva, with additional water, is mixed with the mineral pigment. A vehicle similar to this last recipe may have been used in the smallest group of green paints in the collection. The only instance of the use of water alone as a vehicle with a green pigment is that cited by Stephen (1936: 737) and Hough (1902: 471) for the Hopi, who use a green sandstone or "arenaceous clay colored by carbonate of copper" as the colorant.

Brown

Brown paints consisting mostly of resin were used on 22 percent of the Chetro Ketl pieces. Brown is the second most frequent color. The use of a tree gum as a varnish has been reported archaeologically (Cosgrove 1947: 140; Kidder and Guernsey 1919: 147) and it has been used by historic Pueblo peoples as a varnish and pigment binder. The use of tree resin as a paint is apparently rare, however, and the only definite report of its use as such is in decorations on reed arrowshafts described by Cosgrove (1947: 64).

Examined microscopically, 10 percent are resin unmixed with other material; the best example is the transparent, lustrous red-brown on the large horn (Fig. A.10 *a*). Sixty-five percent of the resin browns appear to be mixed with varying amounts of fine sand, evenly distributed, the effect being a lessening of the reddish cast and the production of a more opaque, true brown. Twenty-five percent contain not only sand but also recognizable charcoal. Certain amounts of both inclusions are probably contaminants in these once sticky resins, but the evenness of distribution through the paints and the resulting variety of shades strongly suggest intentional mixing. The previously mentioned opaque, matte brown on the effigy arrows (Fig. A.35) is an outstanding example of this mixture. A sample from the arrow fletching was assayed (Table B.1, Sample III) and found to be composed of 33 percent silicon. It may be possible that a brownish iron-stained sand was used as one ingredient, for iron was 2.3 percent of the sample. Any element present in a one percent quantity or more is considered spectrographically to be a "major" constituent of a sample (Shepard 1961: 145), and, therefore, a possible colorant (Gettens 1962a: 560). Except for the matte

brown on the arrows, all resin brown paints retain a luster and are generally crackled where thickly applied.

Pine, pinyon, and juniper trees could all have furnished the gum or resin for these brown paints, as they were present in Chaco Canyon during the eleventh century. Pinyon was probably used most often, however. Pepper (1920: 37) reports several small balls of pinyon gum and one large piece from Pueblo Bonito, and Brand and others (1937: 51) state that the occurrence of pinyon gum is common in Chaco ruins. Among modern Pueblo groups, pinyon gum is the only tree resin mentioned for use as a binder, a varnish, or a glue (Hough 1902: 471; Bunzel 1932: 861; Lange 1959: 145; Parsons 1939: 341; Stephen 1936: 1192-4).

Black

Black is the third most frequently used color, present on 18 percent of the painted objects. Finishes are generally matte to slightly lustrous. Four samples that appeared to differ in texture and finish and therefore also in possible color source were submitted for spectrographic analyses. Results of the analyses, plus microscopic examination, indicate the use of charcoal, one or two iron oxides, and a possible shale for black pigment.

Forty-four percent of these black paints appear to be made entirely of crushed charcoal; of these, two-thirds have a slightly oily to resinous base; others are matte in finish. On only one piece (Fig. A.4 *a*) has flat (charcoal) paint been overlaid with varnish, presumably resin. The total inorganic content of the sample tested from this group (Table B.1, Sample IV) was only 6.9 percent and the inorganic elements that were present, such as iron or manganese, either would not produce a black color in a mineral form or are in too small a quantity to do so. Impurities probably account for most of the inorganic material.

Twenty-two percent of the black paints contain no recognizable charcoal, but compare very credibly with microscopic characters of finely crushed black shale taken from a collection of expertly identified geological specimens. The spectrographic sample from this group (Table B.1, Sample V) does to some extent support this possibility. Shales are composed principally of clay (aluminum silicate) and some sand (Pough 1953: 21) and can be stained with dark carbonates or oxides of iron and magnesium. All of these elements were present in our tested sample in amounts above one percent; silicon was well over 10 percent. Further, shales are very common at Chaco, and the dark carbonaceous variety is said to be preponderant (Brand and others 1937: 62; Bryan 1954: 4). Paints in this group tend to have a slightly oily to resinous base.

In a third group of black paints (13 percent), some charcoal can be found along with fine particles resembling those of shale. All but one example is thin and matte in finish and all contain much fine sand.

Eleven percent of the black paints (5 objects) are composed mainly of specular iron. The finish is matte black sprinkled with refractive particles. In the assayed sample (Table B.1, Sample VI), iron made up 54 percent of the total inorganic material. Based upon visual characteristics and the analysis, the pigments of these paints fit well the description of the specular or "micaceous" variety of hematite (Dana 1964: 484). Iron oxide deposits are easily accessible throughout the Chaco area (Brand and others 1937: 58; Judd 1954: 285).

One other paint, composed mainly of iron oxide, appears to have been originally a pure black which later became unevenly oxidized, producing a range of color from deep black to reddish-brown (Fig. A.21). The speculation that black was the intended color seems reinforced by the presence throughout of particles of charcoal. On both sides of the plaque, the dark color is flat or matte in finish but may have been dulled when its vehicle was absorbed by the white undercoat. The test run on a sample of this paint showed iron present in an amount well over 10 percent (Table B.1, Sample VII); other elements present would not contribute to the color. Black or blackish-brown varieties of certain oxides, hematite, goethite, and possibly limonite (Dana 1964: 484, 503, 505) are all available at Chaco Canyon (Brand and others 1937: 58, 60). The remaining examples of black paint are too fugitive to be gainfully described.

As for the historical use of these materials, of the black paints found in the Awatovi murals, almost all of the tested samples contained some form of carbon. Charcoal was found in a few examples; and the presence of phosphate in other samples suggested the use of bone black. Minerals detected were iron (used together with carbon) and a possible manganese compound in a paint with no carbon present (Smith 1952: 24). No phosphorus was found in the four Chetro Ketl samples, and manganese was present in minor amounts in each. Cosgrove (1947: 140) describes the black used on wooden pieces from the Upper Gila and Hueco area caves as "possibly carbon."

Modern Pueblo Indian sources for black paints used for ceremonial purposes are many. Watson Smith (1952: 26-7) has published an extensive but not complete list of both organic and mineral sources for black pigment.

Of the pigment materials listed by Smith, corn smut seems to be especially sacred and highly valued, at least among the Hopi (Colton 1949: 10; Stephen 1936: 708). Shale paint is particularly frequent on Hopi prayersticks (Stephen 1936: 65, 108, 607, 624-5, 739, 898) and masks (Stephen 1936: 240, 396), and is used on the water serpent effigies (Stephen 1936: 311).

Again for the Hopi, lignite coal, charcoal, soot, and corn smut pigments "are never mixed together, but are used separately for different occasions" (Stephen 1936: 1195). No mention is made by Stephen of shale being mixed with other black pigments. However, at Zuni, a black paint used "to color sticks of plume offerings" is prepared from Rocky Mountain beeweed (*C. serrulata*) and a black mineral (Stevenson 1915: 96). Coal and lignite are readily found in Chaco Canyon (Bauer and Reeside 1921: 155-237; Brand and others 1937: 59) and have been reported from five rooms in Pueblo Bonito (Pepper 1920: 373).

Among fluid vehicles and binders recorded as being used specifically with black pigments, water alone is mixed with charcoal (Stephen 1936: 1195) and specular iron (Stephen 1936: 90) for painting prayersticks at Hopi. At Zuni water is mixed with corn smut for a body paint (Bunzel 1932: 860). "Medicine water" is used with shale pigment for Hopi Antelope prayersticks (Stephen 1936: 607). Again at Hopi "seeds of appropriate kinds" (Stephen 1936: 305) are chewed and the resultant saliva mixed with the dry pigments—cotton seeds with lignite (Stephen 1898: 264); muskmelon seeds with lignite (Stephen 1898: 264), coal (Stephen 1936: 470), shale (Parsons 1939: 341; Stephen 1936: 296, 470, 898-9), and charcoal (Stephen 1936: 751); and squash seeds with "black" pigment (Stephen 1936: 542). Masks used in a Hopi Powa'mû ceremony "are covered with charcoal and melted pinyon gum" (Stephen 1936: 211-2). Tewa mix a shiny black quartz, sphalerite, and galena pigment with pinyon gum or yucca juice for masks (Roediger 1961: 100), and at Zuni, corn smut is mixed with yucca syrup (Bunzel 1932: 860) for a mask paint. Honey is combined with shale pigment (Stephen 1936: 624) for Hopi Antelope prayersticks. Soot is mixed with egg white (White 1932: 131) as a mask paint at Acoma, the eyes being painted with a soot and egg yolk combination.

Yellow

Yellow makes up 12 percent of all the paint on the Chetro Ketl wooden objects, but areas covered are generally small. On the basis of the range of hues and microscopic differences, yellow paints seem to fall into three groups. Sixty-three percent are pure to golden-yellow (Maerz and Paul 1950: Pls. 9L2-9L7), contain varying amounts of irregular, bright orange crystals and fine sand, and have a generally resinous to slightly oily base. One example from this group is varnished over, probably with resin. Twenty-seven percent are slightly oily to watery stains of dull yellow (Maerz and Paul 1950: Pl. 11G3), and 10 percent are pale, opaque, matte yellows (Maerz and Paul 1950: Pl. 11G3) with a slightly oily base, in two cases applied over white. No orangish crystals are found in the last two groups.

Two samples were assayed (Table B.1, Samples VIII, IX), and results seem to indicate that the major colorant is an organic substance (mixed with sand or clay) rather than a mineral. Among the Hopi, a bright yellow paint is made from the flowers of rabbitbrush (*Chrysothamnus graveolens*), white sandstone and "an impure almogen [alunogen?]" (Hough 1902: 470). Corn pollen is mixed with boiled yucca juice to produce a glossy yellow paint for painting mask designs at Zuni (Bunzel 1932: 860).

It may be significant to note that of the 15 paint samples tested, only the two yellows contained the element arsenic, albeit in relatively minor amounts (0.88 percent in Sample VIII and 0.42 percent in Sample IX, Table B.1). It did not occur in other color samples as a minor or trace element as did titanium and manganese, which were found in all 15 samples. Arsenic in the two yellow paints may, of course, simply be a coincidence, but its presence in a mineral form could account for the deep orange inclusions and golden hues of the greatest percentage of yellow pigments. A possible source is orpiment (arsenic trisulfide), a yellow mineral occurring in some clays in the Southwest and used commercially as a pigment. It is commonly associated with the less stable monosulfide form, realgar, which is red to orange-yellow and which, upon exposure to light, changes into the lighter yellow trisulfide (Dana 1964: 409). In thick applications of the paints containing orange crystals, the outer surface tends to be a clear yellow but becomes increasingly orange underneath (this is especially noticeable when paint is scraped off and the recesses of the wood grain are exposed). This suggests that these yellows may be an altered state of an originally orange paint.

A characteristic of the group of metals to which arsenic belongs is the insolubility of their sulfides in dilute hydrochloric acid (Engelder, Dunkelberger, and Schiller 1940: 154). The individual orange crystals and other orange and yellow particles in these paints were found to be insoluble in this acid, with no loss of color. Still, arsenic is present in very small amounts, and organic colors have been found highly resistant to acids with rention of color brightness. (See the discussions of Maya Blue, a possible "clay-organic complex" colorant, by Gettens [1962a: 557-63] and Shepard [1962: 565-6]).

The yellow iron oxide limonite could have been used in the smallest group of yellows; certainly its use would be expected since limonite is so readily available in Chaco Canyon and found with frequency in Chaco ruins (Brand and others 1937: 60; Judd 1954: 284-5; Pepper 1920: 373). It is the sole mineral source of yellow pigment recorded among recent Pueblo peoples, and its use is extensive (for example: Acoma [White 1932a: 131]; Cochiti [Lange 1950: 144]; Hopi [Bourke 1884: 121; Hough 1902: 471; Stephen 1936: 55, 271]; and general Pueblo [Parsons 1939: 274]). Vehicles used with yellow ochre are egg yolk at Acoma (White 1932a: 131), and plain water and "water in which squash has been boiled" at Hopi (Stephen 1936: 541, 521). The latter is said to produce "a fine, rich yellow, almost orange."

At Zuni, limonite and yellow flower petals (buttercups and other bright flowers) are ground with abalone shells and mixed with water to produce a paint for the body and for masks and prayersticks (Bunzel 1932: 860). Also, ground flowers of a thistle (*Psilostrophe tagetina*) are mixed with yellow ochre and urine for yet another Zuni mask and body paint (Stevenson 1915: 97). Both rabbitbrush, mentioned earlier, and this thistle grow in or near Chaco Canyon, and various infusions of these and other yellow flowering plants may well be the dyestuffs used to produce the yellow stains coloring that 27 percent of the objects which are dull yellow.

White

There are 22 instances of the use of white paint in the collection (9 percent of the objects). Exactly one-half of the visible whites were applied first as an undercoat, then used as a ground color for subsequent paints; remaining white paints were applied as separate design elements or zones. There is no instance of white being varnished over since it would probably be darkened. Figure A.4 *d* is a good example. The black and yellow are varnished with a resinous fluid while the white is left matte and chalky. White on the tail in Figure A.3 is the only example where the pigment clearly seems to have an oily or resinous base, giving it an uneven, brownish stain. All other white paints tend to be chalky or powdery and matte in finish. Some are thick and others are fugitive. Most appear to have had a watery or slightly oily base. In all cases, white appears to have absorbed to some degree the darkening vehicles of adjacent paints.

Microscopically, all but the most fugitive examples of white contain varying amounts of fine sand and crushed white crystals together with fine, powdery particles. In six examples, crushed white crystals appear to compose the entire paint layer. Spectrographic analysis of two samples of white (Table B.1, Samples X, XI) show a calcium compound to be the pigment source. Samples identical to the two above were tested in hydrochloric acid and both reacted as a sulfate and were definitely negative for carbonate (Pough 1953). Thus gypsum (calcium sulfate) is probably the main source for white. Dana (1964:759) states that gypsum is often impure with clay or silica, which may account for the percentage of silicon in both samples and for aluminum in Sample X (Table B.1).

Gypsum occurs in several forms in Chaco Canyon and has been found carved, mixed in wall plaster, and in unaltered form in Chaco ruins (Brand and others 1937: 58; Dutton 1938: 68; Pepper 1920: 373). At Cochiti, it is used on walls (Lange 1959: 145), and Stephen (1936: 898) writes that "gypsiferous clay," mixed with saliva produced when muskmelon seeds are chewed, is a Hopi white paint for prayersticks. Kaolin and chalk (calcium carbonate) may also have been used on the wooden items. Hopi use kaolin extensively for white paint (Hough 1902: 469; Stephen 1936: 396, 411, 542), and Zuni trade for it from Acoma for the same purpose (Bunzel 1932: 859). Chalk is also used at Hopi, alone with water or ground and mixed with clay (Hough 1902: 471; Stephen 1898: 264). Except for the one instance of mixing with saliva generated by seed chewing, white pigments generally seem to be mixed only with water.

Blue

Twelve wooden pieces in the collection (5 percent) are decorated with a blue paint, which is generally applied in small bands. The majority are fairly clear blues (Maerz and Paul 1950: Pl. 33K9); those mixed with what is probably resin are darker (Maerz and Paul 1950: Pl. 38L6). Three examples of blue are matte in finish, probably mixed only with water; six are mixed with a resinous base, and two are clearly varnished over with resin. One blue could have either a resin base or varnish. Two samples were assayed (Table B.1, Samples XII, XIII); copper was reported as 29 percent of the first sample and 18 percent of the second. Specimens from the same two objects were also tested in acid, and, unlike the green paints, proved to be positive for a carbonate (Pough 1953: 170). Solution in cold, dilute hydrochloric acid was rapid and with effervescence, thus eliminating silicates and sulfates (Pough 1953: 190, 278). No calcium sulfate crystals formed upon the addition of calcite to the acid solutions of the two blue pigments. Azurite, the blue copper carbonate, is, therefore, the colorant in the two tested samples. Like malachite, this blue copper mineral is found frequently in Chaco ruins, both powdered and unaltered (Brand and others 1937: 55; Judd 1954: 102, 285; Kluckhohn and Reiter 1939: 54; Pepper 1920: 373).

There are numerous references for the Hopi use of "copper ore water," "blue malachite," and a copper carbonate for painting masks and prayersticks. Usually the intended color is blue-green, but depending upon the composition of the copper ore available, a range from pale green through dark blue is used (Bourke 1884: 120; Hough 1902: 469; Stephen 1898: 263; 1936: 55, 65, 311, 397, 606, 624, 894). Azurite is used at Zuni (Bunzel 1932: 859), and at Zia blue-green

malachite is listed for making mask paint (White 1962: 21). Vehicles used with copper ore pigments were pinyon gum, saliva, medicine, plain water. At Hopi, squash seeds are chewed and the saliva mixed with azurite pigments for blue paints (Stephen 1898: 265; 1936: 1193).

Red

Generally fugitive, dull red paint (Maerz and Paul 1950: Pl. 5K9) occurs on only 10 items in the collection (4 percent). Four pieces have edges painted a dull orange-red; three have design areas that were painted red first, then covered with nearly opaque brown resin, apparently intended either as a varnish or a second paint. Traces of red occur on a single surface of one piece, and a narrow, dull red line was used to guide the placement of paints on each of two rosettes. A sample of red paint was removed from the fairly heavy coat on one paint-applicator stick (Fig. A.40 *j*) and was submitted for analysis (Table B.1, Sample XIV). Iron is the obvious color-producing element, probably in the earthy, red oxide form of hematite. Clay is often mixed with the mineral in the reddle and red chalk forms (Dana 1964: 484). This would account for the percentages of silicon and aluminum in the tested sample.

Hematite, like limonite, occurs commonly in ruins and is found sporadically throughout the Chaco area in sandstones and shales (Brand and others 1937: 58, 60; Dutton 1938: 68; Judd 1954: 285; 1959: 193; Kluckhohn and Reiter 1939: 54; Pepper 1920: 373). Its use among historic tribes is widely recorded (for example: Acoma [White 1932: 131]; Cochiti [Lange 1959: 132, 144]; Hopi [Hough 1902: 469; Stephen 1936: 90, 199, 588]; Jemez [Parsons 1925: 112]; Zia [White 1962: 18, 153, 162]; Zuni [Bunzel 1932: 859]). At Hopi and Zuni, red ochre is rubbed down with water to form the paint (Bunzel 1932: 859; Stephen 1936: 1195). Stephen (1936: 542) records one instance of squash seeds being chewed and the saliva spat into a mortar for mixing with the ground red pigment. The blade of a wooden sword swallowed in a ceremony at Zia is smeared with deer tallow, then with red ochre (White 1962: 153). Parsons mentions one instance of dry red ochre being rubbed on prayersticks (1939: 274).

The two squash or gourd fragments (Fig. A.41 *k-l*) found with the material from Room 93 are painted with a red-orange color that does not appear to contain hematite. It may be similar to an "orange-colored juice" used "to decorate artificial squash blossoms" at Hopi. This paint is made from the root of the painted cup (*Castilleja linariaefolia*), chewed together with juniper bark and mixed with white clay (Whiting 1939: 91).

Red-Purple

A distinctive reddish-purple stain (Maerz and Paul 1950: Pl. 45L9) was used to color the central area of one of the discs (Fig A.18 *b*), and the same hue was found in irregular traces on three other objects. These represent only 2 percent of the specimens. The color in all cases is dull and flat, and, under microscopic investigation, black to purplish irregular crystals can be seen along the stained wood grain. A sample was taken from the pieces illustrated in Figure A.18 *b* for analysis. As shown in Table B.1, Sample XV, no element was present in a concentration over 1 percent that would indicate a mineral of a red to purple color from which a pigment could be made. Neither iron nor manganese, both of which were found in a maroon or purple color used in the Awatovi murals (Smith 1952: 23), were in sufficient quantities to produce a color. Aluminum, calcium, and magnesium minerals (oxides, fluorides, silicates) are either too hard and crystalline or do not occur in the Southwest, and, moreover, apparently do not react in the same way chemically as the unknown sample (Dana 1964: 463, 472, 488, 516; Pough 1953: 122, 141, 153). Samples of the purplish paint were found to be insoluble in hot hydrochloric acid, but crystals and stained bits of wood from the scrapings immediately lost the purple color and turned an amber-yellow upon contact with the cold acid. The original purple color was again restored with addition of an alkaline (ammonium hydroxide).

Silicon made up 35 percent of the spectrographic sample, or 78 percent of the inorganic part. It is therefore probable that the crystals and other particles are fine sand and clay that were mixed into and stained by an organic dye. The color change in acid and alkaline solutions suggests that the purple coloring matter, haematoxylin, could have been obtained from tropical logwood trees (*Haemotoxylon brasiletto* and *H. campechianum*). This dye was used by the Aztecs and it is still in use today (Emmart 1964: 83-5). The dye when extracted is yellow but becomes red and purple when boiled with alum. One form of alum (aluminum sulfate with ammonia) might furnish the necessary alkalinity to change the dye color, and, judging from the amount of aluminum in our sample, it could be present. Hopi have long used alum as a mordant in dyes and derive it from an impure alum-bearing clay in their country (Hough 1902: 469). This is not to say that a logwood dye necessarily was traded to Chaco from Mexico; a similar plant dye could be involved.

A "pink-purple" body paint is made at Hopi from water in which purple corn kernels have been boiled, and which is then poured over dried sumac (*Rhus trilobata*) berries and mixed with "potato clay" (Hough 1902: 469; Stephen 1936: 1194). A Zuni body stain of purple is obtained from chewed stalks and husks of black corn (Bunzel 1932: 861; Roediger 1961: 101), and purple prayerstick dye is made from purple cornhusks or cactus flowers (Parsons 1939: 274). Also at Zuni, crushed fruits of the barberry (*Berberis fremontii*) are used for coloring the skin and ceremonial objects purple (Stevenson 1915: 88). Sunflower seeds furnish a purple dye for Hopi basketry (Whiting 1950: 69). All of these dye sources would have been available to the Chaco peoples—barberry, sumac, and the prickly pear cactus in particular (Brand and others 1937: 53-5)—and may well have furnished the magenta color on the small disc form.

DECORATIVE TECHNIQUE

Paint brushes, mixing sticks, and probably raw material for pigments (four azurite nodules and one piece of what appeared to be chrysocolla), were found on the floor of Room 93, but no mortars, palettes, or paint receptacles were present. The two leaf brushes, one of yucca (Fig. A.40*h*) and one of sotol (Fig. A.40*i*), were stripped of their sharp or spiny leaf edges, then shredded on one end, freeing the plant fibers to form bristles; the close fibers of the yucca brush made it a rather precise tool for the painter. The two shaped sticks in Figure A.40 were apparently also used to apply paint. Specimen *j* is split from a smoothed round stick; one end is cut off squarely and the opposite end has been thinned and worn to a rounded point; this end is covered with dull red and above it are many prints left by fingers sticky with the same paint. Specimen *k* is a thin lath, smoothed on both sides; the squared ends are thinned and worn along the edges and both were dipped into black paint. The central area where the painter would have had to grasp the tool for good control when using either end is somewhat polished and darkened, just as any other unsealed wooden handle becomes. Specimens *l-o* could also have been used to apply paint, particularly those illustrated in *l*. They are thinly split twigs, worn slightly at the paint-dipped end. The remaining sticks could have been used to mix or stir paints. The presence of these items in Room 93 does not necessarily signify that decoration of the painted wood artifacts was being carried out in the room, nor have we attempted to infer such room activities by noting their presence.

Yucca leaf brushes have been reported from other sites (Tularosa Cave [Hough 1914: 11] and Cordova Cave [Martin and others 1952: 402, 408]), but no references were encountered regarding shaped sticks used as paint applicators. A strip of yucca chewed at one end to free the fibers is a frequently recorded tool among recent Pueblo peoples for decorating pottery (for example: Cochiti [Lange 1959: 148;]; general

[Guthe 1925: 28]; Tewa [Robbins, Harrington, and Freire-Marreco 1916: 52]; Walpi, Zuni, Santa Ana, San Ildefonso [Gifford 1940: 51]). Sedgwick (1927: 280) recorded the use at Acoma of "two or three strands of yucca fiber about three inches in length" as a pottery brush. At Hopi, Stephen observed the same type of brush for painting prayersticks (1936: 55, 606, 607, 625, 820, 899, 902), masks (396, 411, 523), kachina dolls (211, 305), and body decorations (908). Other known methods of paint application include a strip of green cornhusk bent over the finger (Stephen 1936: 874, wall painting), a beanstalk (Stephen 1936: 230, prayerstick paint), and a finger (Stephen 1936: 92, prayerstick; 411, headdress). A general method of applying the blue-green copper ore mask paint at Hopi and at Acoma is to spurt it from the mouth (Stephen 1936: 396, 470, 478, 520-3; White 1932: 131).

References to the use of applicator sticks or other inflexible tools are sparse. Stevenson lists the use of "yucca needles" for pottery paint brushes at Zuni (1904: 375), and Parsons (1932: 351) mentions the use of a "stick covered with wool" at Isleta, where the potters later changed to the yucca brush tradition of Laguna. Only one reference was found concerning the painting of masks with a stick. Black soot paint is "applied with a stick, such as is used to paint pottery" at Acoma (White 1932a: 131). For ceramic decoration at least, the use of a stick applicator is more frequent among other southwestern tribes. A stick brush is used by the Navajo, Apache, and Papago groups investigated by Gifford (1941: 51); a pointed stick is used by a Pima potter (Sayles 1948: 30); the unaltered tip of devil's claw (*Martynia*) is used by the Papago (Fontana and others 1962: 78).

Leaf brushes were probably used to paint most of the Chetro Ketl pieces, for the large majority of paint surfaces have visible brush strokes. The thick, grainy white paints, especially those on the small rectangular fragments (Fig. A.16 *i-l*) and on the long slats in Figure A.25 *a-f*, appear to have been daubed on, but this could have been done with a brush also. Sticks could have been used to apply narrow bands and lines and would function well to lay on large smooth areas of color. The black polka dots on one side of the set of plumes shown in Figure A.29 very possibly were applied with the tip of a finger. Thick applications of resin tend to be smooth or crackled and show no brush marks, probably having become smooth and even upon drying like most modern lacquers.

With the possible exception of one object, paints were applied after construction and after component parts were joined together. The two parts of the plaque shown in Figure A.21 seem to have been painted separately. The carefully rendered stepped frets on both sides of each half are placed indepen-

dently of the layout on the opposing semicircular piece. Paints continue over the adjacent straight edge of each piece in a way that would seem difficult to execute if the two were sewn together first. Sinew fragments are slightly stained but not covered over with paint. On all other pieces in the collection stitches are painted over, or, when they are missing, unpainted areas around or extending from perforations indicate their former existence and position.

Other features of original construction are revealed because the objects were decorated after being assembled. Unpainted areas show that some pieces were joined to and overlapped by others. Examples are the small tail (Fig. A.4 *c*) and components of the two large wands (Figs. A.23 and A.24). The presence of an oval-shaped backing at the joint of the two elements in the well-carved bird wings in Figure A.6 *a-d* would probably not have been evident if the pieces had not been painted after construction.

Pieces painted on one side only are few, which suggests that these were intended to be seen only from the decorated side. The oval form (Fig. A.12) and the hoop fragments (Fig. A.13) were probably mounted to be seen from one general angle. The small black disc fragment (Fig. A.16 *g*) and the whole disc (Fig. A.17 *a*) are painted only on one side and were probably mounted on a backing before being decorated. The two groups of long slats (Fig. A.25 *a-n*) appear to be painted for orientation toward one direction. Two other pieces may have been mounted so that only one side would generally be seen. The carved fragment in Fig. A.9*c* is covered with an irregular coat of resin on the reverse of the side illustrated, and the semicircular fragment (Fig. A.19*d*) is painted solid black on the opposite surface.

The outlining of areas that were to be painted is clearly evident on only three objects in the collection, but was probably done on many more pieces, particularly those with individual motifs. The remaining pieces of what seems to have been a large circle of wooden plumes (Fig. A.32) have narrow black lines along the edges of the upper and lower bands. These were later covered with the green and brown paints. Two rosettes in Fig. A.18 *a-b* definitely show a narrow dull red line marking the limits for the central and outer band paints.

As mentioned earlier, in half of the instances where white paint was used in decoration, it was first applied over the whole surface of the object as a ground color, as is done in Zuni masks (Bunzel 1932: 859) and on Hopi masks and kachina dolls (Stephen 1936: 211, 519-20). On the Chaco artifacts white was applied as an undercoat on only one side of five objects and on both sides of six other pieces.

The large majority (78 percent) of flat-carved pieces have carefully painted edges, edges that received intentional and not accidental covering. The edges on 21 percent are unevenly painted and coverage seems incidental to the decoration as a whole. The remainder are either unpainted or fugitive.

Annual renewal or refurbishing of altar slats and masks before their use in ceremonies is traditional at Hopi. Old paints are generally scraped away or washed off with water before new paints are applied (Stephen 1936: 116, 160, 211, 395, 519, 606). The large slats in Figure A.25 *g-n* suggest this sort of treatment. Both sides are stained a pale watery green, and the black and white paints on one side were then applied over this initial color. Five small pieces may have been renewed or at least may have undergone an attempted cleaning. In all cases, resin-green paint appears to have been brushed over with water that softened the resin and permitted the redistribution of the color over a formerly crackled and chipped surface, filling in bare spots and dulling the luster.

DECORATIVE STYLE

Painted decoration is generally simple throughout the collection, consisting mainly of solid areas and broad or narrow bands of one or two colors. Isolated elements are an L form (Fig. A.26 *a*) and a single scroll (Fig. A.15 *a-b*). Multiple narrow bands or stripes (Figs. A.1 *b*, A.5 *a-d*, A.6 *a-d*, A.15 *c-d*), parallel rows of pendent triangles or sawteeth (Fig. A.16 *i-l*), trapezoids (Fig. A.32 *a*), bullseyes in squares (Fig. A.32 *b*), and polka dots (Fig. A.29) make up the list of simple, repeated design elements. There are two instances of a checkerboard pattern (Figs. A.12, A.19 *d*).

Among the more complex designs are the three lace-like bands of small solid and open triangles (created by horizontal lines drawn through diamond cross-hatching) on the long plumes in Figure A.25 *a-f* and the zigzag design on both sides of one slat fragment (Fig. A.33 *e*). The major design element on both sides of the disc or plaque shown in Figure A.20 is a curved, stepped fret or scroll; the placement or layout differs somewhat on the two sides. As mentioned earlier, the best example of draftsmanship is seen on the larger plaque (Fig. A.21). On both sides, the green and black interlocking, stepped frets are evenly placed, basically in relation to the outer curve of each half section, but independent of the layout on the opposite piece.

The painted designs seem basically decorative rather than symbolic, just as they are when they occur on contemporaneous pottery. Small pendent triangles, dots, checkerboards, open squares with one dot in the center, and interlocking oblique sawteeth are typical elements on McElmo Black-on-white pottery (Judd 1954: Pl. 57; 1959: Pls. 21-23; Vivian 1959: Figs. 30-32). Frets in several forms occur on McElmo and Chaco Black-on-white (Judd 1959: Pl. 21A; 1954: Pl. 57; Vivian 1959: Fig. 32). Two stepped or sawtooth scrolls appear on a Chaco Black-on-white bowl from Kin Kletso (Vivian and Mathews 1965: Fig. 38). The interlocking, stepped frets on the large plaque from Chetro Ketl are similar to those on the painted stone mortar and the painted board recovered by Pepper from Pueblo Bonito (1920: Fig. 110, Pl. 8).

Although designs do not appear to be symbolic, the carved forms that they embellish (birds, flowers, plaques, plumes, wands) undoubtedly had meaning beyond certain recognizable shapes. Painting completed the objects, "finished" them, and the pigments are what made them "sacred, valuable" (Parsons 1939: 341).

BINDINGS

Materials

Sinew

The frequent use of sinew in construction of the carved wooden objects (173 instances) is of interest in considering primitive technology. Sixty-five percent of all sinew not too heavily covered with paint for the twist to be identified was initially S-twisted (70 are single-ply; five are two-ply [S, Z]). Fourteen two-ply cords consist of two untwisted elements S-plied together. Thirty single-ply cords are not twisted at all, and only one single-ply is slightly Z-twisted. Six two-ply cords are first Z-twisted then S-plied. Eighty-five percent are single-ply; 13 percent are two-ply and only one cord is three-ply. The diameters of all sinew cordage average 1 mm and range from 0.5 to 2.0 mm. Methods of tying and joining the wooden pieces together with sinew are discussed in Chapter 2.

Bark

Fragments of cordage made of what appears to be a soft reddish fiber, possibly juniper bark, occur along all five non-functional bow pieces (Fig. A.36). Most appear to be two-ply, Z-plied and all average 2 mm in diameter. One loose wad or bundle of the same material occurs in the collection and among the short pieces are several loosely Z-twisted lengths of cotton cordage (Fig. A.43 *d*).

Cotton

Only seven lengths of cotton cordage were recovered from Room 93; six are one-ply, Z-spun, and one is three-ply, Z-spun, S-plied. Z-spun cotton is the usual form in the Southwest (Kent 1957: 476; Wasley 1962: 384).

Hard Plant Fiber (Bast)

Of the 148 instances of yucca-type cordage, only 35 are employed in the construction of the wooden objects. Sixty-two percent of all hard plant fiber in the collection is S-spun, which appears to be a lower percentage than usually encountered from southwestern sites. Kent (1957: 478) states that yucca thread is nearly always two-ply, S-spun, Z-plied. From Tularosa Cave, for example, about 70 percent of hard fiber from two test squares was S-spun; in later levels that was the only type of hard fiber yarn (Martin and others 1952: 206).

Five pieces of cordage are single-ply, S-spun. One hundred twenty-eight or 86 percent are 2-ply, of which 84 are S-spun, Z-plied; 42 are Z-spun, S-plied; one is loosely S-twisted, and one is loosely Z-twisted. One 3-ply cord has two elements Z-spun, S-plied and one element S-spun only; all are Z-replied together. Thirteen cords are 4-ply: four have two 2-ply, Z-spun S-plied elements Z-replied; three have two 2-ply, S-spun Z-plied elements S-replied together; two have two 2-ply, unspun, S-plied elements Z-replied; two have four elements Z-spun, S-plied; one has four elements S-spun, Z-plied; and one has two 2-ply Z-spun S-plied elements Z-replied with two 2-ply, unspun, S-plied elements. One cord is 5-ply, with all elements S-spun, Z-plied. Diameters range from 0.5 to 5 mm, with an average of 1 mm for the bindings used on the wooden objects, and 2.5 mm for the larger cordage possibly used to suspend the objects.

Six lengths of cordage are shaped in such a way as to suggest use as wrappings around flat objects from 6 to 8 cm wide. One has multiple knots along its length forming loops suggesting a former function of joining a series of rods, perhaps, in a tight row (Fig. A.43 *e*).

Other forms utilizing bast fiber were recovered from Room 93. One is a simple over-one, under-one, three-element flat braid (Fig. A.42*g*); elements are 0.5 cm wide; braid width is 0.9 cm, thickness 0.5 cm, and length 16 cm. One end is held together in an overhand knot.

Of particular interest are two short lengths of similarly formed composites of cordage and feather quills (Fig. A.43*f-g*). Each basically consists of one two-ply, Z-spun, S-plied cord looped around two supporting, parallel elements in a manner identical to the "twined splint" from Ruin 2 in northeastern Arizona reported by Kidder and Guernsey (1919: 115, Fig. 43). Differences in the Chetro Ketl pieces are the use of three cordage elements and incorporation of split quills. The foundation cords of one composite (brown colored) are two-ply, S-spun, Z-plied; held together with one of these cords are two small feathers. The second composite (white) consists of one two-ply, Z-spun, S-plied cord on one side and two split quills unaccompanied by a cord as the other supporting element; the second piece also differs in having a third cord (two-ply, Z, S) sewn through and around its length.

Construction Techniques

The most frequently used binding types are described below.

Type I. The cord is looped through two holes (one in each wooden piece) and tied in a single knot:
   a. single loop through the holes
   b. two loops
   c. three loops
   d. four loops

Type II. The cord is looped through two holes and one end is tucked under one loop:
   a. single loop
   b. two loops
   c. four loops

Type III. The cord is looped twice through two holes and one end is wrapped several times around one loop.

Type IV. The cord is looped through two holes and both ends are tucked into one hole and trimmed on each side:
   a. single loop
   b. two loops
   c. three loops

Type V. The cord is looped twice through two holes and both ends are tied in an overhand knot *inside* of one hole; ends are trimmed on both sides.

Thirty-four percent of the individual uses of sinew are Type IV bindings and, in all but three cases, are looped twice through the perforations. Six percent were found definitely to be Type V. This was determined only where the perforations were broken across and the overhand knot revealed. It is quite possible that many or most of the Type IV bindings are actually Type V, but this could not be determined. Twenty-two percent are a form of Type I, generally looped twice, and 14 percent are of Type II, in all but two cases looped twice. Seventeen percent are too fragmentary to be specifically typed. Thirty-one square knots, one granny knot, and twelve overhand knots were identifiable among the sinew ties. Thick paint obscures the remaining 16 knots.

In addition, unusual methods of tying with sinew are employed on several of the specimens. Figure B.1 *a-b* illustrates the multiple-part central binding (occurring between two simpler ties) on the "handle" of one of the bird tails (Figs. 2.3, A.3). Figure B.1 *c* illustrates the tying method used at the proximal end to secure the wooden fletching to the arrow mainshaft in

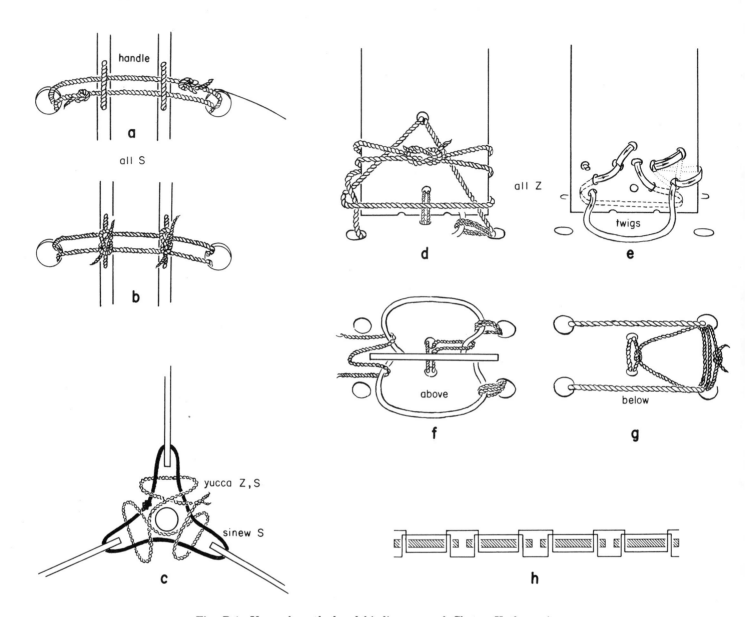

Fig. B.1. Unusual methods of binding several Chetro Ketl specimens. Sinew binding on bird tail: *a*, middle binding on side illustrated in Figure A.3; *b*, reverse side. Bindings on arrow mainshaft (Fig. A.35 *a*): *c*, attachment at proximal end, cross-section. Bindings on oval form with handle (Fig. A.12): *d*, *f-g*, plant fiber cordage; *e*, split twigs.

Figure A.35 *a*. Bindings on the other two non-functional arrows (Fig. A.35 *b*, *c*) appear to have been the same.

Bast or plant fiber cordage is utilized in only 13 individual bindings. Of these, only 7 are complete; one is Type Ia, four are IIa, and two are IIb. The remaining plant fiber cordage is used in less common tying methods: the "toggle" (Fig. A.42 *n*); the wrappings on the oval form with handle (Fig. A.12), diagramed in Figure B.1 *d, f-g*; Holbein stitching on the rectangular fragments (Fig. A.16 *j-l*), diagramed in Figure B.1 *h*; and wrappings on both ends of the feathers on the wood-fletched arrows (Fig. A.35 *a-c*),

proximal end of Figure A.35 *a* diagramed in Figure B.1 *c*.

The third kind of flexible binding material used on the flat carved objects is split twig. Two lengths of twig 2-4 mm wide were used to form the two wide loops on either side of the handle piece projecting from the oval form (Fig. A.12), as diagramed in Figure B.1 *e*. Each of the two similar discs (Fig. A.18 *d-e*) has a double split-twig binding, each averaging 1 mm in width, along the outer edge. One broken twig binding 2 mm wide is placed through the upper edge of one of the slats composing the large "plume circle" (Fig. A.32 *a-b*), and may have functioned to suspend the object.

Appendix C

THE DENDROCHRONOLOGY OF ROOM 93 CHETRO KETL

Bryant Bannister and William J. Robinson
Laboratory of Tree-Ring Research, University of Arizona

Although no roofing beams were recovered from the second story of Room 93, the ceiling of the first story, which formed the floor on which the painted wood artifacts were found, was intact and provided some basis for the dating of this portion of Chetro Ketl. William J. Robinson and Jeffrey S. Dean cored most of the beams in this ceiling; the results of their efforts are given in Table C.1.

There was also an attempt to provide dates for the wooden artifacts from tree rings exposed on the edges of some pieces. The results of this study are tentative, but, we believe, interesting.

ROOM 93: LOWER ROOM CEILING

Nearly every beam in the room was sampled—a total of 49 separate cores. Of these all but five were dated. Though a clearer building sequence was hoped for, one fact was obvious. All the savinos dated A.D. 1052 have incomplete outer rings; that is, they were cut during the growing season (roughly June and July). The savinos dated 1051, on the other hand, are all *complete*, suggesting that the cutting of the savinos for the room took place near the beginning of the growing season with some trees still dormant (1051) and others having commenced growth (1052). This would probably pin the time to around June 1, 1052, give or take a few weeks. The dates from the main beams and from the door and vent lintels suggest that the masonry construction and original roofing of the room took place a few years earlier—possibly around 1045. This would substantiate the architectural remodeling evidence, though it is interesting that no more than six years elapsed before remodeling began.

PAINTED WOODEN ARTIFACTS

Because some of the painted wooden fragments contain appreciable tree-ring series, a study was con-ducted to see if any of these records were of sufficient length and character to be datable. From 213 cataloged items, five uncataloged pieces, and three small boxes of miscellaneous fragments housed at the Southwest Archaeological Center in Globe, approximately 50 specimens appeared to contain a dozen or more rings. Eight pieces that could be further studied with minimal damage to existing surfaces were selected, and of these three specimens were dated. Number C2492 (Fig. A.10 *a*), a somewhat scimitar-shaped piece in its present state, yielded a series extending from A.D. 1002 to 1073vv. A small flattish stick, Number C2593 (not illustrated), covered the period A.D. 1062 to 1110vv, while another curved wing-shaped sample, Number C2477 (Fig. A.7 *c*), was tentatively placed at A.D. 959 to 1003vv. Number C2501 (Fig. A.14 *a*) was the longest series plotted (86 rings), but the crossdating is weak, and a tentative placement was not established. Numbers C2467 (Fig. A.5 *a*), C2475 (Fig. A.7 *b*), C2499 (Fig. A.12), and C2569 (Fig. A.30 *d*) were all undatable because of short or complicated records.

For several reasons, this collection presented some very unusual problems of analysis. The majority of the ring records were exceedingly short and fragmentary and most of the samples tended toward complacency. In order to avoid undue defacement of the artifacts, only the most rudimentary surfacing techniques were used. Some of the plots, for example, were made from viewing the long-axis side of the tracheids with kerosene surfaces—a dangerous practice at best. While dates obtained are fairly reliable (particularly the 1073vv specimen), the nature of the material precludes positive quantitative documentation.

Specimen C2593 (an unpainted stick) was submitted to Austin Long at the Department of Geosciences, Laboratory of Isotope Geochemistry, University of Arizona, for a radiocarbon assay. Long provided the following statement (August 21, 1972):

A-1228 Chaco Canyon, New Mexico 1080±155
A.D. 870

Wood from Chetro Ketl (36° 03′ 45″ N Lat, 107° 57′ W Long) Chaco Canyon National Monument, San Juan County. Sample was C2593, a single wooden object from a cache of similar objects carved from a single tree (*Pinus ponderosa*) found in room 93. These were tentatively dated dendrochronologically by Dr. Bryant Bannister at A.D. 1050. Collected (in) 1947 by Gordon Vivian, submitted by Tom Mathews and Jon Young. Comment: In this time range, C^{14} dates band on the Libby half-life (as the present one is) and tree ring dates agree very closely. This analysis thus substantiates the probable prehistoric origins of the carved objects.

In conclusion, and subject to the above qualifications, it appears that the collection of carved and painted wood is prehistoric, and from the evidence at hand, local Chaco wood was used. Furthermore, a case may be made for a manufacturing date in late Classic times, that is, the first quarter or so of the twelfth century. It is possible, of course, that reused logs are a factor or that by coincidence the dated samples represent only a small part of the total collection.

There is an impression that many of the fragments came from one original tree—a rather complacent Ponderosa pine. This would be most difficult to prove, and duplication and species identifications were not the primary focus during the study. Ponderosa pine dominates the collection, however.

TABLE C.1

Tree-Ring Dates from First Story Ceiling, Room 93

Component	Specimen Number	Species	Dates
Main beams	CK-1054	PP	890p-1036++L
	CK-1052	PP	972p-1041L
	CK-1053	WF	983-1043L
Shelf supports	CK-1056	DF	1009p-1051L
	CK-1057	WF	1013p-1064L
Lintel, south niche	CK-1058	PP	991-1047L
Savino	CK-1079	PP	995p-1037+L
	CK-1099	PP	978p-1041+L
	CK-1061	PP	004p-1043++L
	CK-1100	PP	1008p-1044++L
	CK-1089	PP	1005p-1048++L
	CK-1098	PP	995-1048++L
	CK-1063	PP	1014p-1050+L
	CK-1070	PP	990p-1050+L
	CK-1073	PP	1010p-1050L
	CK-1059	PP	1003p-1051L
	CK-1060	PP	1012-1051L
	CK-1065	DF	1020p-1051L
	CK-1066	PP	1013-1051L
	CK-1067	PP	1013p-1051L
	CK-1068	PP	1016p-1051L
	CK-1069	PP	1016p-1051L
	CK-1071	PP	999p-1051L
	CK-1072	DF	1014p-1051L
	CK-1075	PP	992p-1051L
	CK-1076	PP	1006-1051L
	CK-1077	PP	1018p-1051L
	CK-1078	DF	1007p-1051L
	CK-1080	PP	1018-1051L
	CK-1081	PP	1009p-1051L
	CK-1084	PP	1017p-1051L
	CK-1085	PP	1008p-1051L
	CK-1086	DF	1030p-1051L
	CK-1090	PP	994p-1051L
	CK-1062	PP	1009p-1052L
	CK-1064	PP	1015-1052L
	CK-1074	PP	1017-1052L
	CK-1082	PP	1019p-1052L
	CK-1083	PP	1010p-1052L
Door lintel (north wall)	CK-1093	PP	956p-1020++L
	CK-1094	PP	1020p-1045L
Vent lintel (east end, south wall)	CK-1095	PP	988p-1045L
Vent floor (east end, south wall)	CK-1096	WF	966p-1041v
Vent lintel (east end, north wall)	CK-1097	WF	1020-1043vv

PP   Ponderosa pine
WF   White fir
DF   Douglas fir
p   pith ring
v   no evidence of cutting date criteria and possibly a few rings lost from exterior
vv   no evidence of cutting date criteria and probably many rings lost from exterior
L   condition of outer surface of specimen indicates probable cutting date
+   outer rings crowded and possibly a few absent rings in series
++   outer rings very crowded and probably many absent rings in series

Note: Dates in parentheses are considered tentative.

Appendix D

SPECIES IDENTIFICATION

Arthur E. Dennis and Jeffrey Zauderer
Western Archeological Center, National Park Service

Some of the wood specimens from Room 93 were further examined in 1974. Bannister's impression (Appendix C) that many of the fragments came from one original tree was substantiated. The flat carved pieces were identified as pine (probably *Pinus ponderosa*); however, several other kinds of wood also are represented in the collection.

The non-functional bows (Fig. A.36 *a-e*) are of oak, probably *Quercus gambelii* (Gambel's oak). Three of the non-functional arrowshafts (Fig. A.35 *b-d*) are *Salix* sp. (willow), while a fourth (Fig. A.35 *a*) is *Rhus trilobata* (squawbush). The wood fletching in all cases is pine. The arrowshaft shown in Figure A.37 *a* is *Salix* sp., while the one shown in Figure A.37 *b* is an unidentified herbaceous plant. The wooden foreshafts (Fig. A.37 *f-g*) are *Atriplex* sp. (saltbush).

The two carved prayersticks (Fig. A.39 *a-b*) are probably *Acer negundo* (box elder); however, the three large prayerstick butts (Fig. A.39 *c-e*) are *Amelanchier utahensis* (serviceberry). Cottonwood (*Populus* sp.) was used for the carved cone (Fig. A.39 *f*), and the 27 lightning lattice segments (Fig. A.38) are all *Rhus trilobata*. The 35 smoothed sticks in Figure A.39 *g* are *Fendlera rupicola* (Fendler bush).

All the specimens in Figure A.40 were examined and are identified in the following list.

Fig. A.40 *a*: *Salix* sp.
  b-c: *Sarcobatus vermiculatus* (greasewood)
  d: probably *Fendlera* sp.
  e: all four specimens, *Pinus* sp.
  f: *Salix* sp.
  g: *Quercus* sp.
  h: *Yucca baccata* (blue yucca, banana yucca)
  i: *Dasyliron wheeleri* (sotol)
  j: *Salix* sp.
  k: *Pinus* sp.
  l: both specimens, *Fendlera* sp.
  m: top two specimens, *Pinus* sp.; bottom specimen, *Quercus* sp.
  n: top specimen, *Prunus* sp. (wild plum or cherry); bottom specimen, *Salix* sp.
  o: both specimens, *Salix* sp.

The various pieces used in binding and tying, such as those shown in Fig. A.42 *i-j*, are *Salix* sp., *Rhus* sp., or *Quercus* sp. Because of their flexibility these three plants were frequently used prehistorically for these purposes.

Appendix E

THE EXCAVATION OF ROOM 92
CHETRO KETL

Charles B. Voll
Navajo Area Lands Group, National Park Service

Room 92 was excavated incidental to ruins stabilization by Charles B. Voll and Martin T. Mayer during the fall of 1964. Room 92 is located in the northwest rear section of the main (north) house block, and is bordered by Room 93 on the north, which separates it from the rear wall of the ruin, Room 91 on the south, Room 102 on the east, and Room 103 on the west (see Fig. 2.1). Of the adjacent rooms only Room 93 was excavated, and in that room no excavation was carried below the first-story floor.

All of the immediately surrounding rooms and others in this section of the ruin exhibit the same style of masonry, which Hawley classes as Type II, narrow banded with core (1934: Pl. 12).

Room 92 is divided into two parts. The first part consists of the first and second stories and fill of wall debris and fallen ceilings, and the second part consists of the lower story and fill of intentionally deposited, trashy sand.

The masonry of the first- and second-story walls is identical and continuous. It is classed as Type II, narrow banded with core (Figs. E.1, E.3).

The second-story walls stand approximately 5 feet above the first-story ceiling except for the east half of the south wall, which is broken to below the ceiling level (see Fig. E.2). White plaster over a thick tan adobe plaster base adheres to the southwest corner and the north and east walls. In the north wall near the northwest corner, and 1.1 feet above the floor, is a plaster wall niche, 1.5 x 1.7 x 0.3 feet. One doorway is in the center of the west wall and a second slightly east of the center in the south wall. The east wall is set back from the east wall of the first story 0.8 feet (Figs. E.2, E.3).

In the north and south walls of the first story are two evenly spaced viga sockets 9 feet above the floor, and two sets of four shelf pole sockets at either end of

the room approximately 4.5 feet above the floor. In the center of the south wall is located the only doorway in this story (Fig. E.3, Plan). The rectangular doorway contains slanted secondary jambs of masonry and adobe 0.2 feet wide in its lower half. Eleven savino sockets were discernible in the east and west walls at ceiling level. The walls of the first story are plastered with tan adobe.

The fill of the first and second stories occurred in two layers. The upper division of 10 feet was dry and contained a large amount of both wall and fallen ceiling debris. The lower division of three feet differed in that it was damp and contained considerably less fallen ceiling material but still a great amount of wall debris (Fig. E.3, Section). The two divisions appear to have no cultural significance.

From the fill of the first and second stories 65 tree-ring specimens and a great amount of juniper bark and reeds were removed, in addition to about 1630 cubic feet of masonry and adobe wall material. Of the 65 wooden ceiling pieces, only eight large logs, evidently vigas, were assigned to particular stories, and only one of these, the first-story west viga, was found in place (Fig. E.4). From the number of vigas, their stratigraphic relationship to one another, and the volume and nature of the wall debris, it is believed that four ceilings and stories are represented, and that the walls of the four stories were all of the same type of masonry. It also appears that the walls and ceilings of the second, third, and fourth stories collapsed at once and crashed through the first-story ceiling.

Very few potsherds and artifacts and little trash were found in the fill of the first and second stories. Most, if not all, of the 73 potsherds recovered are believed to be wall spalls, and two of the three stone artifacts, one fragmentary and the second a small uniface sandstone mano, are believed to have been

[137]

Fig. E.1. Type II masonry of first story, north wall, Room 92.

Fig. E.2. Room 92 (*foreground*), facing east wall. South wall (*right foreground*) has doorway and is broken below first-story ceiling.

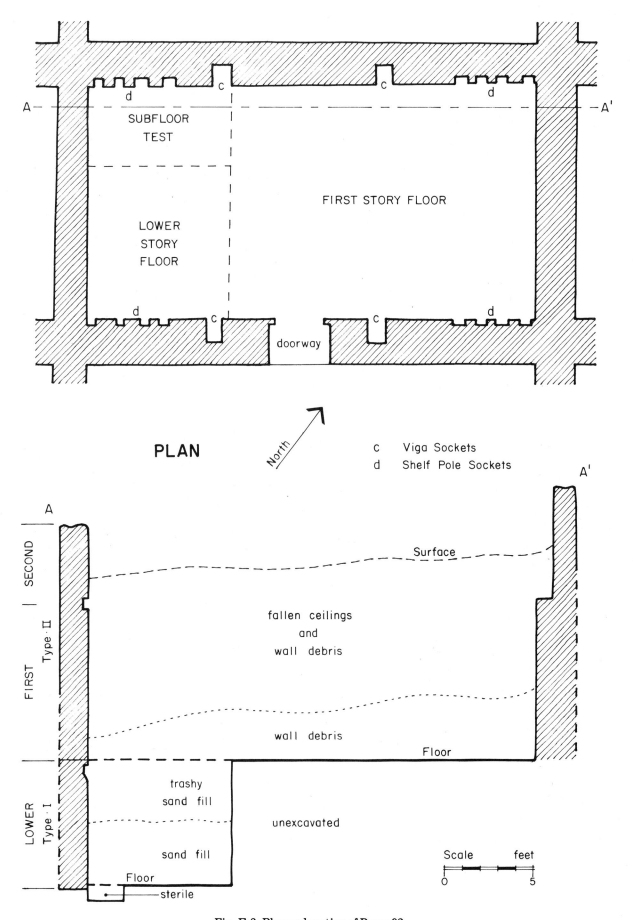

PLAN

North

c   Viga Sockets
d   Shelf Pole Sockets

Fig. E.3. Plan and section of Room 92.

[140]

Fig. E.4. Remains of ceilings, Room 92. The viga found in place is horizontal at center.

used in the masonry. The third artifact is a crude, small, circular sandstone jar lid or disc. Two short strands of what appears to be yucca fiber cordage, several corncobs, squash seeds, pinyon nuts, and four mammal bones, possibly rabbit, were recovered.

The dessicated remains of 10 articulated cottontail rabbits, trapped in a void in the fill near the middle of the north wall at a depth of 5 feet, and the proximal end of a right humerus of a very juvenile Great Horned Owl (*Bubo virginianus*), identified by L. L. Hargrave (personal communication) were recovered and are considered to be post-occupational.

The floor of the first story was featureless and consisted of packed gray earth. Recovered from the floor next to the west wall in the northwest corner were two fragments of thin, green painted, worked wood. These pieces were compared to those found by Gordon Vivian in Room 93 in 1947 and are believed to be part of the same lot.

Below the first story, a lower-story room was found (Fig. E.5). Shallow tests made along all four walls showed that the first-story walls rest directly on the lower-story walls. The excavation of the western one-third of the lower story revealed that it was filled intentionally.

The walls of the lower story differ from those above in that they are built of Type I, unfaced slab masonry, which is covered with a heavy layer of tan adobe plaster (Fig. E.6). The irretrievable, rotted, very punky stub of a lower-story viga was found socketed in the south wall near the southwest corner. No viga stub or socket was found opposite it in the north wall.

The fill of the lower story also occurred in two layers (Fig. E.3, Section). The upper three-foot layer consisted of sand that contained the articulated front legs and skulls of four deer, the majority of the 118 potsherds recovered from this room, a few squash seeds, a small turquoise pendant, and four fragments of mammal bone. The articulated deer remains extended from immediately below the first-story floor to the base of the upper layer, and for this reason the upper layer is believed to have been deposited at one time.

The lower layer of 5 feet consisted of sand that contained a very few potsherds and a few flecks of charcoal. This division, because of its homogeneity, is also believed to have been deposited at one time. The floor of the lower story was made of compacted gray earth upon which the sand fill rests.

The fact that the fill of the lower story rested directly on the floor without any intervening layer of water or wind-deposited material, or any layer of occasionally deposited trash, indicated that the lower-story room was filled intentionally, the ceiling removed, and the walls used as foundations for the first-story room. It is believed that little time elapsed between the upper and lower deposits of the lower-

story fill, for the nature of the sand in these two divisions is the same.

A test 1.0 foot deep was excavated through the lower-story floor in the northwest corner of the room. Only sterile soil was observed.

From the evidence obtained from the excavation of Room 92, it appears that in this section of Chetro Ketl an earlier structure, built of Type I, unfaced slab masonry, was intentionally robbed of ceiling materials, filled with sand, and built over by a series of Type II, narrow banded with core, masonry rooms.

Hawley (1934: 77), in her summary of the history of Chetro Ketl, finds it divided

> . . . into three periods, of which the first and at present the least known is the largest. We recognize the existence of this period through discovery of timbers the cutting dates of which fall between the years 945 and 1030. These beams were subsequently re-used in walls of later construction. No walls of the first period have yet been uncovered at Chetro Ketl, as deep excavation is only begun, but logs of the same dates are found to come, consistently, from walls of crude masonry I in other Chaco pueblos.

Bannister (1965: 147-9), on the basis of new and additional data, refines Hawley's conclusions:

> On the whole, Hawley's conclusions require little modification in the light of new tree-ring dates. Only refinement is indicated. Perhaps the greatest changes would come in her first period, from 945 to 1030. Hawley assumes, for instance, that this was a period of 'unfaced slab' masonry because the pre-1030 dates from Chetro Ketl match the dated timbers from this type of masonry in other Chaco pueblos. An analysis of the tree-ring dates, however, shows that Hawley is in error. In the first place, none of the 31 dated specimens definitely associated with 'unfaced slab' masonry in Chaco Canyon ruins date later than 950. . . . As a group, these early dates range from 828 to 950, with the majority of the cutting dates near the upper end of the range. This evidence strongly suggests that the 'unfaced slab' masonry was used during the period from before 900 to about 950.

Turning to Chetro Ketl and considering all of the pre-1030 cutting dates, the following data can be assembled (figures in parentheses indicate the number of specimens . . .):

945	1066?	1020 (6)
989	1006+	1021 (7)
990	1007	1024 (2)
994	1008 (3)	1026 (4)
995+	1009 (5)	1028 (4)
1000 (2)	1015	1029 (4)
1000 +	1016++	
1002	1018	

It is evident that the one 945 date stands apart from the main group, and this single date can hardly be considered justification for assuming that the 'unfaced slab' masonry was used until 1030. The few pre-1030 non-cutting dates with an estimated small number of rings lost tend to reinforce the clusters apparent in the dates listed. Significantly, all of the dates, with the exception of 1006? (GP-2439), are known to have come from the north part of the north block of the numbered Chetro Ketl rooms. Five distinct clusters of dates can be distinguished, with the later ones the strongest. These clusters are: 989-995+, 1000-1002, 1006-1009, 1020-1021, and 1024-1029. That the last is not an artificial cluster is attested to by the fact that there is only one Chetro Ketl cutting date at 1030 and only a slight sprinkling of dates in the early 1030's. Another feature of importance is that all of the pre-1030 cutting dates were derived from reused timbers, since in every case the early specimens were found associated with greater numbers of pieces that dated later. The weight of evidence, then, would indicate the earlier existence of a structure (or structures) which was built intermittently from the 990's through 1029. Its location may have been under or close to the present north portion of Chetro Ketl, and, although the masonry used is unknown, in all likelihood it was not of the 'unfaced slab' type, hence, either an unnamed masonry type or a backward extension of Hawley's 'narrow banded with core' type (1030-1070) is indicated. It may be that this hypothetical structure was similar to some of the smaller house units on the south side of the canyon. Granting the existence of such a structure, it was probably razed around 1038 or 1039; no archeological evidence of it has yet been found in the Chetro Ketl excavations.

On the basis of Bannister's discussion it appears that the postulated earlier structure at Chetro Ketl dates from the 990s through 1029, and that there is only one tree-ring date (945) at Chetro Ketl dating from the period "before 900 to about 950."

Bannister, unlike Hawley, however, denies the existence of Type I, unfaced slab masonry at Chetro Ketl on the basis that nowhere in Chaco Canyon is it found dating from the late tenth and early eleventh centuries. He also speculates that the postulated underlying late tenth and early eleventh century structure is similar to some of the smaller house units on the south side of the canyon.

Judd (1964: 57-77) details the occurrence of Type I, unfaced slab masonry at Pueblo Bonito. There he finds the extensive remains of a ". . . double row of rectangular rooms, grouped crescentically and facing southeast. Close within the crescent and below its foundations were several circular, ceremonial chambers or kivas" (Judd 1954: 30). Judd also publishes a long list of cultural traits assigned to this village and describes the associated ceramic assemblage (1954:36-8, 231). The types which make up this ceramic assemblage today are called Kana-a Grey (Neckbanded) and Red Mesa Black-on-white. Later, Judd states: "Together, Transitional and Degenerate-Transitional were not only the principal pottery products of the old Bonitians, but the predominant ware of Pueblo Bonito" (1959: 146). The Transitional pottery is the Red Mesa Black-on-white of present nomenclature (Judd 1954: Pl. 48), and Vivian (1959: 22) equates Degenerate-Transitional with the Escavada Black-on-white of present nomenclature.

Bannister (1965: 183) reviews the tree-ring material from Pueblo Bonito. He concludes that the early tenth century dates associated with Type I, unfaced slab masonry, date the first building period at Pueblo Bonito to the early part of the tenth century, and that the second period of construction, which is associated with faced masonry, dates to the later part of the eleventh century.

Judd implies throughout his reports on Pueblo Bonito that the site was occupied continuously from its founding in early Pueblo II through its abandonment in Pueblo III. Thus Judd considers that the Type I, unfaced slab masonry building at Pueblo Bonito was occupied at least from the early tenth century (his Old Bonitian) until the middle or later part of the eleventh century (the beginning of his Late Bonitian), a period of approximately 150 years.

Ceramic evidence from Roberts's sectioning of the refuse at Peñasco Blanco also indicates a continuous occupation from early Pueblo II until abandonment in Pueblo III (1927: 63-4). Tree-ring data gathered from Type I, unfaced slab masonry at Peñasco Blanco and reviewed by Bannister indicate a first period of construction during the early tenth century. Other tree-ring data indicate later construction at the same time as other major Chaco Canyon pueblos (Bannister 1965: 179).

From Una Vida and Kin Bineola comes additional tree-ring evidence for an early tenth century date for the construction of Type I, unfaced slab masonry (Bannister 1965: 168, 196).

Generalizing to the extent possible from the published data and from personal observations, it appears that Type I, unfaced slab masonry villages at Pueblo Bonito, Peñasco Blanco, Una Vida, and Kin Bineola were first constructed from before A.D. 900 to about 950. They were occupied continuously at least from the tenth century until the beginning of faced masonry in the mid-eleventh century, and consisted of both small and large multi-storied rooms that served as a nucleus for later, surrounding and overlying faced masonry rooms. Further, the Type I, unfaced slab masonry construction was associated with Red Mesa and Escavada Black-on-white.

Fig. E.5. Lower story, Room 92.

Fig. E.6. Walls of lower story, Room 92.

TABLE E.1

Tree-Ring Dates From Room 92

Specimen Number	Provenience or *Assignment*	Component	Species	Dates	Comments
CK-970	2nd Story Fill	Savino	DF	1008p-1046cL	Same as CK-1051
CK-971	*2nd Story*	Viga	PP		
CK-972	2nd Story Fill	Savino	WF	1018p-1043cL	
CK-973	2nd Story Fill	Savino	PP	974p-1007vv	Same as CK-996
CK-974	2nd Story Fill	Shake or Savino	DF	986p-1033rL	
CK-975	*2nd Story*	Viga	PP	976p-1069cL	
CK-976	2nd Story Fill	Savino	WF	1017p-1056rL	
CK-977	*4th Story*	Viga	PP	981p-1039+cL	Possibly one absent ring near end
CK-978	2nd Story Fill	Savino	PP	(1033p-1054cL)	
CK-979	2nd Story Fill	Savino	PP	912p-1034++LGB	Many absent rings near end. Ring count from 989.
CK-985	2nd Story Fill	Savino	PP	1028p-1054cL	
CK-987	2nd Story Fill	Savino	PP	1025p-1053cL	Same as CK-988
CK-988	2nd Story Fill	Savino	PP	1025p-1053cL	Same as CK-987
CK-990-1	2nd Story Fill	Savino	PP	997p-1054cL	
CK-990-2	2nd Story Fill	Savino	PP	1015p-1054r	Same as CK-1045
CK-991	*1st Story?*	Savino	PP	(1024p-1054rL)	
CK-992	2nd Story Fill	Savino	PP	998p-1053r	Same as CK-1046
CK-995	*2nd Story?*	Viga	WF	938p-1065v	
CK-996	2nd Story Fill	Savino	PP	947p-1007vv	Same as CK-973
CK-999	1st Story Fill	Savino	WF	962p-1052rL	
CK-1011	*1st Story*	Viga	PP	(998p-1033cL)	
CK-1012	1st Story Fill	Viga or Savino	WF	964p-1066v	
CK-1013	1st Story Fill	Savino	PP	1018p-1054cL	
CK-1014	1st Story Fill	Savino	PP	1000p-1054cL	Same as CK-1015
CK-1015	1st Story Fill	Savino	PP	1000p-1054cL	Same as CK-1014
CK-1017	1st Story Fill	Savino	PP	(1027p-1054cL)	
CK-1018	1st Story Fill	Savino	PP	1016p-1054cL	
CK-1020	1st Story Fill	Savino	PP	(1016p-1052cL)	
CK-1022	*4th Story*	Viga	WF	953p-1066v	
CK-1023	1st Story Fill	Viga	WF	968p-1067rL	
CK-1024	1st Story Fill	Viga	WF	1000p-1067r	
CK-1025	1st Story Fill	Savino	PP	1022p-1054cL	
CK-1026	1st Story Fill	Viga	WF	956p-1067rL	
CK-1028	*2nd Story?*	Viga	WF	954p-1067v	Probable cutting date
CK-1029	*3rd Story*	Viga	PP	1010p-1070r	
CK-1030	*2nd Story?*	Viga	WF	965p-1052rL	Same as CK-1044
CK-1031	*3rd Story*	Viga	WF	978p-1053r	
CK-1032	*1st Story (In Situ)*	Viga	PP	955-1033cL	
CK-1038	1st Story Fill	Savino	WF	(989p-1062vv)	
CK-1044	*1st Story?*	Viga	WF	965p-1052rL	Same as CK-1030
CK-1045	2nd Story Fill	Misc. Savino	PP	1015p-1054r	Same as CK-990-2
CK-1046	2nd Story Fill	Misc. Savino Fragment	PP	998p-1053rL	Same as CK-992
CK-1047	2nd Story Fill	Misc. Savino Fragment	PP	960p-1029vv	
CK-1048	2nd Story Fill	Misc. Savino	PP	988-1050rL	
CK-1049	2nd Story Fill	Misc. Savino	PP	(1007p-1040rL)	
CK-1050	2nd Story Fill	Misc. Viga (?) Fragment	WF	1012-1052vv	
CK-1051	2nd Story Fill	Misc. Savino Fragment	DF	1008p-1046cL	Same as CK-970

PP	Ponderosa pine	c	outer ring consistent about circumference of specimen and probable cutting date
WF	White fir		
DF	Douglas fir	L	condition of outer surface of specimen indicates probable cutting date
p	pith ring		
v	no evidence of cutting date criteria and possibly a few rings lost from exterior	+	outer rings crowded and possibly a few absent rings in series
vv	no evidence of cutting date criteria and probably many rings lost from exterior	++	outer rings very crowded and probably many absent rings in series
r	outer ring consistent over significant portion of specimen and probable cutting date		

Note: Dates in parentheses are considered tentative.

TABLE E.2

Story Assignment of Room 92 Tree-Ring Specimens

Certainty of Assignment	Specimen Number	Story Assignment and Component	Date
	CK-1032	1st Story Viga (*in situ*)	1033cL*
	CK-1011	1st Story Viga	(1033cL)
Good	CK-971	2nd Story Viga	
degree	CK-975	2nd Story Viga	1069cL
of	CK-1029	3rd Story Viga	1070r
certainty	CK-1031	3rd Story Viga	1053r
	CK-977	4th Story Viga	1039+cL
	CK-1022	4th Story Viga	1066v
	CK-991	1st Story	(1054rL)
Some	CK-1044	1st Story	1052rL (same as 1030)
degree			
of	CK-995	2nd Story	1065v
certainty	CK-1028	2nd Story	1067v
	CK-1030	2nd Story	1052rL (same as 1044)

*See key below Table E.1

TABLE E.3

Pottery From Room 92

TYPE	1st and 2nd Stories		Lower Story		Total	
	Number	Percent	Number	Percent	Number	Percent
Corrugated	17	23.2	39	33.0	56	29.3
Red Mesa Black-on-white			6	5.0	6	3.1
Escavada Black-on-white	10	13.6	16	13.5	26	13.6
Gallup Black-on-white	2	2.7	1	0.8	3	1.5
Chaco Black-on-white	30	41.0	30	25.4	60	31.4
McElmo Black-on-white	4	5.4	3	2.5	7	3.6
White Sherds	10	13.6	16	13.5	26	13.6
Puerco Black-on-red			1	0.8	1	0.5
Wingate Black-on-red			2	1.6	2	1.0
Red Sherds			1	0.8	1	0.5
Red Smudged			3	2.5	3	1.5
Total	73	99.5	118	99.4	191	99.6

The evidence from the lower story of Room 92 at Chetro Ketl is meager. No pottery, artifacts, or tree-ring material were recovered from this period, but the architectural evidence in the form of masonry and room size and the stratigraphic evidence indicate a very close relationship to the Type I, unfaced slab construction of the other large villages. The only difference occurs in the assignment of tree-ring dates. These place the Chetro Ketl Type I, unfaced slab masonry construction at a later time—A.D. 900 to 1029. Nevertheless, it appears that the periods of occupation of the Type I rooms in all the large pueblos overlap and are contemporaneous during the later tenth and the early eleventh century.

Bannister (1965: 150), in his reexamination of the tree-ring dates of Chetro Ketl, modifies Hawley's original time span for Type II, narrow banded core with masonry: "Judging from tree-ring evidence alone, then, it would seem that the Chetro Ketl building period confined to 'narrow banded with core' [Type II] masonry started about 1038 and continued through three waves of activity until about 1054."

He further states: "Since most of the dates come from timbers of primary usage, that is, they are not from reused or repair timbers, it appears that the 1036-1040 interval represents the first major building period of the presently visible Chetro Ketl pueblo. Although it cannot be definitely proved, an analysis of the data suggests that construction in the north block of rooms probably started in 1038 or 1039, and that, if a former structure did exist in the immediate vicinity, it was torn down at that time, and the earlier logs reused" (Bannister 1965: 149-50).

The results of dating the tree-ring specimens from Room 92 are presented in Table E.1.

In Table E.2 the tree-ring specimens from Room 92 are classed according to the degree of certainty of their story assignment (specimens that cannot be given a story assignment are excluded). On the basis of tree-ring dates alone one can make a case for the construction of the first story at about A.D. 1054, and the other three stories at about A.D. 1067 and 1070. However, in view of the homogeneity of the architecture, it is most likely that all four stories were built at one time—A.D. 1067 to 1070.

This dating indicates that Bannister's upper date of A.D. 1054 for Type II masonry can be extended to A.D. 1070, which agrees with Hawley.

All of the pottery from Room 92 (Table E.3) is considered to be a unit deposited in the fill and walls during the period of construction of the Type II walls of Room 92, which are dated by the tree-ring material at A.D. 1067-1070.

McElmo Black-on-white occurs as 3.6 percent of the total ceramic assemblage or 6.8 percent of the black-on-white types. Chaco Black-on-white makes up 31.4 percent of the total ceramic assemblage or 58.8 percent of the black-on-white types. It appears that at the time of the construction of the Type II Room 92 walls, Chaco Black-on-white was at its height of popularity, and McElmo Black-on-white was beginning to appear.

The suggestion here is that the McElmo phase began in Chaco Canyon shortly after the beginning of the Bonito phase in Chetro Ketl. This conclusion compares very favorably with Vivian and Mathews' beginning dates of A.D. 1050 for the McElmo phase and A.D. 1030 for the Bonito phase (1965: 109), and suggests that the Chaco propensity for building and remodeling is not the result of the infiltration of a McElmo phase people into the Chaco Canyon, but rather is related to some other factor—perhaps the diffusion of Mesoamerican traits, as suggested by Ferdon (1955).

REFERENCES

Adams, William Y., A. J. Lindsay, Jr., and C. G. Turner, II
1961   Survey and Excavation in Lower Glen Canyon, 1952-1958. *Museum of Northern Arizona Bulletin* 36 (Glen Canyon Series No. 3).

Alexander, Hubert G., and P. Reiter
1935   Report on the Excavation of Jemez Cave, New Mexico. *University of New Mexico Bulletin* Vol. 1, No. 3.

Bannister, Bryant
1965   Tree-Ring Dating of Archeological Sites in the Chaco Canyon Region, New Mexico. *Southwestern Monuments Association, Technical Series* Vol. 6, Part 2: 116-206.

Bartlett, Katherine
1934   The Material Culture of Pueblo II in the San Francisco Mountains, Arizona. *Museum of Northern Arizona Bulletin* 7.

Bauer, Clyde M., and J. B. Reeside, Jr.
1921   Coal in the Middle and Eastern Parts of San Juan County, New Mexico. *U.S. Geological Survey Bulletin* 716: 155-237.

Bourke, John G.
1884   *The Snake Dance of the Moquis of Arizona, being a narrative of a journey from Santa Fe, New Mexico, to the villages of the Moqui Indians of Arizona, with a description of the manners and customs of this peculiar people, and especially of the revolting religious rite, the Snake Dance.* New York and London.

Brand, Donald D., F. M. Hawley, F. C. Hibben, and D. Senter
1937   Tseh So, A Small House Ruin, Chaco Canyon, New Mexico: Preliminary Report. *University of New Mexico Bulletin, Anthropological Series* Vol. 2, No. 2.

Bryan, Kirk
1954   The Geology of Chaco Canyon. *Smithsonian Miscellaneous Collections* Vol. 122, No. 7.

Bunzel, Ruth
1932   Zuni Katcinas. *Bureau of American Ethnology, 47th Annual Report:* 837-1086.

Colton, Harold S.
1949   *Hopi Kachina Dolls.* University of New Mexico Press.

Cosgrove, Cornelius B.
1947   Caves of the Upper Gila and Hueco Areas. *Papers of the Peabody Museum of American Archaeology and Ethnology, Harvard University* Vol. 24, No. 2.

Dana, Edward S.
1964   *A Textbook of Mineralogy.* John Wiley and Sons, New York.

DiPeso, Charles C.
1974   *Casas Grandes: A Fallen Trading Center of the Gran Chichimeca.* Amerind Foundation, Dragoon, Arizona.

Dockstader, Frederick J.
1954   The Kachina and the White Man. *Cranbrook Institute of Science Bulletin* 35. Cranbrook Institute of Science, Bloomfield Hills, Michigan.

Dorsey, George A., and H. R. Voth
1901   The Oraibi Soyal Ceremony. *Field Museum of Natural History, Anthropological Series* Vol. 3, No. 1.

Dumarest, Father Noel
1919   Notes on Cochiti, New Mexico. Translated and edited by Elsie Clews Parsons. *American Anthropological Association Memoirs* Vol. 6, No. 3: 135-236.

Dutton, Bertha P.
1938   Leyit Kin, A Small House Ruin, Chaco Canyon, New Mexico. *University of New Mexico Bulletin, Monograph Series* Vol. 1, No. 5.

1963   *Sun Father's Way: The Kiva Murals of Kuaua.* University of New Mexico Press.

Ellis, Florence Hawley, and L. Hammack
1968   The Inner Sanctum of Feather Cave, A Mogollon Sun and Earth Shrine Linking Mexico and the Southwest. *American Antiquity* Vol. 33, No. 1: 25-44.

Emmart, Emily W.
1964   Notes on Aztec Dye Plants. In "Dye Plants and Dyeing, A Handbook," *Brooklyn Botanical Garden Special Printing of Plants and Gardens* Vol. 20, No. 3: 83-85.

Engelder, C. J., T. H. Dunkelberger, and W. J. Schiller
1940   *Semi-micro Qualitative Analysis.* John Wiley and Sons, New York.

Ferdon, Edwin N., Jr.
1946   An Excavation of Hermit's Cave, New Mexico, *Monographs of the School of American Research* No. 10, Santa Fe.

1955   A Trial Survey of Mexican-Southwestern Architectural Parallels. *Monographs of the School of American Research* No. 21, Santa Fe.

Fewkes, J. Walter
1898   Archaeological Expedition to Arizona in 1895. *Bureau of American Ethnology, 17th Annual Report* Pt. 2: 519-742.

1899   The Alosaka Cult of the Hopi Indians. *American Anthropologist* n.s, Vol. 1, No. 3: 522-544.

1900   Tusayan Flute and Snake Ceremonies. *Bureau of American Ethnology, 19th Annual Report* Pt. 2: 957-1011.

1909   Antiquities of the Mesa Verde National Park: Spruce Tree House. *Bureau of American Ethnology Bulletin* 41. Smithsonian Institution.

1916   The Cliff-ruins in Fewkes Cañon, Mesa Verde National Park, Colorado. In "Holmes Anniversary Volume," pp. 96-117.

1924   The Use of Idols in Hopi Worship. *Smithsonian Institution, Annual Report for 1922:* 377-397.

Fewkes, J. Walter, and J. G. Owens
1892   The Lalakonta: A Tusayan Dance. *American Anthropologist* Vol. 5, No. 2: 105-129.

Fontana, Bernard L., W. J. Robinson, C. W. Cormack, and E. E. Leavitt, Jr.
1962   *Papago Indian Pottery.* University of Washington Press.

Fulton, William S.
1941   A Ceremonial Cave in the Winchester Mountains, Arizona. *Amerind Foundation, Inc.* 2, Dragoon, Arizona.

Gettens, Rutherford J.
1962a Maya Blue: An Unsolved Problem in Ancient Pigments. *American Antiquity* Vol. 27, No. 4: 557-564.
1962b Mineral in Art and Archeology. *Smithsonian Institution, Annual Report for 1961*: 551-569.

Gifford, Edward W.
1941   Culture Element Distribution: II. Apache-Pueblo. *University of California Publications in Anthropological Records* Vol. IV, No. 1: 1-207.

Goldfrank, Esther Schiff
1927   The Social and Ceremonial Organization of Cochiti. *American Anthropological Association Memoir* No. 33: 1-129.

Guernsey, Samuel J.
1931   Explorations in Northeastern Arizona. *Papers of the Peabody Museum of American Archaeology and Ethnology, Harvard University* Vol. 12, No. 1.

Guthe, Carl E.
1925   Pueblo Pottery Making. *Department of Archaeology, Phillips Academy, Papers of the Southwestern Expedition* No. 2.

Harrison, G. R., R. C. Lord, and J. R. Loofbourow
1949   *Practical Spectroscopy.* Prentice-Hall, New York.

Haury, Emil W.
1934   The Canyon Creek Ruin and the Cliff Dwellings of the Sierra Ancha. *Medallion Papers* 14, Gila Pueblo, Globe, Arizona.
1945   The Excavation of Los Muertos and Neighboring Ruins in the Salt River Valley, Southern Arizona. *Papers of the Peabody Museum of American Archaeology and Ethnology, Harvard University* Vol. 24, No. 1.

Hawley, Florence M.
1934   The significance of the Dated Prehistory of Chetro Ketl, Chaco Cañon, New Mexico. *Monograph of the School of American Research* No. 2 (*University of New Mexico Bulletin* Vol. 1, No. 1).

Hewett, Edgar L.
1936   *The Chaco Canyon and Its Monuments.* Handbooks of Archaeological History, University of New Mexico Press.

Hibben, Frank C.
1938   A Cache of Wooden Bows from the Mogollon Mountains. *American Antiquity* Vol. 4, No. 1: 36-38.
1975   *Kiva Art of the Anasazi at Pottery Mound, New Mexico.* K.C. Publications, Las Vegas, Nevada.

Hough, Walter
1902   A collection of Hopi Ceremonial Pigments. *United States National Museum, Annual Report for 1900*: 463-471.
1907   Antiquities of the Upper Gila and Salt River Valleys in Arizona and New Mexico. *Bureau of American Ethnology Bulletin* 35.
1914   Culture of the Ancient Pueblos of the Upper Gila. *United States National Museum Bulletin* 87.

Judd, Neil M.
1930   The Excavation and Repair of Betatakin. *United States National Museum Proceedings* Vol. 77, Art. 5, Publication 2828.
1954   The Material Culture of Pueblo Bonito. *Smithsonian Miscellaneous Collections* Vol. 124.
1959   Pueblo del Arroyo, Chaco Canyon, New Mexico. *Smithsonian Miscellaneous Collections* Vol. 138, No. 1.
1964   The Architecture of Pueblo Bonito. *Smithsonian Miscellaneous Collections* Vol. 147, No. 1.

Kent, Kate Peck
1957   The Cultivation and Weaving of Cotton in the Prehistoric Southwestern United States. *Transactions of the American Philosophical Society, New Series* Vol. 47, Pt. 3.

Kidder, Alfred V.
1932   The Artifacts of Pecos. *Department of Archaeology Phillips Academy, Papers of the Southwestern Expedition* No. 6.

Kidder, Alfred V., and S. J. Guernsey
1919   Archaeological Explorations in Northeastern Arizona. *Bureau of American Ethnology Bulletin* 65.

Kluckhohn, Clyde, and P. Reiter
1939   Preliminary Report on the 1937 Excavations, Bc 50-51, Chaco Canyon, New Mexico. *University of New Mexico Bulletin* No. 345, *Anthropological Series* Vol. 3, No. 2.

Lambert, Marjorie F., and J. R. Ambler
1961   A Survey and Excavation of Caves in Hidalgo County, New Mexico. *Monographs of the School of American Research* No. 25, Santa Fe.

Lange, Charles H., Jr.
1959   *Cochiti: A New Mexico Pueblo, Past and Present.* University of Texas Press.

Maerz, A., and M. R. Paul
1950   *A Dictionary of Color.* McGraw-Hill, New York.

Martin, Paul S., J. B. Rinaldo, and E. A. Bluhm
1954   Caves of the Reserve Area. *Fieldiana: Anthropology* Vol. 42.

Martin, Paul S., J. B. Rinaldo, E. A. Bluhm, H. C. Cutler, and R. Grange, Jr.
1952   Mogollon Cultural Continuity and Change: The Stratigraphic Analysis of Tularosa and Cordova Caves. *Fieldiana: Anthropology* Vol. 40.

McGregor, John C.
1943   Burial of an Early American Magician. *Proceedings of the American Philosophical Society* Vol. 86, No. 2.

Mera, Harry P.
1938   Reconnaissance and Excavation in Southeastern New Mexico. *American Anthropological Association Memoir* 51.

Morris, Earl H.
1919a The Aztec Ruin. *Anthropological Papers of the American Museum of Natural History* Vol. 26, Pt. 1.
1919b Preliminary Account of the Antiquities of the Region between the Mancos and La Plata Rivers in Southwestern Colorado. *Bureau of American Ethnology Bulletin* 33.
1928   Notes on Excavations in the Aztec Ruin. *Anthropological Papers of the American Museum of Natural History* Vol. 26, No. 5.
1939   Archaeological Studies in the La Plata District, Southwestern Colorado and Northwestern New Mexico, *Carnegie Institution of Washington, Publication* 519.
1941   Prayersticks in the Walls of Mummy Cave Tower. *American Antiquity* Vol. 6, No. 3: 227-230.

Nordenskiöld, Gustaf E. A.
1839 *The Cliff Dwellers of the Mesa Verde, Southwestern Colorado, Their Pottery and Implements.* Translated by D. Lloyd Morgan. Royal Printing Office, Stockholm.

Parsons, Elsie Clews
1920 Notes on Ceremonialism at Laguna. *American Museum of Natural History, Anthropological Papers* Vol. 19, Pt. 4: 85-131.
1925 The Pueblo of Jemez. *Department of Archaeology, Phillips Academy, Papers of the Southwestern Expedition* No. 3.
1929 The Social Organization of the Tewa of New Mexico. *American Anthropological Association Memoirs* No. 36.
1932 Isleta, New Mexico. *Bureau of American Ethnology, 47th Annual Report:* 193-466.
1939 *Pueblo Indian Religion.* Two volumes. University of Chicago Press.

Peckham, Stewart
1963 Highway Salvage Archaeology, Number 18, The Red Willow Site. In *Highway Salvage Archaeology, Volume 4,* assembled by Stewart Peckham. New Mexico State Highway Department and Museum of New Mexico.

Pepper, George H.
1909 The Exploration of a Burial Room in Pueblo Bonito, New Mexico. *Putnam Anniversary Volume:* 196-252, New York.
1920 Pueblo Bonito. *Anthropological Papers of the American Museum of Natural History* Vol. 27.

Pough, Frederick H.
1953 *A Field Guide to Rocks and Minerals.* Houghton Mifflin Co., Boston.

Richert, Roland
1964 Excavation of a Portion of the West Ruin, Aztec Ruins National Monument, New Mexico. *Southwestern Monuments Association, Technical Series* No. 4.

Robbins, Wilfred W., J. P. Harrington, and B. Freire-Marreco
1916 Ethnobotany of the Tewa Indians. *Bureau of American Ethnology Bulletin* 55.

Roberts, Frank H. H., Jr.
1927 The Ceramic Sequence in Chaco Canyon and its Relationship to the Culture of the San Juan Basin. Ph.D. dissertation, Harvard University.

Roediger, Virginia More
1961 *Ceremonial Costumes of the Pueblo Indians.* University of California Press.

Rohn, Arthur H., R. A. Luebben, and L. Herold
1960 An Unusual Pueblo III Ruin, Mesa Verde, Colorado. *American Antiquity* Vol. 26, No. 1: 11-20.

Sayles, Ted, and G. Sayles
1948 The Pottery of Ida Redbird. *Arizona Highways,* January, pp. 28-31.

Sedgwick, Mrs. William T.
1927 *Acoma, The Sky City.* Harvard University Press, Cambridge.

Shepard, Anna O.
1961 Ceramics for the Archaeologist. *Carnegie Institution of Washington,* Publication 609.
1962 Maya Blue: Alternative Hypothesis. *American Antiquity* Vol. 27, No. 4: 565-566.

Smith, Watson
1952 Kiva Mural Decorations at Awatovi and Kawaika-a, with a Survey of Other Wall Paintings in the Pueblo Southwest. *Papers of the Peabody Museum of American Archaeology and Ethnology, Harvard University* Vol. 37.

Smith, Watson, R. B. Woodbury, and N. F. S. Woodbury
1966 The Excavation of Hawikuh by Frederick Webb Hodge: Report of the Hendricks-Hodge Expedition, 1917-1923. *Contributions from the Museum of the American Indian Heye Foundation* Vol XX.

Steen, Charlie R., L. M. Pierson, V. L. Bohrer, and K. P. Kent
1962 Archaeological Studies at Tonto National Monument, Arizona. *Southwestern Monuments Association, Technical Series* Vol. 2.

Stephen, Alexander M.
1898 Pigments in Ceremonials of the Hopi. *International Folklore Association, Archives* Vol. 1: 260-265.
1936 Hopi Journal of Alexander M. Stephen, edited by Elsie Clews Parsons. *Columbia University, Contributions to Anthropology* Vol. 23 (2 volumes).

Stevenson, James
1883 Illustrated Catalogue of the Collections Obtained from the Indians of New Mexico and Arizona in 1879. *Bureau of American Ethnology, 2nd Annual Report,* 1880-1881.

Stevenson, Matilda Cox
1894 The Sia. *Bureau of American Ethnology, 11th Annual Report:* 3-157.
1904 The Zuni Indians: Their Mythology, Esoteric Fraternities, and Ceremonies. *Bureau of American Ethnology, 23rd Annual Report:* 1-608.
1915 Ethnobotany of the Zuni Indians. *Bureau of American Ethnology, 30th Annual Report:* 31-102.

Vivian, Patricia Bryan
1961 Kachina: The Study of Pueblo Animism and Anthropomorphism Within the Ceremonial Wall Paintings of Pottery Mound, and the Jeddito. M.A. Thesis, Department of Art, State University of Iowa, Iowa City.

Vivian, R. Gordon
1949 Pre-historic Handy Man. *New Mexico Magazine* Vol. 27, No. 6: 15, 39-41.
1959 The Hubbard Site and Other Tri-Wall Structures in New Mexico and Colorado. *Archaeological Research Series* No. 5. National Park Service, U.S. Department of the Interior, Washington.

Vivian, R. Gordon, and T. W. Mathews
1965 Kin Kletso: A Pueblo III Community in Chaco Canyon, New Mexico. *Southwestern Monuments Association, Technical Series* Vol. 6, pt. 1: 1-115.

Vivian, R. Gordon, and P. Reiter
1960 The Great Kivas of Chaco Canyon. *Monographs of the School of American Research and the Museum of New Mexico* No. 22, Santa Fe.

Vivian, R. Gwinn
1970 An Inquiry into Prehistoric Social Organization in Chaco Canyon, New Mexico. In *Reconstructing Prehistoric Pueblo Societies,* edited by William A. Longacre, pp. 59-83. University of New Mexico Press.

Voth, Henry R.
1901 The Oraibi Powamu Ceremony. *Field Museum of Natural History, Anthropological Series* Vol. 3, No. 2: 61-158.
1903 The Oraibi Oaqöl Ceremony. *Field Museum of Natural History, Anthropological Series* Vol. 6, No. 1: 1-46.
1912 The Oraibi Marau Ceremony. *Field Museum of Natural History, Anthropological Series* Vol. 11, No. 1: 1-88.

Waring, C. L., and C. S. Annell
1953 Semiquantitative Spectographic Method for Analysis of Minerals and Ores. *Analytical Chemistry* Vol. 25, No. 8: 114-119.

Wasley, William W.
　1962　A Ceremonial Cave on Bonita Creek, Arizona. *American Antiquity* Vol. 27, No. 3: 380-394.

Wheat, Joe Ben
　1955　Mogollon Culture Prior to A.D. 1000. *Memoirs of the Society for American Archaeology* 10.

White, Leslie A.
　1932a　The Acoma Indians. *Bureau of American Ethnology, 47th Annual Report:* 17-192.
　1932b　The Pueblo of San Felipe. *American Anthropological Association Memoirs* No. 38: 1-69.

　1935　The Pueblo of Santo Domingo, New Mexico. *American Anthropological Association Memoirs* No. 43: 1-210.
　1942　The Pueblo of Santa Ana, New Mexico. *American Anthropological Association Memoirs* No. 60: 1-360.
　1962　The Pueblo of Sia, New Mexico. *Bureau of American Ethnology Bulletin* 184.

Whiting, Alfred F.
　1939　Ethnobotany of the Hopi. *Museum of Northern Arizona Bulletin* 15. Flagstaff.